Paved Roads and Public Money

Bridge Detail on the Merritt Parkway
Courtesy of the Connecticut Highway Department

Merritt Parkway Route Map
Courtesy of the Connecticut Highway Department

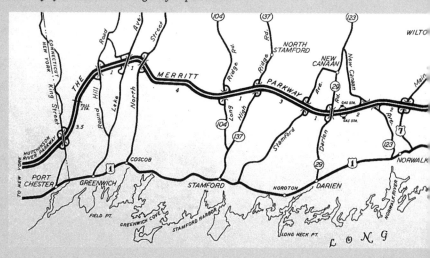

Connecticut

Transportation in

the Age of Internal

Combustion

Richard DeLuca

Paved Roads and Public Money

WESLEYAN UNIVERSITY PRESS

Middletown, Connecticut

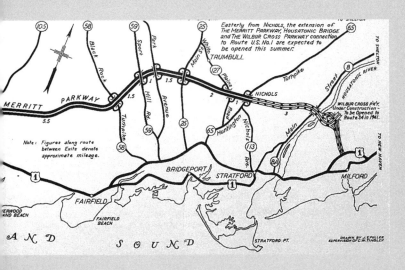

Wesleyan University Press
Middletown CT 06459
www.wesleyan.edu / wespress
Manufactured in the United States of America
Typeset by Nord Compo

The Driftless Connecticut Series is funded by the
Beatrice Fox Auerbach Foundation Fund
at the Hartford Foundation for Public Giving.

Library of Congress Cataloging-in-Publication Data
NAMES: DeLuca, Richard, author.
TITLE: Paved roads and public money: Connecticut transportation in the age
of internal combustion / Richard DeLuca.
DESCRIPTION: Middletown, Connecticut: Wesleyan University Press, [2020]
| Series: Driftless Connecticut series | Includes bibliographical
references and index. | Summary: "A complete history of modern
Connecticut transportation infrastructure, from bicycles paths to
highways"— Provided by publisher.
IDENTIFIERS: LCCN 2020015368 (print) | LCCN 2020015369 (ebook) |
ISBN 9780819573032 (cloth) | ISBN 9780819573049 (ebook)
Subjects: LCSH: Transportation—Connecticut—History. |
Roads—Connecticut—History. | Roads—Connecticut—Finance—History. |
Transportation and state—Connecticut—History.
CLASSIFICATION: LCC HE213.C6D448 2020 (print) | LCC HE213.C6 (ebook) |
DDC 388.109746—dc23
LC record available at https://lccn.loc.gov/2020015368
LC ebook record available at https://lccn.loc.gov/2020015369

5 4 3 2 1

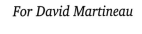

For David Martineau

Contents

As a companion volume to my earlier book *Post Roads & Iron Horses: Transportation in Connecticut from Colonial Times to the Age of Steam,* published by Wesleyan University Press in 2011, this work completes an attempt to provide a four-hundred-year overview of how transportation technology and policy have shaped, *and continue to shape,* the history of our state. The story in the first volume was fairly straightforward, with new technologies replacing older ones as the nineteenth century progressed, culminating in a system of rail, trolley, and steamboat services controlled by the privately owned transportation monopoly that was the New Haven Railroad. This volume presents a more complex story line, where the new technologies of the automobile and the airplane replaced the railroad as the predominant modes of transportation, while the federal government, in partnership with the state of Connecticut, became major actors in the drama of twentieth-century travel, providing public financing for the infrastructure required by the new modes of transport—to the detriment of the existing rail system. In addition, the federal government used its funding influence to promote a policy of scientific management and long-range planning that came to define how states addressed the problems of population growth and land use. However, despite the complexities of this second volume, the story of Connecticut transportation in the twentieth century contains the same three themes that are woven through the earlier book: the evolution of transportation technology and its impact on the physical landscape, the difficulties of regulating and financing transportation systems, and the various attempts by agents of the state to alleviate those difficulties and mitigate that impact. These three story lines provide a unique overview of the first four hundred years of Connecticut history, and a primer on the continued importance of transportation to our state's future.

It bears repeating that a project of this magnitude is never accomplished alone, and I was fortunate to receive more than my fair share of help from many different quarters: from mentors and colleagues, from librarians and research staff, and especially from writers of Connecticut history who came before me, and whose work influenced my own. Their works are cited in the bibliography, and this book could not have been written without them. In particular, I extend heartfelt thanks to the following persons and institutions: Walter Woodward, Connecticut State Historian, for his steadfast belief in this project; Laura Smith at the Dodd Research Center at the University of Connecticut for guiding me through the labyrinthine archives of the New Haven Railroad; Patty and Bruce Stark, Cecelia Bucki, Guocun Yang, Matt Warshauser, Kit Collier, and fellow members of the Association for the Study of Connecticut History for welcoming into their midst a freelance historian hungry for peer support, and for providing opportunities to share my research as it progressed; the management team of the Connecticut Department of Transportation who took the time to talk to me about their work and their world, including James P. Redeker, Commissioner; Robert Card, Finance Administrator, Thomas J. Maziarz, Chief of Policy and Planning, and Richard Armstrong, Principal Engineer; the staffs of the Connecticut State Library, the Connecticut Historical Society Museum, and the Law Library at Quinnipiac University; and Suzanna Tamminen, Director and Editor-in-Chief of Wesleyan University Press for her patient support of this project. Lastly, I would like to acknowledge my longtime friend and fellow planner, David Martineau, to whom this book is dedicated. Our friendship is one of the joys of my life and incontrovertible proof that the best things in life can never be planned. And as always to Phyllis, my wife of nearly fifty years, for whom no amount of thanks can ever be sufficient. Your sudden passing soon after this manuscript was completed was a supreme tragedy. My consolation is knowing that your love continues to make my life possible.

Paved Roads and Public Money

T he conversion of energy into motion is at the heart of all transportation. Indeed, the history of transportation— from the horse-drawn wagon and wind-powered sailing ship to automobile and the jet-powered aircraft—can be thought of as the discovery through time of different sources of energy and the invention of the means to convert that energy into a mode of transport. In much the same way that the technology of coal-fired steamboats and locomotives transformed the nation in the nineteenth century, so would gasoline-powered automobiles and airplanes in the twentieth century. While the advent of steam power was contemporary with the idea of internal combustion, the evolution of the internal combustion gasoline engine followed a long and circuitous route through the workshops of numerous nineteenth-century inventors on both sides of the Atlantic. In Europe, Gottlieb Daimler developed the first horseless carriage using an internal combustion engine in 1883. In America, the Duryea Brothers of Springfield, Massachusetts, did not produce this country's first viable horseless carriage until 1895. But from these modest beginnings the early auto age soon developed. Yet a generation before the accomplishments of Daimler and the Duryea Brothers, an interim mode of transport helped lead the way toward automobility: by developing technology integral to automotive design, by sparking a popular desire for independent travel, and by creating a public outcry for better roads. This frequently under-appreciated member of the transport revolution was none other than the man-powered, pedal-driven, mechanical horse called the bicycle.

A Celebration of Progress and Technology

With the Centennial Exposition of 1876, progress and technology came to be seen as inseparable aspects of American culture.

From May to November of 1876, the city of Philadelphia hosted a grand celebration of industry and science larger in size and broader in scope than previous industrial fairs held in London or Paris. The International

Exposition of Arts, Manufactures and Products of Soil and Mine—as the Centennial Exposition was officially known—was America's first of such a caliber, held to commemorate the founding of the republic in Philadelphia's Independence Hall a century before. Situated on several hundred acres of parkland along the banks of the Schuylkill River among "deep-wooded ravines, groves of century elms and oaks and immense meadows," the fairgrounds contained more than one hundred buildings filled with exhibits of all kinds representing the arts, science, and technology produced in dozens of American states and territories, and fifty foreign nations. Before the fair ended, nearly ten million visitors from around the country and the world would tour the exhibits, brought to the fairgrounds on the final leg of their journey by the Pennsylvania Railroad, one of the nation's largest. To accommodate such a large number of visitors, the railroad constructed a new branch line to the fair, several storage sidings, and a large gothic-style station just outside the fair's main entrance gates.[1]

The workhorse of the industrial revolution being celebrated at the fair—the one piece of technology that made the growth and prosperity of the nineteenth century possible—was the steam engine. It was the coal-fired steam engine that powered the mills and factories that made the manufactures on which the nation's economy depended; and it was steam power that propelled the riverboats, coastal steamers, and railroads that brought raw materials to the factories and distributed the finished products to wholesalers around the nation via a railroad network, which by 1876 extended into the heart of communities large and small from coast to coast.

It was appropriate, therefore, that the one exhibit that became symbolic of the fair as a whole was the Corliss Steam Engine, which stood like a giant at the very center of Machinery Hall, itself one of the largest buildings at the fair where the finest in machinery from around the world was on display. Built by the Corliss Company of Providence, Rhode Island, and used to provide power for hundreds of exhibits in Machinery Hall, the Corliss engine was the largest steam engine in the world. Standing thirty-five feet tall and weighing seven hundred tons, it required sixty-five railroad cars to transport its component parts to the fair for final assembly. One flywheel alone measured thirty feet in diameter and weighed more than fifty tons. The steam generated by the engine's twenty boilers created a total of two thousand horsepower, which was distributed to

The Corliss Engine became the symbol of the Centennial Exposition of 1876 in Philadelphia.
Leslie's Illustrated Historical Register, *1876*

individual exhibits in all four quadrants of the hall via a network of shafts and belts that totaled more than a mile in length.[2]

Clearly the size and power of the Corliss Steam Engine—like the size and scope of the fair of which it was the centerpiece—was meant to suggest the size and power of the new American republic. While still in the process of settling the western half of a nation that now extended from the Atlantic seaboard to the Pacific Ocean—and only recently rid of the curse of slavery that had plagued the country's reputation since its founding—America was fast becoming one of the great nations of the world. As President Ulysses S. Grant commented on opening day, during the past one hundred years Americans had not only settled a new nation through "great primal works of necessity . . . felling forests, subdividing prairies and building dwellings factories, ships, docks, warehouses, roads, canals [and] machinery"; they had also come to rival "older, more advanced nations in law, medicine and theology; in science, literature, philosophy and the fine arts."[3] In truth, the Centennial Exposition of 1876 celebrated far more than the founding of a new nation. It marked the arrival of that nation on the world stage.

By relating the founding of the nation to the progress made through the application of American ingenuity and technology, the Centennial Exposition of 1876 also celebrated the idea of technological determinism in American culture. Promoted in the early days of the republic by Secretary of State Alexander Hamilton, technological determinism equated the nation's growing economy—so essential to its very survival *as* a nation—to the machine-based system of manufactures and factory-based system of production developed by American businessmen. Since the beginning of the nineteenth century, the spread of technological inventions had sown deep into the subconscious minds of most Americans the idea that progress and technology were one and the same. A popular lithograph by Currier and Ives sold at the fair commemorated this belief in visual form. Titled "The Progress of the Century," the lithograph depicted scenes of steam-powered technology—a large printing press, a steamboat, and a steam locomotive—while a man seated at an electric telegraph was busy sending a message that read, "Liberty and Union, Now and Forever, One and Inseparable."[4]

By 1876, the belief that economic prosperity and advances in technology went hand in hand had become an important part of the American psyche and was on display for the world to see (and imitate) at the Centennial Exposition. Indeed, technological determinism would remain a force in the American consciousness for nearly another century, through the advent of electricity, internal combustion, and nuclear power, before being challenged during the 1960s by an accumulation of evidence showing Americans that growth, technology—perhaps even the prosperity they made possible—all had their limits.

But in 1876, technological determinism, the age of steam, and the industrialization they made possible were far from over. The steam-powered railroad and the steamboat, for example, would remain commonplace means of transport for decades to come. However, despite these advances, there remained one aspect of transportation in which the power of steam was at a severe disadvantage: personal, independent transport of the kind provided by a horse and buggy. Because the steam engine was an external combustion engine—where fuel was burned in a chamber outside the engine to heat the water and create the steam that powered the machinery—the steam engine along with the boilers where the steam was created formed a large and heavy apparatus, whose power could only be increased by making the size and heft of the engine even larger, until one reached the immense size of the Corliss Steam Engine itself.

While some mechanics did pursue the application of steam power to personal transport, most inventors understood that the key to propelling a horseless carriage by mechanical means was to reduce the size and weight of the engine while at the same time increasing the amount of power it produced. The solution they devised was the internal combustion engine, where a small amount of vaporous fuel was ignited inside the engine cylinder in an explosion akin to gunpowder in a cannon or musket. But instead of the explosive energy being imparted to a cannon or musket ball that flew from the chamber, the force created by the internal combustion of fuel was held within the cylinder and transferred via the up-down motion of a piston to the axle of a wheeled vehicle.

In Europe, English inventor Robert Street devised the first internal combustion engine as early as 1794, while Swiss engineer Isaac de Rivaz built the first horseless carriage in 1813; however, his vehicle was a four-wheel cart with barely enough engine power to move at three miles per hour. From these modest beginnings experimentation continued on both sides of the Atlantic. But it took many more years, and the discovery of the four-stroke engine cycle (intake-compression-ignition-exhaust) by German mechanic Nikolaus Otto in 1876, to make the idea of internal combustion a practical reality. Still, many technological problems remained to be solved before the internal combustion engine could be successfully adapted to an automotive vehicle. The first horseless carriage in the world using an internal combustion engine of the Otto design was developed by Gottlieb Damiler and appeared in Germany in 1883. In

America, the first horseless carriage, more primitive than its European counterpart but functional nonetheless, was introduced in 1895, manufactured by the Duryea Brothers of Springfield, Massachusetts. On August 5, 1895, Charles Duryea arrived in Hartford driving a horseless carriage that he and his brother Frank had designed and built in their shop in Springfield. Duryea had made the twenty-mile, one-way trip in about two hours, his open carriage automobile "taking the hills and grades with comfort." The historic journey made Charles Duryea the first person to operate a gas-powered auto in Connecticut.[5]

However, there was already on exhibit in Philadelphia in 1876 a new mechanical vehicle that for the coming generation would ease the way to automobility while providing a means of personal transportation for millions of Americans. That vehicle, an import from England, was on display in the Centennial's Wagon & Carriage Exhibition Building, right next to the latest in English horse-drawn carriages. It was called the "ordinary bicycle." Despite its name, the rather odd-looking machine was far from ordinary. It had a large front wheel, fifty-six inches in diameter, to which the drive pedals were attached at the hub; while at the other end of its S-shaped iron frame was a much smaller rear wheel, twenty-four inches in diameter. Metal pegs protruding from the spine of the frame allowed the rider to climb up the back of the cycle onto a small leather saddle seat situated atop the front wheel, where the rider perched himself precariously above the driving pedals.

One of the millions of visitors to Philadelphia in 1876 was Albert A. Pope, a Civil War veteran who still carried the title of Colonel with pride. At thirty-five years of age, Pope was already a successful entrepreneur who had amassed a million dollars in personal wealth by manufacturing tools and nonleather supplies for the thriving shoe industry in Massachusetts, and was looking about for a new business opportunity. Seeing the small display of English ordinary bicycles at the Centennial Exposition, Pope became enamored with the product. As he recalled, "They attracted my attention to such an extent that I paid many visits to this exhibit, studying carefully both the general plan and the details of construction and wondering if any but trained gymnasts could master so strange and apparently unsteady mount."[6]

On the train back to Massachusetts, Colonel Pope considered the possibility of importing such ordinary bicycles from England through his Boston-based company and selling the odd-looking machines in the

Colonel Albert A. Pope's success in Hartford earned him the title "Father of the American Bicycle Industry." One Hundred Years of American Commerce 1795–1895, *1896*

States. Or perhaps he would manufacture his own version of the bicycle, thereby eliminating licensing and import fees and increasing his profit accordingly. A keen man of business, Pope considered as well the risks inherent in such an enterprise. Just how popular could such an unconventional vehicle become? Who, exactly, would buy one? Who could even ride one! Yet ordinary bicycling was already a popular pastime in England, and Pope's instinct told him that the bicycle might also find an audience among athletic young men in America looking for a new sport to master.

It is here, in the ruminating mind of Colonel Albert Pope, on the train ride home to Boston from the Centennial Exposition of 1876, that the story of Connecticut transportation in the twentieth century begins.

The Bicycle Comes to Connecticut

In the 1880s and 1890s, Boston entrepreneur Albert Pope made Hartford a national center of high-quality bicycle manufacturing.

Nearly two years after visiting the Centennial Exposition, in May 1878, Colonel Albert Augustus Pope arrived at Hartford's Asylum Street station on a New Haven Railroad day coach from Boston. He brought with him not luggage, but a Duplex Excelsior ordinary bicycle that he had recently imported from England. When Pope retrieved the vehicle from the train's baggage car, the 56" high-mount bicycle was the first of its kind to appear in Hartford. Drawing quizzical stares from station onlookers, Pope skillfully mounted the Duplex Excelsior and rode off in the direction of the Weed Sewing Machine Company on nearby Capitol Avenue, a cadre of curious children traipsing behind him.[7]

Since returning from the Centennial Exposition, Pope decided to pursue the business of manufacturing and selling ordinary bicycles—having first learned to ride and enjoy the vehicle himself at his home in Boston—and had purchased a batch of fifty ordinary bicycles from England, with which he intended to test the market. However, rather than retool his factory in Boston to manufacture bicycles, Pope thought it best to find a business partner to make the bicycles for him, while he focused his talents as a salesman on promoting the product. As he himself once said, "I could not make a bicycle if my life depended on it, but I know how to sell them."[8]

The Weed Sewing Machine Company, headed by George A. Fairfield, a fellow Civil War colonel, was a logical choice. The firm was well respected in the shoe manufacturing industry with which Pope was familiar, and had in place a skilled workforce that was experienced in making interchangeable parts. As it happened, the sewing machine business was then in a slump, and whether Pope was aware of it or not, the Weed Company was looking for a new source of revenue. So when Pope approached Fairfield with an offer to make a batch of fifty ordinary bicycles for him based on the Duplex Excelsior—to be sold under the American trade name Columbia—Fairfield accepted.

Even with a prototype at hand, however, manufacturing the bicycles proved a daunting task. To replicate the English model, Weed Company engineers had to design and forge seventy-seven unique parts, some of which required large and expensive dies costing hundreds of dollars. Each part also had to have a production tolerance small enough to be interchangeable from one bicycle to another. Only the solid rubber tires were to be purchased from an outside supplier.

The bicycles were completed by fall, and to Pope's delight the first batch of fifty ordinary bicycles made in America sold out quickly, along with the fifty Duplex Excelsior cycles that Pope imported from England. With one hundred units sold and a rash of unfilled orders still in hand, Pope increased production and during the following year sold an additional one thousand ordinary bicycles through Columbia agents that he established in cities such as Hartford, Boston, New York, and Chicago. By the end of 1879, both Pope and Fairfield were convinced that a new American industry had been born in Hartford, Connecticut.[9]

The Columbia ordinary was not the first "bicycle" to be ridden in Connecticut. Its earliest ancestor, a European invention called the "dandy horse" velocipede, appeared in American cities as early as 1819, including New Haven, where it excited the interest of Yale students. Unlike the ordinary bicycle, this earlier model looked more like the bicycle we know today. It had reasonable thirty-inch wheels front and back "and a saddle between them on which the rider sits." There were, however, no pedals to propel the dandy horse, which moved only when the rider, "touching his feet to the ground, sets the wheels in motion, and keeps them rolling by now and then lightly touching the ground."[10] Seeing an opportunity to make some quick money, local carriage makers produced cheap copies of the dandy horse and rented them out to interested riders by the day or month, until dandy-horse bicycles were seen around New Haven "in great numbers."[11] But as its name implied, the dandy horse was viewed more as an amusement than a mode of transportation, and so the fad soon faded.

A half century later, a second bicycle craze took place in Connecticut, after a French mechanic named Pierre Lallement had modified the velocipede's design by adding foot pedals to the hub of the machine's front wheel and a steerable front column that allowed the rider to power and direct the bicycle by pedaling. Unable to arouse interest in his invention in Paris, Lallement came to Connecticut in 1865 where he took a job at a machine shop in Ansonia. Once established, he assembled the bicycle he had brought with him to America, and pedaled his way into New Haven, where a newsman saw him and recorded the event for posterity. "An enterprising individual propelled himself about the Green last evening on a curious frame sustained by two wheels, one before the other, and driven by foot cranks."[12]

Though Lallement's velocipede was a smart improvement on what had come before, its iron-rimmed, wooden wheels made for an uncomfortable ride, and the machine was soon dubbed the "boneshaker." Despite this limitation, Lallement's bone-shaking velocipede sparked a second bicycle fad throughout the Northeast. This time, riding academies and cycling rinks appeared in cities around the state, including New Haven.

At Yale, a student noted in the college's *Literary Magazine* that business at several indoor rinks was brisk and that he had to wait in line for two hours to take a fifteen-minute ride on a boneshaker, which cost him one cent per minute. Some riders went so far as to pay a premium to usurp the time slot of a person who had lined up ahead of them.

Despite the boneshaker craze, Lallement was unable to find an American investor or manufacturer willing to turn his prototype invention into a commercial product, in part because he was "a pleasant young man . . . incapable in every way of promoting his invention." So Lallement returned to Paris "no closer to fortune than when he had left," and America's second velocipede craze came to a close.

In the 1870s, the bicycle manufacturers of England developed the high-mount ordinary design, mainly out of engineering necessity. Since the technology of chain drive and gearing had yet to be perfected, the only way to increase the power and speed of a bicycle like Lallement's boneshaker—with pedals attached to the hub of its front wheel—was to increase the diameter of the front, or power, wheel. This led to the odd-looking design of the ordinary bicycle, with a front wheel fifty inches or more in diameter, which was kept from twisting out of roundness by a mesh of metal spokes. It was just such a top-of-the-line, English-made ordinary bicycle, on display at the Centennial Exposition of 1876, that had captured Colonel Pope's imagination.

With production well underway and his first thousand ordinary bicycles sold, Pope instructed Fairfield to design an improved model that utilized lighter tubing and smoother bearings for an improved ride. As a result of ubiquitous advertising and a team of salesmen who traveled the country demonstrating and promoting the improved Columbia ordinary bicycle, sales continued to rise, and within a few years the Weed Sewing Machine Company in Hartford became the largest bicycle factory in the world, having increased production to one thousand ordinary bicycles *each month*, and selling them at an affordable retail price of one hundred dollars apiece. By now, of course, other manufacturers entered the lucrative cycling market. But such was the high quality and popularity of Pope's product that the improved Columbia accounted for two-thirds of all ordinary bicycles sold in America.[13]

Perhaps the most notorious owner of a Columbia ordinary was Hartford's own Mark Twain, who purchased his bicycle directly from the Weed factory, along with lessons from an instructor who taught him to ride in the privacy of his own backyard. Twain described the experience with usual humor, equating the high-mount bicycle to the familiar horse it was intended to replace:

> Mine was not a full-grown bicycle, but only a colt—a fifty-inch, with the pedals shortened up to forty-eight—and skittish, like any other colt. The Expert explained the things points briefly, then he got on its back and rode around a little, to show me how easy it was to do. He said that the dismounting was perhaps the hardest thing to learn, and so we would leave that to the last. But he was in error there. He found, to his surprise and joy, that all he needed to do was to get me on to the machine and stand out of the way . . . Although I was wholly inexperienced, I dismounted in the best time on record.[14]

In the 1880s, English bicycle manufacturers developed an effective chain drive and gearing system, which allowed them to detach the drive pedals from the hub of the front wheel, equalize the diameter of the bicycle's two wheels at a reasonable size, and let the rider utilize both wheels in propelling the vehicle. The new design was called the "safety bicycle"—the ride, and the dismount in particular, being much safer than that of an ordinary bicycle—and subsequent improvements, including pneumatic tires, lightweight tubular frames, and coaster brakes, now made bicycling accessible to the masses and for the first time opened the market to women and children.

Keeping up with technological advances, in 1888 Pope introduced his own Columbia safety bicycle complete with a low-mount frame, chain drive and gearing, and adjustable handlebars and seat. The first Columbia safety weighted fifty pounds and cost one hundred fifty dollars, and as

An advertisement for the Pope Ordinary bicycle of the 1880s.
Courtesy of the Library of Congress

a result of Pope's penchant for high-quality production, it soon became the industry standard. The success of the mass-produced Columbia safety bicycle in the 1890s allowed Pope to purchase the Weed Sewing Machine Company outright, making it a fully owned subsidiary of the Pope Manufacturing Company. By the turn of the century, the Pope factory complex in Hartford was producing six hundred safety bicycles *each day* for sale by more than three thousand Columbia agents worldwide. By then, mass production had reduced the price of the Columbia safety to one hundred dollars, and improvements in metallurgy—the Pope complex had its own metal-working laboratory, the only one of its kind in New England—had reduced its weight to a more manageable twenty-two pounds.[15]

In the course of two decades, Colonel Pope had earned himself a new moniker—Father of the American Bicycle Industry—and the bicycle itself, incorporating in its design the latest in gearing systems, metal-working technology, and pneumatic tires, had become a mode of transportation for millions of Americans. As one visitor to sleepy Old Saybrook at the turn of the century attested, "An odd thing about the town, and one that rather offsets its sentiment of antiquity, was the omnipresence of bicycles. Everybody—young and old, male and female—rode this thoroughly modern contrivance. Pedestrianism has apparently gone out of fashion, and I got the idea that children learned to ride a wheel before they began to walk."[16]

The Bicycle and the Good Roads Movement

Albert Pope, together with the League of American Wheelmen, led a populist movement to establish federal and state agencies dedicated to improving public highways for bicycle use.

No sooner had Pope begun to sell his first ordinary bicycles than the young men who bought them began to organize themselves into wheel clubs so as to socialize with fellow cycling enthusiasts. In Connecticut, clubs of ordinary-bicycle owners were established early on in Hartford (1879), New Haven (1880), Bridgeport (1880), and Waterbury (1881). By the mid-1880s, ten additional ordinary-bicycle clubs had been formed in towns large and small around the state, including Stamford, Cheshire, and New London.[17]

In May 1880, realizing that promoting the culture of cycling was a surefire way to increase sales, Albert Pope helped to organize the League of American Wheelmen (LAW), comprised of thirty-one cycling clubs from around Southern New England. The LAW was established as a national organization of cycling enthusiasts with chapters in each state; its aim was to promote the general interests of cycling, to protect the rights of wheelmen, and to facilitate touring. Membership in the LAW increased steadily over the decades, especially after the introduction of the safety bicycle in 1888, and peaked at more than 100,000 in 1898.[18]

An important recruitment event for the LAW was the annual state gathering at which races, tours, and other events were organized and where proposed cycling legislation was debated. One such gathering—the Third Annual Cycling Tournament sponsored by the Hartford Wheel Club—was held in that city's Charter Oak Park on September 2–3, 1889. The weekend program included a four-mile bicycle race to the state prison in Wethersfield, a tour of the prison facilities, and in the evening, an open-air concert with music by the Weed Company Military Band.[19]

As stated in its charter, one of the group's main activities during the 1880s was the promotion of long-distance touring, which had captured the imagination of many adventurous cyclists. One of the most note-worthy touring cyclists of the time was former Yale student Karl Kron, who undertook numerous forays throughout New England riding his Columbia no. 273, one of the early ordinary bicycles manufactured by the Weed Company. Kron wrote of his cycling adventures in detail in a book titled *Ten Thousand Miles on a Bicycle,* which included several jaunts around and through Connecticut at speeds averaging five or six miles per hour. The following quote describes a portion of one such trip that originated in Boston in the summer of 1883 and during which Kron traveled the shoreline Post Road through Rhode Island and eastern Connecticut to New Haven—the same route traveled on horseback by Madam Sarah Kemble Knight in 1704. The quote is memorable, to be sure, for the effort that it documents but also for its snapshot of existing transportation modes in Connecticut—from turnpike and steamboat to railroad, electric street railway, and roads paved with oyster shells—that Kron's description inadvertently captures. The distances mentioned were measured using a Pope-made odometer that Kron had attached to his Columbia ordinary bicycle (m. = miles, h. = hours):

> I had an extremely pleasant ride to New Haven, the following forenoon (27 m. in 5 h.), through the clear, bracing air and bright sunshine, on roads quite free from dust and mud. From the corner in Clinton to the flagpole in Madison (4m.), I kept mostly on the sidewalks, and I was 1 h. in wheeling thence to the green in Guilford (5 m.), where I decided to leave the turnpike in favor of the shore road, and so followed the telegraph line out from the s. w. corner of the green and turned l. with the poles

at the first fork. The road across the marshes supplied goodish riding, though it is overflowed when the tides are very high. On a hill on Leete's Island (3 m.), I stopped before a little gravestone at the left of the road to copy the inscription: "Simeon Leete, shot here by the Enemy, 18 June 1781, age. 29," and then I hastened on to the station at Stony Creek (2 m.), whence to the green in Branford (4 m.) I found the riding almost continuously good, in spite of the hills. From there I went without stop to the summit of the big hill (2 m.), and again without stop to the watering trough near Tomlinson's bridge (3.5 m.), by which I entered New Haven. The dock of the New York steamboats is just beside this bridge; and I rode from it without dismount to the city hall on Church St., facing the green,—my route being alongside the car tracks to Wooster St., through that, l., and its prolongation, over the railway bridge, then a few rods l., to the head of Crown St., which soon crosses Church St. at right angles. All three of these streets, and many others in the city are macadamized; and, as a very large number of the New Haven sidewalks are without abrupt curbs at the crossings, long rides may be taken continuously on their bricks or flagstones. Oyster-shells [from the thriving oyster fishery in nearby Fairhaven] supply a smooth surface for several of the suburban roads.[20]

As an extension of the touring activities of its members, the LAW published a cyclist's travel guide to Connecticut, a pocketsize, leather-bound volume titled *The Cyclist's Road-Book of Connecticut*. The guidebook included seventeen long-distance road trips—including one from New York to Boston via the upper Post Road through New Haven, Hartford, and Springfield—mapped out on eight county road maps of Connecticut. The routing for each tour was highlighted in red, and each section of the route was rated (from one to five) by its gradient (from level to mountainous) and by the quality of its surface (from first class to very poor). The road book also included a list of hotels along each route where cyclists could spend the night, some of which advertised reduced rates for LAW members.[21] With books such as these, the LAW provided useful touring information for its members and also helped to publicize the surface condition of many Connecticut roadways. Indeed, in 1891, the Connecticut division of the LAW offered prizes for "the best collection of photographs showing the need for improved roads."[22]

As a logical extension of his work with the LAW, in 1889 Pope began an unrelenting advocacy on behalf of good roads with a speech before the Carriage Builders' National Convention in Syracuse, New York, where Pope,

Pope's Good Roads petition of 1893 to Congress is stored in the National Archives in Washington, D.C.
Courtesy of the National Archives

ever the businessman, equated good roads with good business, in particular the sale of carriages, wagons, and bicycles. Pope continued to preach the gospel of good roads in subsequent speeches and in print, calling for a national commission to deal with the matter. The "good roads" movement, as it came to be called, peaked in 1893 as Pope delivered to Washington, D.C., a massive petition that listed the support of 150,000 individuals and organizations, including seventeen governors, for an ongoing nationwide program of road improvements. In response to the activism of Pope and other good-road advocates, Congress that year established an Office of Road Inquiry (ORI) within the federal Department of Agriculture.[23]

As the name implied, the main role of the ORI was educational, and it fulfilled its mission in two ways: by collecting and disseminating information on how to build good roads to towns and cities across the nation, and by building short segments of "object lesson" roads in select cities, including Pope's hometown of Boston, to demonstrate what a good road could be like and thereby whet local appetites for the construction of additional good-road mileage. While the ORI had no funds to build a continuous network of good roads (that degree of federal support would have to wait two more decades), the ORI did become a permanent institutional presence within the federal government and as such soon replaced the LAW as the nation's most vocal advocate for road improvement.

As might be expected, the good roads movement led by Pope, the LAW, and other advocates had its impact on state governments, first in New Jersey and Massachusetts, where the nation's first two state highway commissions were established in 1891 and 1893, respectively, to address the ongoing issue of improved roadbuilding. In Connecticut, the momentum for good roads legislation peaked in the winter of 1894–95, as farmers from the state's 122 Grange chapters at their annual meeting passed a resolution supporting legislation to provide for good roads throughout the state, and vowed their "continued agitation" until such action was taken.[24] Meanwhile, the *Hartford Courant* published articles on good-road activities in other states, thereby keeping the issue alive in the consciousness of the state's citizens and their elected representatives. In June 1895, the Connecticut Legislature created the state's first Highway Commission (and the nation's third). At the beginning, the Connecticut Highway Commission was comprised of a three-man board of commissioners, with James H. MacDonald its first chairman. Two years later, in an effort to centralize responsibility for roadbuilding even further, the legislature revised the structure of the commission, reducing it to a single commissioner, James H. MacDonald, who alone was now responsible for implementing a highway improvement program for Connecticut. As we shall see, it was through MacDonald's efforts as highway commissioner over nearly two decades that the Connecticut Highway Department was eventually organized in 1913, along with a statewide network of paved trunk line highways for which the department was responsible.[25]

The bicycle craze of the 1880s and 1890s left two important legacies, one technological, the other social. The technology of the bicycle included much that would prove useful to makers of the automobile (and later the airplane), including advanced metallurgy, improved ball and roller bearings, variable speed transmissions, shaft drive, pneumatic tires, and certain techniques for the mass production of precision parts. Whereas their French and British counterparts were responsible for inventing the boneshaker velocipede, ordinary, and safety bicycles, American inventors made significant contributions to "the development of tools for affordable mass production," such as improved lathes for wheel and frame manufacturing. And, of course, it was American industrialist Albert Pope who showed the world how to sell bicycles—and the related culture of bicycle touring.

The social legacy of bicycle touring introduced the public to the reading of road maps, the need for route signing, and the possibility of long-distance touring, complete with tour books and discounted lodging, all of which would later become essential elements of auto travel. In addition, the bicycle promoted the need for good roads between towns and in the process turned the idea of roads improved for all-weather, long-distance travel from a low-priority government activity, historically carried out in haphazard fashion by individual towns, into a public right whose time had finally come. As a result of the efforts of Albert Pope, the LAW, and other cycling advocates, the struggle for good roads became a national political issue, and for the first time in American history agencies were created in our national and state governments to promote and provide for adequate roads.

Most importantly, bicycle touring encouraged the *desire* for independent travel long before the advent of the horseless carriage. So powerful was this contribution to the public consciousness that one Pope engineer believed it was the bicycle that "directed men's minds to the possibilities of independent, long-distance travel over the ordinary highway. We thought the railroad was good enough."[26] But though people had lived for half a century with the omnipresence of mass transportation via the railroad, "the bicycle created a new demand which it was beyond the ability of the railroad to supply. Then it came about that the bicycle could not satisfy the demand, which it had created. A mechanically propelled vehicle was wanted instead of a foot-propelled one."[27] The unprecedented craze of bicycle riding and touring in the 1880s and 1890s had created the desire for the automobile years before the horseless carriage itself appeared.

Ultimately, it was automobility—the interconnected system of automotive technology (vehicle, engine, and fuel) together with the smooth running surface of paved highways—that made high-speed, door-to-door travel possible year round. And it was automobility (the vehicle *plus* the infrastructure over which it would operate, not one or the other alone) that would radically alter the course of Connecticut history, have a significant impact on the landscape through the redistribution of the state's population, and have an adverse effect on the state's established system of railroad and steamboat transportation—as we shall see in the first chapter. It was also automobility that by the climax of this story in the 1960s would make visible to the general populace the dangers to the natural environment—from air, noise, and water pollution, traffic congestion, and suburban sprawl—inherent in automobility itself. This conundrum of technology (if some is good, why isn't more even better) would make visible the limitations of all technology and strike at the heart of America's long-held belief in growth through technological progress, so proudly exhibited for all the world to see at the Centennial Exposition of 1876 in Philadelphia.

Chapter One The Early Auto Age

In 1895, Connecticut created it first Highway Commission, which was to become the third state highway agency in the nation after those of New Jersey and Massachusetts. Over the next forty years, the one-man office of the Connecticut Highway Commission evolved into the bureaucracy of the Connecticut Highway Department (CHD) using public funds to transform a network of nineteenth-century earthen turnpikes into a trunk line system of modern paved highways to satisfy the demands of the automobile, truck, and motor bus. In the process, the CHD became the most powerful agency of state government. Between 1916 and 1921, the national government in Washington likewise began to use public tax dollars to build the nation's first network of two-lane interstate highways. This was accomplished by creating a megagovernment partnership with state highway departments around the country. The partnership relied on such state departments to construct the federal system, thereby adding to the power and influence of these agencies. Meanwhile, Connecticut's existing system of steamboats, railroads, and electric street railways, consolidated and operated under the corporate structure of the New Haven Railroad, floundered under the burdens of heavy debt incurred by Morgan and Mellen during their attempt to create a New England transportation monopoly in the 1910s, and under antitrust regulation by the Interstate Commerce Commission. By 1935, as the early auto age ended, Connecticut had completed a three-tiered system of modern highways—federal, state, and town—that used public money to promote automobility at the expense of privately owned mass transportation, and as a result transformed the relationship between Connecticut cities and the rural towns that surrounded them. That same year, with revenues declining heavily and unable to cover the interest on its long-term debt, the New Haven Railroad filed for bankruptcy.

Paving the Way

In the first decades of the twentieth century, state and federal governments created a highway network based on a hierarchy of road types and funding responsibilities that continues to this day.

TOWARD A STATE HIGHWAY SYSTEM

Ever since Connecticut's earliest days as an English colony, the construction and maintenance of all highways had been the responsibility of individual towns. In the English tradition, the task was accomplished through the use of statute labor, whereby men of a certain age were required by law to work a specified number of days each year on building and repairing the roads in their town. As might be expected, improvements were at best uneven, and at worse nonexistent. Following the Revolution, the responsibility for improving and maintaining major highways in Connecticut was given to privately owned turnpike companies, chartered by the state, who for their efforts were allowed to collect tolls from passing travelers. While this method fostered travel by stagecoach, which helped to stitch the newly independent colonies into an economic whole, it too proved problematic. Such was the ongoing cost of maintenance that some 90 percent of Connecticut turnpike corporations failed to earn enough income to provide their investors with any significant return on their investment. Therefore, as the nineteenth century wore on, companies found ways to abandon their unprofitable routes, after which responsibility for the roadway reverted back to the local community. The last privately owned turnpike in Connecticut, the Derby Turnpike into New Haven, returned to public use on February 9, 1897, after nearly one hundred years in private hands, precisely because it had been one of the few profitable toll roads in Connecticut.[1]

With all highways in the state back in public hands, the legislature went about formulating a statewide program to improve Connecticut roads. To gauge the scope of the work to be done, the legislature appointed a committee of nine men—one state senator together with one representative from each of the state's eight counties—to hold public hearings and collect information from selectmen around the state as to the number of miles of road that needed rebuilding in each town. The committee's report, published two years later, noted that there were 2,300 miles of road in the state in need of improvement, half to be improved by a macadam surface of crushed stone, compacted in layers and held together by a sprinkling of oil or tar, and half to be improved as simple gravel roads. The total cost of such a program was estimated at six million dollars. To finance the program, the committee recommended that in wealthier towns with grand lists in excess of one million dollars, the cost be paid two-thirds by the state and one third by the town; in smaller towns with grand lists less than one million dollars, the state would pay three-quarters of the cost and the town one quarter. The choice of which roads to improve, and the advertising of bids for construction, were to be handled by the towns, with the state commissioner having the power to inspect the results and force additional repairs if necessary. After each highway was improved, it was to be kept in good repair by town authorities. The committee recommended a funding level of $250,000 per year, which meant that the six million dollars of recommended improvements would not be completed for twenty-four years.[2]

As proposed by the legislative committee of 1897, the state's first highway program had one disturbing characteristic. Instead of investing control of the program in James MacDonald as the state's first highway commissioner, the program looked backward to the long-held tradition of town responsibility with regard to highway improvements. *Which* routes were to be modernized, what *surface* would be used on the roadway, and *maintenance* of the improved roads were all left to the towns, historically the source of poor road conditions.

It should also be noted that the slow pace of the program, which at recommended funding levels would take more than two decades to complete, suggested that the program was undertaken in response to the demands of the bicycle and the good roads movement, and not the automobile. Neither the state's first good roads law in 1895 that established the Connecticut Highway Commission, nor the legislature's first road program as conceived in 1899, took much heed of the horseless carriage, which in all fairness had yet to appear in sufficient numbers to reveal its full significance.

Connecticut's town-oriented highway program continued under the supervision of Commissioner MacDonald for more than a decade, by which time the difficulties inherent in the program from the beginning had become apparent. The issue came to a head in March 1907, when MacDonald testified before the legislature's Committee on Appropriations and Roads, Bridges and Rivers responsible for the road program. In his address, MacDonald made several points. First, he complained that the roads that had been improved during the previous twelve years were not being maintained by the towns and were "fast passing into a bad state of repair." Why continue in the same manner, MacDonald asked, "if the roads upon which we have been expending our money are neglected?" Rather than continue to spend good money to no good end, MacDonald asked that the legislature make highway maintenance the responsibility of the state highway commissioner.[3]

Also by 1907, the automobile had become a phenomenon to be reckoned with in Connecticut. In that year, the state established a Department of Motor Vehicles to regulate the sale and ownership of the nearly three thousand automobiles now owned and operated by Connecticut residents. Higher-speed automotive travel was wreaking havoc with roadway surfaces, so that even well-made improvements were not lasting as long as they might have otherwise under horse-and-buggy travel. Clearly, the durability of improvements had to match the changing traffic conditions, which ultimately meant asphalt paving for all roadways in the state to accommodate the high speeds and gross weight of automobiles and trucks.

Equally important, town selection of projects had produced, rather than a network of contiguous highway improvements, a patchwork of disjointed improvements around the state, many segments chosen specifically to appease local interests. To rectify that situation, MacDonald formulated a trunk line system comprised of 1,070 miles of the state's most important thoroughfares, whose improvement from this point forward would become the program's top priority. Designation of a trunk line network redirected the focus of the highway program to routes that not only provided for longer-distance travel across and through Connecticut, but also included among their number the most heavily traveled thoroughfares in the state.

MacDonald's attempt to redirect the focus of his program toward a statewide trunk line system was also prompted by a proposal from businessmen in Connecticut and Massachusetts looking to solve the problem of long-distance travel by harking back to the days of the privately owned toll road. In January 1907, two months before MacDonald's speech to the road committee, two groups of investors, one in Boston, the other in Hartford, submitted petitions to their respective state legislatures to incorporate the "New York & Boston Automobile Boulevard," a privately owned toll highway that was to run from Mount Vernon, New York, through Greenwich, New Haven, and Middletown in Connecticut, and on to Boston in a line that approximated a direct airline route between the two terminal cities. The plan was to build a mostly limited access highway consisting of "two broad roadways, one for cars going east and the other for cars going west . . . [with] entrances every few miles for its entire length."[4]

On July 18, 1907, the charter bill received an unfavorable report from the legislative committee that reviewed it—no doubt influenced by the change in policy advocated by MacDonald the previous March—and within a week was withdrawn from both the House and the Senate.[5] Of course, rejection of the toll road charter in Connecticut doomed the entire enterprise, but the effort remains significant as one of the earliest attempts to address the issue of long-distance interstate travel by constructing an unprecedented new kind of roadway, the controlled-access highway, something that would not come to fruition in Connecticut until the construction of the Merritt Parkway in the 1930s.

Last of all, MacDonald addressed the matter of funding, which he requested be doubled to $500,000 per year. In addition, he suggested that legislative appropriations be made in multiyear intervals, so that his office together with the towns could plan for future improvements. To help pay for the additional funding, MacDonald suggested that the income generated by the registration and licensing fees collected by the Department of Motor Vehicles be used exclusively for the highway program. It was an early example of a user tax applied to the age of automobility. Much the way those who crossed a bridge might pay a toll to help repair the bridge, it was considered only fair that those who owned the cars that ran on and damaged the state's highways should pay for the repair of those highways. As had been the case since the program's inception, the remainder of the funds for Connecticut's good roads program would continue to come from the general funds of the state.[6]

With these important modifications agreed to by the legislature in 1907—state responsibility for project selection and ongoing maintenance, the designation of a high-priority trunk line system for cross-state traffic, and the funds collected by the Department of Motor Vehicles to be used only for highway improvements—MacDonald released the state's good roads program from the shackles of history and created the state's first truly modern highway program, one with a forward-looking agenda.

The legislature confirmed this new approach by adopting the commissioner's designated trunk line system into law as the state's official highway network. Over the years, this network of state highways would continue to expand, reaching 1,340 highway miles by 1913 and 1,566 miles by 1923. However, at the core of the state system from the start were fourteen major cross-state routes. These included three east-west corridors: Route 1 from Greenwich to Rhode Island; Route 6 from Danbury across the central portion of Connecticut to Killingly; and in the northern portion of the state, Route 44 from Salisbury to Putnam. And there were three north-south corridors: Route 7 from Norwalk to North Canaan; Routes 5 and 10 in the center of the state from New Haven to Suffield and Granby, respectively; and in eastern Connecticut, Routes 2 and 32 from New London to Stafford and Thompson, respectively.[7]

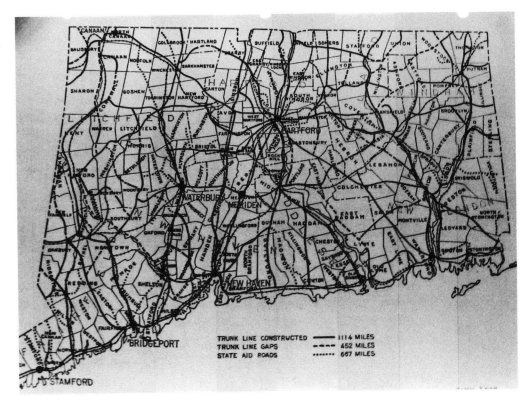

Trunk line system, 1923. Highways function best when part of a system of local feeder roads, secondary highways, and main through routes.
Connecticut Highway Department

In addition, various secondary roads that functioned as collectors of traffic headed to or from trunk line routes were also added to the system. A combination of state and local funds was used to improve these secondary highways, which in the early years of the program were designated as "state-aid" roads. Those roads that were left at the bottom of the highway hierarchy were considered town roads, and they remained the responsibility of the local community.[8]

From the beginnings of the state-controlled program in 1907 to about 1923, MacDonald's objective was simple: to pave over as many miles of dirt highways in the state as possible, with routes included in the trunk line system being given the highest priority. The objective in these early years of the new program was simply to keep pace with the growth of traffic created by the increasing number of automobiles and trucks registered in the state, which grew from 2,700 autos and 60 trucks in 1907 to 153,000 autos and 30,000 trucks by 1923—with no letup in sight. And that did not include traffic created by out-of-state vehicles entering Connecticut from New York and Massachusetts, an important element of travel in the region since the earliest days of the Connecticut colony.

BRIDGES AND FERRIES IN THE EARLY AUTO AGE

Preparing the state's major river crossings to accommodate automobility presented its own set of difficulties. First, there was the matter of seven toll bridges around the state, some of which were still in private hands as of 1887. These seven toll bridges included three over the Housatonic River: the Washington Bridge at Stratford, the Zoar Bridge at Oxford, and Bennett's Bridge at Southbury. Since the first two toll bridges were already town owned, and Bennett's crossing abandoned by its private owner, the General Assembly in 1889 was able to enact a simple bill that allowed for the transfer of these bridges into the hands of Fairfield and New Haven counties, who were to maintain the crossings from that point forward, sharing the costs equally.[9]

More problematic were the three privately owned bridges across the Connecticut River in Hartford County: the Dixon Bridge at Suffield, an old timber crossing last rebuilt in 1832; a new suspension bridge at Warehouse Point that had only been completed in 1886 by the Windsor Locks & Warehouse Point Bridge and Ferry Company; and Hartford Bridge at Hartford, a covered wooden bridge last rebuilt in 1818. The seventh toll crossing, Rope Ferry Bridge, spanned the Niantic River in East Lyme.

Unlike turnpike roads, most of these toll bridges were profitable enterprises that paid dividends to their stockholders. To free such a bridge, a dollar value would have to be determined for the assets of the corporation—bridge, toll house, perhaps some adjacent lands—that was satisfactory to all concerned, and the assets purchased by a public agent of the state, often the town(s) involved. And then there was the matter of maintenance, which in the case of a bridge meant not only small ongoing repairs but also the eventual rebuilding of the structure, a much more expensive undertaking.

The most important of these Connecticut River toll bridges was the one at Hartford. As an important crossing on the upper Post Road to Boston, Hartford Bridge was well used throughout the nineteenth century. But as commerce and traffic increased following the Civil War, so did the public's weariness at having to stop and pay a toll as they crossed the river. As one newspaper suggested, "The public . . . are sick of groping for pennies in their pockets and chafe in these days of easy communication at the idea of barriers across the highways."[10]

In 1887, a petition containing ten thousand signatures was submitted to the legislature asking that the Hartford Bridge be freed at once. As a

The Hartford covered bridge as it appeared in the 1890s.
Crossing the Connecticut, *by George E. Wright, 1908*

result, and consistent with the tradition of town responsibility for highways, a law was passed that session appointing three commissioners to estimate the cost of purchasing the existing bridge, decide which towns benefited most from the bridge, and assess the cost of the purchase against those towns "in such proportion as said commissioners shall find to be equitable." Though existing law would have assessed the bridge purchase against Hartford and East Hartford, the towns on either shore, the legislature was apparently looking for a way to spread the burden among any and all towns that benefited from the bridge, leaving it to the commission and the Superior Court to decide which towns those might be. Once the corporation had been bought out and the bridge freed, the act authorized the creation of a "Board for the Care of Highways and Bridges across the Connecticut River," composed of representatives of the chosen towns, to maintain the structure.[11]

After holding several public hearings on the matter, the commissioners filed their report with the superior court on August 14, 1888. The report set damages to the bridge company at $210,000, and assessed the damages against the five towns of Hartford, East Hartford, Glastonbury, South Windsor, and Manchester in the amounts of $95,000, $66,000, $25,000, $12,000, and $12,000, respectively. However, when the five towns objected to the arbitrariness of the assessments, which had been determined without regard to any particular formula using, say, population or grand list, the court postponed any further action.[12]

To ease the burden on the five towns, the following spring the legislature enacted a law requiring the state to contribute 40 percent (or $84,000) toward the total cost of the bridge purchase. With the assessments of each of the five towns reduced accordingly, the new scheme was approved by the courts, and when the last town assessment was received by the state treasurer on September 11, 1889, Hartford Bridge became a free crossing.[13]

"Quite a crowd had gathered by this time, and a line of sprinters had been formed, from those who were eager for the distinction of being first over the free bridge. Patrick Turley was the Mercury of this band and he easily won the contested honor . . . a curiosity gatherer, purchased the last silver dollar, paid to the bridge man for toll, for $1.50. There was plenty of fun-making by the spectators . . . everyone was evidently in the best of spirits." Except perhaps for the bridge company shareholders, who were sorry to see their investment come to an end.[14]

Once Hartford Bridge became a free crossing, however, problems began to appear. The five-town Board for the Care of Highways and Bridges across the Connecticut River soon entered into a contract with the Hartford & Wethersfield Horse Railway Company to build and operate a horse railroad across the bridge from Hartford to East Hartford. The horse railway company was to install its tracks on new planking and afterwards maintain the bridge deck for two feet on either side of its tracks, thereby easing the cost of maintenance for the five bridge towns. However, two years later, when the railway company decided to electrify the line, an inspection of the bridge indicated that the wooden structure, by then more than seventy years old, was "in rather poor shape" and in places was beginning to move away from its brick foundation piers, likely a result of vibrations caused by the operation of the horse railroad.[15]

Once it became apparent that the crossing would have to be replaced sooner rather than later, the board hired a law firm to lobby the legislature on behalf of a bill that would transfer ownership of Hartford Bridge to the state for the sole purpose of reconstruction. In June 1893, the General Assembly acquiesced to the board's wishes, and a new law declared that Hartford Bridge and its approaches "hereafter be maintained by the state of Connecticut at its expense." That July, the legislature appointed three commissioners to oversee the rebuilding of the bridge, and they in turn contracted with the Berlin Iron Bridge Company to construct a new steel span.[16]

With the bridge replacement project underway, a scandal erupted when it was discovered that the commissioners had used $35,000 in public bridge funds to lobby for the bill transferring ownership to the state, an action contrary to their status as agents of the state. In addition, it was discovered that the contract for a new bridge had been entered into without the commissioners keeping proper records of their actions. As a result, Morgan G. Buckeley, former governor of Connecticut and a well-respected Republican political boss, took legislative charge of the matter and—once again consistent with the Connecticut tradition of town responsibility for highways—introduced a bill to repeal the act of 1893 and return the bridge to town ownership for reconstruction and future maintenance. Hearings were held and arguments were made, pro and con, for weeks. In the end, the Buckeley bill passed the Senate and was to be taken up by the House "Wednesday next."[17]

No sooner had news of the pending action appeared when an early evening fire (accidental or otherwise) destroyed the old wooden bridge.

"Thousands of men and women watched it for four or five hours, from both river banks and from boats." One witness to the grand sight was a teenaged girl from East Hartford named Mabel Goodwin, who rode down to the river on her bicycle to witness the conflagration with her sister: "The old bridge over the Connecticut River caught fire and was completely burned all excepting a little piece on the west side of the river. Jennie and I rode down to see it burn and nearly everybody that possibly could went. It was a glorious sight and the wind blew up the river so that the sparks were all carried that way and so there was not much danger to the buildings near by. Nobody was killed but two fire horses were burned to death."[18]

Two steam-powered ferryboats were soon brought in to carry people back and forth across the river in place of the burned bridge. Despite the disruption of streetcar service, Ms. Goodwin made the trip into Hartford twice during the following week: "We miss the old bridge very much for now one has to transfer from the [street] cars to the boats which now run across the river and then one has to take a car on the other side and it is very inconvenient for they only let so many passengers get on the boats and when there is a crowd one sometimes has to wait for the other boat."[19]

While the destruction of the Hartford Bridge by flames added a sense of urgency to the matter of a new crossing, it did not alter the legislative outcome proposed by Buckeley, as some might have hoped. Buckeley's bill, making the five towns responsible for construction of the new bridge, was enacted soon after the fire. To aid the towns in financing the new span, the bill diverted 50 percent of all taxes paid to the state by any railway company using the new bridge to the towns instead for a period of five years, and 10 percent thereafter. In addition, a second bridge bill was enacted, creating the Connecticut River Bridge & Highway District, to be comprised of the same five towns, which was charged with building a new span up to a maximum cost of $500,000 and with maintaining it once it was completed. Buckeley was appointed as a Hartford representative to the new district and subsequently chosen as its president. Meanwhile, following a recommendation by a superior court judge, the percentages of the cost to be paid by the towns east of the river were lowered considerably, with Hartford now having to bear 79 percent of the total cost, East Hartford 12 percent, and the remaining three towns 3 percent each.[20]

Even so, the towns east of the river thought the idea unjust that they, and not the state, should be held responsible for the new bridge. In 1895, the town of Glastonbury, in protest, refused to pay even its small 3 percent portion of a five-hundred-dollar assessment for normal bridge repairs, on the grounds that the Bridge & Highway District, whose members were not elected by the town, could not force Glastonbury to maintain a bridge that was not even located within its town boundaries. A month later, the Bridge & Highway District sued Mr. Williams, the treasurer of Glastonbury, in superior court to obtain the fifteen dollars in unpaid funds.

When the superior court upheld the right of the bridge district to tax its member towns, Glastonbury appealed the decision to the Connecticut Supreme Court of Errors, where in *Morgan G. Buckeley et.al. v. Samuel H. Williams, Treasurer* (68Conn131) the action of the lower court was upheld by a vote of three to two. As part of the decision, the court restated in no uncertain terms the legal relationship between the state and its member towns. Contrary to popular belief that *the town* was the ultimate source of governmental authority in Connecticut, the court confirmed the long-standing legal position that Connecticut towns "have no inherent rights. They have always been the mere creatures of the Colony or the State, with such functions and *such only* as were conceded or recognized by law."[21] In effect, the state of Connecticut could make any town do its bidding, regardless of existing law, so long as the action had been duly taken by the legislature—to which the town had elected its own representatives. In the most extreme example, the legislature, which had created each town in the first place, could abolish a town's very existence if it saw fit. With regard to transportation, the decision can be seen as consistent with the tradition of town responsibility for highway improvements, a full decade before MacDonald broke with that tradition by asking for state authority over highway construction.

Following the court decision on the powers of the Bridge & Highway District—and with a temporary wooden bridge now in place across the river, complete with an electric streetcar line—it took eight more years before construction began on a new permanent crossing. The delay was caused first by the need for federal approval of the new span. Because the Connecticut River was considered a navigable waterway as far north as the rapids at Enfield, construction of a new Hartford Bridge required an act of Congress. Congress took up the matter in 1893 and authorized the district to build a drawbridge whose design was to be approved by the secretary of war. However, after much grumbling by those who thought a draw unnecessary since navigation above the bridge was unlikely at best, the law was amended two years later to remove the draw requirement—provided the district agreed to put one in at a later date if so ordered by the secretary of war.[22] As a result, the new bridge was built without a draw span.

Adding to the delay, the bridge district and the city of Hartford studied, debated, and studied some more just what kind of bridge to build. Three alternatives were considered: a simple steel girder structure estimated to cost $782,000, a more complicated steel arch design expected to cost $878,000, and a stone arch bridge at a cost of $1,600,000. In conjunction with the bridge, Hartford also decided to build a new approach road along the west side of the river that was estimated to cost an additional $708,000. Finally, in a referendum held on April 2, 1902, the voters of Hartford approved the appropriation of funds necessary to build the more expensive but low maintenance and longer-lasting stone arch bridge across the Connecticut River, together with the proposed approach road, with the city of Hartford to pay all expenses above the $500,000 limit set in the bridge legislation. In keeping with the Supreme Court decision that each town had only the taxing power given it by the state, the following year the legislature approved bills allowing the Bridge & Highway District

The new Hartford stone arch bridge, completed in 1908 and later named for Morgan Buckeley.
Crossing the Connecticut, *by George E. Wright, 1908*

and the city of Hartford to issue bonds in the amounts necessary to cover their portions of the cost of the new bridge and approach road.[23]

Construction of the new crossing began in the summer of 1903 and lasted five years. Perhaps the most difficult part of the job was the construction of the underwater foundations for each of the six regular and two double piers that would support the span as it crossed the river. Under the guidance of chief engineer Edwin D. Graves, the foundations were constructed using large watertight caissons that were sunk around each pier site to provide a workspace—once the water had been pumped out—for the men known as "sand hogs," who removed the dirt and rock from beneath the water's surface. It was filthy, backbreaking labor.

> For a day of eight hours, including a half-hour at the surface for coffee and rest, they were paid $2.50 till a depth of 55 feet had been reached, and then, on account of high air pressure, their day would be decreased to six hours and their wages increased to $2.75. Another raise of 25 cents was given while the concrete filling was being done inside the caisson, as the slaking lime made the temperature high, accompanied by an irritating odor. Burly negroes were generally employed in this exhausting work.[24]

Once the eight piers and the abutments at either end of the bridge were completed, the wooden falsework needed to support the stone arches was constructed within each span, and the exterior and binding stones, some weighing up to forty tons, were hand cut to exacting tolerances and lowered into place. Last of all, the stone understructure of the bridge was filled with concrete to the level of the roadway. The finished roadway was sixty feet wide, with double trolley tracks down the center, and with a ten-foot sidewalk for pedestrians on either side, for a total width of eighty feet.[25]

The new Hartford Bridge was dedicated on October 6–8, 1908, with three days of parades, concerts, and celebrations on both sides of the river, beginning with a reenactment of the arrival of Thomas Hooker and his party of English settlers, who could be watched crossing the river on a raft to meet the "Native Americans" waiting for them in Hartford. The celebrations were attended by some 200,000 residents and out-of-town visitors and concluded with a stunning fireworks display and a nighttime illumination of the bridge and river area.[26]

As the Hartford Bridge neared completion, the General Assembly enacted a law (1907) that freed the remaining toll bridges in the

Sand hogs at work, excavating the piers for the stone arch bridge below the water of the Connecticut River.
Spanning a Century: The Buckeley Bridge 1908–2008. Courtesy of ConnDOT

Stone arch bridges are built around a wood-framed falsework, which is removed once the arch is completed.
Spanning a Century: The Buckeley Bridge 1908–2008. Courtesy of ConnDOT

state that were still privately owned, as well as two new toll crossings that had been erected across the Connecticut River since the Hartford Bridge was first freed in 1889, one in Thompsonville in 1893, the other in Middletown in 1896. With this act, the long and torturous journey to free the last privately owned toll bridges in Connecticut came to an end.[27]

With all private bridge crossings back under public control, the legislature turned its attention to the problem of replacing the state's remaining ferry crossings with bridges especially along major trunk line routes, such as the lower post road to Boston. That ferry crossings could be problematic in the early days of the automobile can be seen in the experience of one driver and his companion who were on an auto tour of Southern New England in the summer of 1901. In his memoir of the adventure, *Two Thousand Miles on an Automobile,* the driver recorded their rather quaint experience crossing the Connecticut River on their way from Providence, Rhode Island, to New Haven:

> At Lyme there is a very steep descent to the Connecticut River, which is a broad estuary at that point. The ferry is a primitive side-wheeler, which might carry two automobiles, but hardly more. It happened to be on the far shore. A small boy pointed out a long tinhorn hanging on a post, the hoarse blast of which summons the sleepy boat. There is no landing, and it seems impossible for our vehicle to get aboard; but the boat has a long, shovel-like nose projecting from the bow, which ran upon the shore, making a perfect gangplank. Carefully balancing the automobile in the center so as not to list the primitive craft, we made our way deliberately to the other side, the entire crew of two men—engineer and captain—coming out to talk with us.[28]

Such antiquated ferry service became more troublesome as time went on and the volume of traffic on the lower post road increased. In 1909, the legislature created the Saybrook & Lyme Connecticut River Commission, specifically to build a new bridge across the mouth of the river between Old Saybrook and Lyme. An existing steam-powered ferry had been handling traffic across the river for more than a decade, but with the volume of traffic crossing the river approaching fourteen thousand vehicles each year, a more modern, more permanent crossing was needed. The commission was authorized to build a low-level drawbridge across the river, to a maximum cost of $500,000, to be paid for with the general funds of the state. It was the first bridge to be built by and paid for by the state of Connecticut.[29]

The Saybrook Bridge was opened on August 24, 1911, by "a monster automobile parade" of five hundred cars. The design of the bridge was a Warren steel truss, 1,800 feet long, with a bascule-type draw near the western side of the span. Since there was some doubt at first as to where to position the draw section, the bridge's chief engineer used the opportunity to conduct a unique experiment. "Two rowboats with red and white flags during the day and white lights at night were anchored at the edge of the proposed channel and all tug boat and steamboat captains using the river were asked to observe this channel and suggest to the engineer any changes desired by them in its location. The rowboats were shifted from time to time until the shipping interests using the river were satisfied with the location." That way the final location of the draw span was determined.[30]

About this time, a new commissioner, Charles J. Bennett, replaced MacDonald as head of the state's highway agency. At his urging—and with automobility now clearly here to stay—the one-man highway commission was reorganized into the Connecticut Highway Department (CHD), a bureaucratic agency more commensurate with the demands of the auto age. A deputy commissioner was hired to oversee all planning and construction, and the state was divided into seven construction districts, each with its own chief engineer. In addition, a superintendent of repairs was put in charge of maintenance, with each district assigned its own supervisor, foreman, and laborers. Meanwhile, a chief clerk was hired to oversee all financial accounts and record-keeping for the department.[31]

Between 1915 and 1918, as part of its expanding duties, the CHD was made responsible for the construction and maintenance of all highway bridges on the trunk line system. With this authority, the CHD began replacing all remaining ferries along the lower post road with new bridges designed and built by state engineers: in Westport in 1917, in Stratford in 1921, in Groton also in 1921 (by converting an existing railroad bridge to auto use), and in Mystic in 1922.[32] By the mid-1920s, with the trunk line system still expanding to include more miles of primary and secondary highways, all major river crossings on the system had been bridged to accommodate automobile and truck traffic. In 1923, bridge tolls were removed from all public crossings still charging them, making

Connecticut, for the first time since its founding, a toll-free state—the only exceptions being those tolls charged by the last three ferries remaining in the state: the Windsor to South Windsor ferry, the Rocky Hill to Glastonbury ferry, and the Chester to Hadlyme ferry, all low-volume crossings on the Connecticut River, and all now under the auspices of the Connecticut Highway Department.[33]

A FEDERAL-STATE PARTNERSHIP IS FORMED

Of course, the coming of the automobile and the need for better highways was hardly a phenomenon unique to Connecticut; it was happening nationwide. Perhaps the best measure of the speed with which automobility took hold of the nation—and the pressure for improved roads that increasing auto traffic placed on highwaymen in every state—were the sales of Henry Ford's Model T, the first car manufactured at an affordable price with the common man in mind. Introduced in 1907 at a price of $850 (when most other automobiles cost several thousands of dollars), by 1915 the sales price dropped to half that amount. By that time, Ford had already sold more than one million Model T automobiles, which he joked, mocking the efficiency of his own mass production techniques, could be had in any color, "so long as it was black." Over the next decade, Ford's assembly line methods lowered the unit price of the nation's most popular automobile even further, until one could be had in 1924 for a mere $290. By that time, ten million Model T Fords had already been sold, and production was approaching two million vehicles a year.[34] With thanks to Henry Ford and his Model T, the automobile went from being a luxury plaything for the rich in the 1910s to a necessity for the everyman in the 1920s. When a woman from Muncie, Indiana, was asked by a Department of Agriculture interviewer in the 1920s, "Why do you own a Model T but you don't own a bathtub?" she replied with a surprised look, "You can't go to town in a bathtub."[35]

As automobility became increasingly common, many other states formed highway departments and initiated statewide road improvement programs. As their number increased, they gathered at annual "road conventions," like the one hosted by Commissioner MacDonald in Hartford in 1904, to share their knowledge and experiences. Some seven hundred highwaymen from twenty-eight states attended the Hartford convention, along with a federal representative from the Department of Agriculture's Office of Road Inquiry.[36] Such gatherings established a social bond among highwaymen and a national consensus on certain policy issues, in particular the need for federal funding of good roads. By 1914, as Congress studied the possibility of a national highway program, state highwaymen created a nationwide organization of their own called the American Association of State Highway Officials (AASHO), which worked closely with federal officials and Congress to sort through the legal, legislative, and engineering details of a national highway effort.

There were several overriding concerns, first and foremost the legality of such a program. After efforts in the early 1800s to create a national highway program were vetoed by three different presidents on the grounds that the national government had no authority to build roads within individual states, the issue was resolved in 1907 by the U.S. Supreme Court in *Wilson v. Shaw*, which stated directly the government's right under the Constitution to build interstate highways: "This power in former times was exerted to a very limited extent . . . and many of our statesmen entertained doubts as to the existence of the power to establish ways of communication by land . . . [but] land transportation has so vastly increased [and] a sounder consideration of the subject has prevailed and led to the conclusion that Congress has plenary power over the whole subject. Congress, therefore, has . . . the power . . . to authorize the construction of a public highway connecting several states."[37]

But what roads should the federal government build? What should the purpose of such a program be? As in many states, the debate centered on whether a highway program should focus on short sections of roadway whose improvement was intended to aid rural farmers in reaching the nearest railroad or market town, or on longer stretches of improvements that would facilitate long-distance interstate travel for everyone. By 1916, when Congress passed the first Federal Aid Highway Act, appropriating $75 million over five years to states with functioning highway departments (on a fifty-fifty matching basis), a decision was made to use federal funds for "such projects as will expedite the completion of an adequate and connected system of highways, interstate in character." In an effort to placate rural citizens, funds were apportioned according to a formula weighted one third on the area of the state, one third on its population, and one third on its rural road mileage. Once the improved highways were built, they were to be maintained by their respective states.[38]

It was a momentous decision. For the first time in the nation's history, the federal government agreed to direct funding of highway improvements. The program itself, however, was much less momentous, mainly because the diversion of manpower and resources to the war in Europe delayed improvements under the new federal program. By the time the five-year program ended in 1921, less than five hundred miles of highway had been improved nationwide, barely a drop in the proverbial bucket.[39]

Yet the Federal Aid Highway Act of 1916 established an important precedent, and when the program came up for renewal—just in time to meet the postwar boom in automobile ownership—it was thoroughly revised to create a more aggressive road-building program. The Federal Aid Highway Act of 1921 created a historic partnership between federal and state governments, with the states building in effect a trunk line system of federal-aid highways, to a maximum of 7 percent of a given state's total road mileage. In addition, three-sevenths of the federal system was to be comprised of roads "interstate in character," on which the state was free to spend up to 60 percent of its federal appropriation. Once again, states were held responsible for ongoing maintenance of the federal highways (at their own expense) as they were for the matching state money required by the program.[40]

To help states define the federal system, the Department of Agriculture formed a Joint Board of Interstate Highways to select the final network from the 7 percent mileage submitted by each state. In 1925, the secretary of agriculture approved and numbered a system that included some 169,000 federal-aid highway miles nationwide.[41] In Connecticut, this network consisted of three east-west routes: U.S. Route 1 along the shoreline from Greenwich to Stonington, U.S. Route 6 across the center of the state from Danbury to Killingly, and U.S. Route 44 in northern Connecticut from Salisbury to Putnam. These were supplemented by four north-south routes: in western Connecticut, U.S. Route 7 from Norwalk to North Canaan; U.S. Routes 5 and 5a in the center of the state from New Haven to Enfield and Suffield, respectively; and U.S. Route 202 from Danbury to Granby.

The designation of an ongoing federal highway program helped states like Connecticut in several ways. First, the influx of federal funds added to the budgetary power and prestige of the Connecticut Highway Department. Second, the highways assigned to the federal system, interstate in character, were by definition more heavily traveled, and therefore more costly than other routes to improve and maintain. Third, federal approval and funding of highway projects allowed the federal government to institute policy requirements, such as design standards, that improved safety and created uniformity from state to state. But most importantly, the Federal Aid Highway Act of 1921 established a megagovernmental model of joint federal-state cooperation and financing that through the years could be expanded to match the state's expanding highway needs. It was also a model that would be adapted to federal funding for other transportation programs, such as aviation, and later to nontransportation social programs as well.

In the 1920s, with the federal-state partnership firmly established by the new highway act and much of the state's trunk line system of roads *and* bridges now firmly in state hands, Connecticut's highway program entered a new phase. As car engines became more powerful, highwaymen turned their attention from paving to other roadway characteristics, such as lane width, gradient, and sight line. Existing roadways were not just paved over but straightened; bridges were widened; hills were flattened to lower the steepness of a grade; and other dangerous situations, such as at-grade railroad crossings were modified or eliminated. At times, the need for such improvements resulted in a complete relocation of a roadway, moved to a new right-of-way and rebuilt to modern specifications. And of course, as trucks became larger, small bridges needed to be rebuilt to accommodate heavier loads.[42]

To pay for this never-ending cycle of highway improvements, Connecticut, like many states, resorted to a tax on gasoline. Connecticut passed its first gas tax law in 1921, imposing a one-cent per gallon tax on all gasoline sold in the state. Two years later, in keeping with the idea that highway users should pay directly for the care of the roads they traveled, gas tax revenue in Connecticut was dedicated to a separate Highway Fund to be used for highway purposes only, at the discretion of the state highway commissioner. As a result, by 1927, the state highway program had three main sources of revenue: the state gas tax (by then 2¢ per gallon), fees charged to register motor vehicles and license drivers, and federal monies from the general fund of the United States dedicated to the construction and maintenance of the state's federal highway system. Such was the increase in motor vehicle registrations and gasoline consumption that by 1928, despite the expanding responsibilities of the Connecticut Highway Department, the state's highway program had become financially self-sufficient, able to fund projects from these three dedicated sources of revenue without the need for money from the state's general fund.[43]

The Connecticut Highway Department was the largest and fastest-growing agency of state government, with an annual budget that grew from $45,000 in 1896 to $16,000,000 in 1928. That year, the department was reorganized into five bureaus: engineering and construction, business administration, maintenance, roadside development, and boundaries and right-of-way. The offices of the newly reconstituted department were then relocated to a new State Office Building constructed on Capitol Avenue in Hartford, its very existence a sign that other areas of state government were growing too in their bureaucracy, albeit not as rapidly as the Connecticut Highway Department.[44]

In 1931, the Connecticut Highway Department expanded its responsibilities yet again by creating a town-aid program through which it passed state funds to towns for use in local highway improvements, in much the way that the national government passed funds to the state for use on federal-aid highways. The town-aid program represented the final piece of an interlocking, three-tiered program of highway improvements (federal, state, and town) held together by a powerful megagovernment bureaucracy controlling interagency financing.[45]

Though highway revenues declined during the Great Depression to a level of about twelve million dollars per year, the Connecticut Highway Department remained one of the most powerful state agencies, still able to fund highway improvements on a pay-as-you-go basis without the need for long-term borrowing by the state. In a span of just four decades, Connecticut highways had gone from a network of unkempt nineteenth-century earthen turnpikes to a modern system of primary, secondary, and local highways (and bridges) built for the auto age, maintained by a three-level megagovernment arrangement of highway agencies, and paid for one hundred percent with public tax dollars.

Only one blemish spoiled this nearly perfect picture. In the state's larger cities, and most especially along the lower post road from Greenwich to New Haven, a new phenomenon appeared on Connecticut highways: bumper-to-bumper traffic. As travel speeds, traffic congestion, and the number of traffic accidents all increased, engineers were suddenly faced with new questions: was there a limit to the amount of traffic a normal highway could handle? If so, how were they to accommodate the seemingly endless desire for travel and commerce unleashed by the automobile, bus, and truck?

The answer they devised involved a new kind of highway, a highway so different from what had come before that it might even be considered a new mode of transportation, one uniquely adapted to the age of automobility. That new kind of highway—where a driver entered and exited a road only at designated interchanges, and in between was able to travel at high speed unaffected by roadside distractions—was in effect a concrete railroad for the automobile, truck, and bus. Highway engineers had a name for it: the controlled-access expressway. In the 1930s, one of the first of its kind in the nation was built across Connecticut as part of the state's first high-speed highway link between New York and Boston. Reminiscent of the privately owned New York & Boston Automobile Boulevard toll road first proposed in 1907, the new controlled-access highway would be owned by the state and built with public funds, though in the end it too would become a toll highway—one known as the Merritt Parkway.

Highways and the Progressive Movement

In the half century from 1870 to 1920, a broad social movement known as progressivism touched many aspects of American life, including highway transportation.

As the twentieth century turned and immigration from Europe continued unabated, the population of Connecticut reached more than 900,000 persons, 56 percent of whom lived in sixteen industrialized cities around the state—on less than 10 percent of the state's land area. Problems of overcrowding, sanitation, and traffic control became commonplace. Traditional politics and boss cronyism could no longer handle such concentrated and chaotic growth effectively. In an effort to create a different, more modern social order, government at all levels became more specialized, more bureaucratic, organized around bureaus or commissions headed by professional managers whose expertise was more technical than political.

The approach was not unlike that adopted by railroads and other big businesses in the decades following the Civil War, as private corporations of all kinds grew larger and more complex. In the world of commerce, this bureaucratic approach transformed traditional market capitalism into a new kind of business model referred to as managerial capitalism.

In much the same way, as town, state, and national governments grew in size and complexity to regulate problems created by urban growth, they created a new kind of model for governing, one that might similarly be termed managerial government.

The establishment of an independent Highway Commission in 1895 and its reorganization into the powerful state agency known as the Connecticut Highway Department in the first decades of the new century provides a perfect example in transportation of the transition from a form of government where elected representatives of the people were responsible for important governmental activity—remember the legislators who traveled the state in 1897 to gather information for the state's first highway improvement program—to a new kind of government, where most governmental duties were now executed by unelected, professional managers whose specialized expertise made them not only preferable but necessary. In the case of highways, the matter was even more entrenched. In much the way that managerial capitalism was further complicated by corporate mergers and interlocking directorates, the new model of managerial government for highway transportation was further complicated by the interlocking relationships of interdependent federal, state, and town highway agencies, in Connecticut and throughout the nation.

This transition to both managerial capitalism and managerial government was itself part of a broad social movement known as progressivism that touched on many aspects of American life in the half century from 1870 to 1920. The progressive agenda included such movements as the fight for healthier housing in the tenements of New York and Chicago; women's suffrage and alcoholic temperance; labor struggles for an eight-hour day and a ban on the use of child workers in factories; an attempt to purify the population through the pseudoscience of eugenics, where persons considered unfit to have children were sterilized to prevent them from diluting the general population with unsuitable offspring; the City Beautiful movement that sought to build grand boulevards, plazas, and civic centers, and thereby improve the moral character of those surrounded by such man-made beauty; the creation of the nation's first national park and forest lands as part of a larger effort to conserve America's natural resources; and numerous other expressions of what was considered progressive thought.[46] However, it is important to note that the progressive movement was hardly a uniform phenomenon. Though heavily promoted by a rising urban middle class eager to replace small-town values with big-city ideals, the old ways continued to exist side by side with the new throughout the progressive era, especially in Connecticut where rural majorities continued to exert antiprogressive influence in the state legislature whenever they could.[47]

In addition to the megagovernment bureaucracy of the state's highway program, there were two additional aspects of progressive thinking that proved significant with regard to transportation. The first was the concept of scientific management developed by Frederick Winslow Taylor in 1911. The principles of scientific management were originally designed to promote efficiency in the workplace, but as Taylor was quick to point out, the technique could be applied to the management of any social activity, from business to home to government. At the heart of scientific management was the measurement, quantification, and tabulation of work processes in a well-thought-out scientific manner, along with an analysis of the data collected by a team of technical experts. Through his association with the progressive movement, Taylor's ideas for the use of technological expertise wherever possible as a means to a better, more progressive society were spread nationwide, and Taylor himself became as popular as Henry Ford.[48]

The application of scientific management to highway transportation in Connecticut was a natural fit. As early as 1926, the Connecticut Highway Department (in partnership with the federal Office of Road Inquiry, now known as the Bureau of Public Roads) completed its first comprehensive survey of the state's existing highway system. Wherever possible state engineers applied the techniques of scientific management to the investigation. For instance, the survey included such items as a detailed organizational chart of the Highway Department and its several management bureaus; a year-by-year tally of the state's increasing motor vehicle registrations in comparison to its total population; an inventory and classification of state highway mileage by type and existing condition; a tabulation of highway revenues and expenditures by town; traffic counts made by field workers at fifty-seven survey stations around the state; and an "O&D" questionnaire given to the traveling public to ascertain the origin and destination of their most frequent trips and the routes they took to get there.[49]

A third way in which progressive thought impacted the development of the Connecticut highway system was in the area of planning. A logical extension of the principles of scientific management, when applied

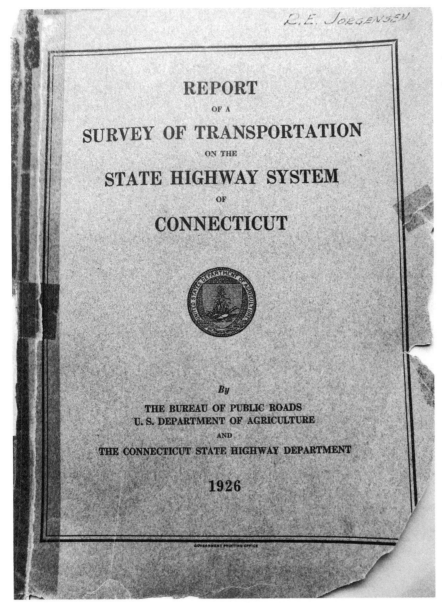

to highway transportation, was to analyze the years of data collected on various subjects (population, motor vehicle ownership, traffic volumes) so as to recognize trends and to project these trends into future needs. Then, by imposing the projected needs onto the existing highway system, engineers could estimate what if any improvements might be required and how much they might cost. As the survey itself stated, "The establishment of scientific plans of highway development . . . requires a careful analysis of highway traffic, the trend of its development, and its distribution over the highway system." In the past, the study noted, highway engineers were handicapped by "the lack of precise knowledge of the character and amount of the traffic using the various roads." No longer. The very purpose of the survey was "to provide a basis for the scientific planning of highway improvements in Connecticut."[50]

The scientific management of transportation improvements represented a major shift in the way highway engineers approached their job. No longer would engineers be lagging behind in their work, trying to solve yesterday's problem only after congestion had become apparent. Using the tools of scientific management, they were now able to look ahead ten, twenty, or more years into the future, identify potential problem areas, and estimate the cost of the highway improvements needed to provide an acceptable level of service. The culmination of this application of scientific management to highway improvement was a turn away from solving today's problems to providing for tomorrow's needs, and from now on a kind of *futurism* would pervade the work of highway engineers—and not always in a sensible way. As we shall see, scientific management was hardly a foolproof methodology, especially when applied to a single-minded highways-only transportation policy.

The Impact of Automobility

The advent of automobility allowed families to move out of crowded urban centers into surrounding rural towns, created a profession of city and town planners looking for progressive ways to shape this emerging urban-suburban environment, and challenged the sustainability of the state's existing railroad, steamboat, and trolley services.

TO THE SUBURBS: RESETTLING THE LAND

With the advent of automobility and the proliferation of good roads, residents who were overcrowded into urban centers around the state began to move outward into the open spaces that existed on the fringes of most cities, resettling the Connecticut landscape yet again.

It is important to recognize that the move to the suburbs typically associated with the postwar boom of the 1960s did not begin in the 1960s. It did not even begin with the construction of controlled-access highways into city centers in the 1940s. In fact, it began with the building of interurban trolley lines in the late nineteenth century, which provided the means for those who could afford it to leave Connecticut's crowded cities for nearby rural areas. At the same time that the proliferation of tall buildings, elevators, the telephone, and the department store concentrated economic activity in an urban core, the trolley doubled, even tripled, the effective size of many urban areas by providing radial access to the core from ever greater distances, allowing the dense population of the walking city to spread out along the direction of each streetcar line. (Steam railroads provided a similar opportunity even earlier, but to a lesser degree; their station stops were farther apart.) Indeed, streetcar companies encouraged this first wave of suburbanization by constructing lines into open country and charging a fixed five-cent fare, which relied on volume, as opposed to a zone system, where fares increased with the distance traveled.[51]

Other factors, too, made the move out of the city to the suburbs feasible in the early auto age, including the development of lighter, timber-frame housing that replaced heavier post-and-beam construction. This modern, balloon-frame house was quicker and easier to build, which translated into lower home prices. In addition, towns and cities themselves stimulated the move to the suburbs by their willingness to extend urban services—paved streets, water and sewer lines, police and fire protection—into outlying areas at public expense, thereby subsidizing the increase in land values along streetcar lines and encouraging the subdivision of rural lands. It should be noted, however, that the movement of affluent and working-class citizens to the periphery of the city was not historically inevitable. It was the product of market forces, government policies, and new technologies, in particular a combination of affordable housing and cheap, convenient transportation. Suburbanization was a uniquely American phenomenon unlike, for example, the European experience.[52]

Suburbanization in Connecticut began in earnest in the 1920s, the decade that automobility first became widespread. And the automobile, together with the extensive road network provided by megagovernment highway agencies, changed the pattern of resettlement significantly from what it had been in the streetcar era. The automobile made it possible for those exiting the city to go almost anywhere they wished with street access. No longer dependent on a linear trolley line for travel to the city, the move to the suburbs now became omnidirectional, the only restraint being the time it took to commute back and forth from a home in the suburbs to work and shopping opportunities in the city.

In Connecticut, the impact of automobility on the movement outward from city to suburb after 1920 can be seen in the increase in population of small towns around the state adjacent to larger cities. One of the largest transformations took place in the town of West Hartford, whose 1920 population of 9,000 grew to 34,000 by 1940. Similar if less dramatic growth occurred in numerous other communities around the state, where population growth over the decades previously measured in hundreds of persons now commonly numbered in the thousands. For example, from 1920 to 1940, the population of Waterford increased from 4,000 to 6,600; Farmington, from 3,800 to 5,300; Stratford, from 12,300 to 22,600; and Hamden, from 8,600 to 23,000.[53]

The percentage of the state's population living in Connecticut cities peaked in 1920 at 63 percent. Thereafter, the percentage declined at a slow but steady pace, as towns that had been rural and agricultural in character, continued to grow more quickly than the state's urban core. The process of suburbanization that began in the 1920s would accelerate in the postwar decades, so that by the year 2000, with the state's total population having increased (fourfold) to 3.4 million, only 37 percent of Connecticut residents would live in cities. By any measure, it was one of the most amazing transformations of the Connecticut landscape in history—and it was automobility (the automobile *plus* megagovernment-sponsored highway building) that made it possible.[54]

There was recognition among engineers and city planners as early as the 1920s that the dispersal of population from Connecticut cities represented more than just a move to the suburbs. They began to see how the movement of people out of the cities created a new political entity on the landscape: the region, a multitown locality that reflected the economic interdependence of the newer suburb and the older city. It can be said that the idea of regional planning took hold in 1922 with the creation of the Committee on a Regional Plan for New York and Its Environs in New York City. Over the next decade, this group surveyed the growth needs of not only the city itself but adjacent portions of New York, New Jersey, and Connecticut as well. Their work sparked early planning efforts in Fairfield County. It would take several decades for the concept of regional planning to spread to the whole of Connecticut, but in the end it is this process of regionalization, creating a new political entity out of city and suburb combined, and not suburbanization alone, that best describes the transformation of the Connecticut landscape in the twentieth century.[55]

CONNECTICUT CITIES: ORGANIZING THE LAND

Even as the move to the suburbs was underway, Connecticut cities began to adopt progressive cures of their own to lessen the ills of urban living for those left behind. By beautifying public places and rebuilding urban centers in a neoclassical style, the progressive reformers believed they could inspire higher moral values among the populace. The first expression of the Beaux Arts style in America—named after the school in Paris where architects were trained in such designs—was at the World Columbian Exposition of 1893 in Chicago, and the concept of city planning in the Beaux Arts style was soon adopted by many American cities, including Chicago in 1896, Washington, D.C., in 1901, and San Francisco in 1906. With impetus from the City Beautiful movement, the city of Hartford created the nation's first City Planning Commission in 1907, and other Connecticut cities soon organized similar commissions: New Haven in 1910, Bridgeport in 1913, and New Britain in 1915. By 1946, twenty-seven cities and towns in Connecticut had planning commissions.[56]

While the planning process helped cities focus on the need for open spaces to provide relief from urban life, and wider streets to accommodate faster-moving automotive traffic, the long-lasting contribution of early city planning was in the concept of zoning, or dividing up the landscape according to how the land was to be utilized. Zoning typically restricted each parcel of land in a community to a specific type of

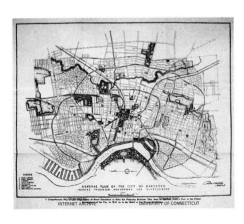

With the Hartford City Plan of 1910, city planning began in Connecticut.
Hartford Commission on the City Plan

use—residential, commercial, or industrial—while establishing building lines and height limits to control the size and location of structures on the building lot, and street lines to delineate the location of new roads. The first zoning laws in the Northeast were adopted in New York City in 1916.

There was, however, immediate concern that restricting the use of privately owned land through zoning might be unconstitutional. For example, were not the creation of building and street lines the equivalent of land taking, and should not a land owner be compensated by the town for that portion of his property that he could no longer build on? The Connecticut Supreme Court tackled the issue early on in *Town of Windsor v. Henry D. Whitney, et al.* In that case, the court determined that such zoning actions were "a legitimate exercise of the police power of the State, as distinguished from the power of eminent domain," under which an owner must be compensated for land taken for public use. In what became a landmark decision on the matter, the court concluded that "the State may regulate any business, or the use of any property, in the interest of public health, safety or welfare, and without making compensation, provided this is done reasonably."[57] The constitutionality of zoning was upheld by the U.S. Supreme Court in *Village of Euclid v. Ambler Realty Company* in 1925, which made zoning a legal expression of a community's policing powers as long as it was applied without prejudice to the entire community and not only to certain property owners.

The Connecticut legislature endorsed zoning for specific Connecticut cities beginning in 1921, and four years later passed general legislation that empowered all Connecticut cities, towns, and boroughs to create zoning agencies to control the bulk and use of structures in their communities, as well as the density of their population. The concept of zoning as an adjunct to progressive city planning proved particularly popular in Connecticut. By 1946, more than half the towns in Connecticut had zoning commissions, many of which were combined into a local planning and zoning commission. As one report noted, "There is no state in which zoning has proved more acceptable."[58]

While planning and zoning allowed cities and towns to organize the landscape according to progressive principles, neither resolved the most egregious problem of city life: unfair and undemocratic representation in state politics. According to the state constitution, Connecticut towns had either one or two representatives in the General Assembly, regardless of population. As a result of the urbanization of large cities after the Civil War, Connecticut's system of representative government, a holdover from colonial times, abrogated the political rights of the majority of the state's residents. For example, by 1889, the demographic changes that occurred during the nineteenth century allowed 11,851 voters living among sixty small towns to elect a total of seventy-six representatives to the state's General Assembly, while the 17,827 voters then living in New Haven could elected only two. And the discrepancy became more disparate as urbanization progressed. In 1900, the town of Union with a population of 400 persons had two representatives in the state assembly, the same number as the city of New Haven with a population of 108,000. It is no wonder that Connecticut's unbalanced system of representation became known in progressive circles as the "rotten borough" system.[59]

In 1901, progressive reformers took up the cause of "rotten borough" politics by calling for a state constitutional convention to address the issue. However, when the convention was organized the following year, its composition reflected the very problem it was called upon to resolve: regardless of its size, each town could send only one delegate to the convention! To no one's surprise, the convention achieved little. One delegate commented boldly on the heart of the problem, if not its legal ramifications: while it is agreed, he said, "that town representation is illogical . . . [and with] no legal justification . . . it is a sentiment which should be cherished and perpetuated."[60] In the end, the convention penned a new draft constitution that increased urban representation slightly, but in a subsequent referendum the voters turned down even this modest improvement.

While Connecticut cities were quick to adopt progressive ideas such as town planning and zoning, the state had failed to redress what after centuries of abuse had become the most egregious problem of life in the city: the unfair representation of city dwellers in the assembly halls of the state capitol. The disparity of the "rotten borough" system of representation would continue well into the 1960s before Connecticut was forced to rectify the situation by a decree of the U.S. Supreme Court. In the meantime, the unearned political control exerted by rural towns under the "rotten borough" system would continue to cast a strong Republican influence over state politics, and in the 1930s would give rise to one of the most flagrant scandals in all of the state's history: the Merritt Parkway land fraud.

The construction of an improved highway network in Connecticut, and the increase in car, truck, and motor bus travel that it made feasible, had a significant impact on the state's existing system of railroad, steamboat, and trolley services operated by the New Haven Railroad. To begin with, there was the direct competition between the fixed route, fixed schedule mass transportation provided by the New Haven, and the more flexible door-to-door service associated with the automobile. The local nature of much of the New Haven's passenger and freight traffic made its rail, steamboat, and trolley operations especially vulnerable to competition from the automobile and the truck. But what railroad managers complained about even more was the unfair nature of that competition. As

Unfair competition. How was a private railroad, responsible for its own infrastructure, supposed to compete with a publicly built highway network? Courtesy of the Hartford Courant

one news cartoon put it, how was a privately owned railroad responsible for its own infrastructure—tracks, stations, bridges, signals, and switching yards—expected to compete with cars, trucks, and buses whose infrastructure, from local streets to secondary collector roads to trunk line highways, was provided for them by the government and paid for with public tax dollars? Yet that was exactly the situation created by the "highways only" policy of the state and federal megagovernment that supported highway construction to the detriment of private transportation corporations such as the New Haven.

As a result of decisions made in 1903 by J. P. Morgan (banker to the New Haven) and Charles S. Mellen (president of the New Haven) to expand the company's operations to other modes of transportation in an effort to create a monopoly over transportation services throughout New England, the debt burden of the New Haven increased dramatically. In the years from 1903 to 1913, Morgan and Mellen increased the capitalization of the New Haven from $93 million to $417 million. Of this increase, only $120 million was spent on rail-related properties and improvements; the remaining $204 million was invested in the acquisition of steamboat and trolley properties, often at prices well above their industry values. To make matters worse, many of the purchases were made in a financially questionable manner, using dozens of subsidiary companies to manipulate New Haven assets and create paper profits designed to deceive stock- and bondholders on the true financial condition of the company.

An investigation of the New Haven's shady dealings by the Interstate Commerce Commission led to a federal court decree in 1914 intended to divest the transportation monopoly created under Morgan and Mellen of its more controversial assets, including its controlling interest in the Boston & Maine Railroad, as well as its steamboat and trolley properties. These assets were placed into the hands of court-appointed trustees and marked for sale. However, before divestiture could be accomplished, the federal government in 1920 reversed its long-held position against the consolidation of railroads as an instrument of monopoly. Instead, in the Transportation Act of 1920, Congress directed the Interstate Commerce Commission (ICC) to devise a plan to deliberately consolidate the nation's major railroads into a number of more efficient, more profitable regional systems. It was hoped that by judiciously combining stronger roads with weaker ones and eliminating duplicate services, financially troubled railroads such as the New Haven could be reorganized into a national network of sustainable, but still privately owned railroads. As a result of this change in policy, the New Haven succeeded in having the court decree of 1914 modified to regain control of most of its divested assets. As the New Haven's annual report notified stockholders in 1925, the court decree "was so modified that all remaining properties taken away from your company in 1914 were returned to it."[61]

Meanwhile, study after study was completed to determine how best to consolidate the New Haven and its various transportation services with other New England railroads and thereby increase its competitiveness with automotive highway services. Two main alternatives emerged: either to combine the New Haven and other New England roads with strong trunk line roads from outside the region, such as the Pennsylvania Railroad or the New York Central, whose systems provided access to cross-country rail service, or to combine all New England roads into one large regional system, thereby increasing the viability of what was essentially a terminal rail network, designed to collect and distribute freight throughout the region.[62]

After more than a decade of shilly-shallying by the railroads, many of which simply refused to discuss the possibility of consolidation, and with the ICC unable by law to impose a consolidation plan on the railroads, the possibility of consolidation as a means to improved rail service disappeared in the 1930s amid the general economic uncertainty of the Great Depression. Which is not to say that the New Haven stood by and did nothing to improve its competitiveness against the onslaught of automobility.

To begin with, the New Haven in the 1920s converted the equipment it operated on many of its branch lines from steam locomotives to self-propelled, diesel-powered rail bus cars. With a top speed of forty-five miles per hour and needing only a two-man crew to transport up to forty-five passengers, these cars were able to provide passenger and freight service at a fraction of the cost of a traditional steam-driven train. By the 1930s, some branch lines were abandoned altogether while others were converted to larger, sixty-five-passenger gas-electric railcars capable of speeds of fifty-five miles per hour.[63]

In 1925, the New Haven Railroad organized the New England Transportation Company, a wholly owned subsidiary created to transport passengers, freight, mail, and express packages throughout the region. The primary purpose of these automotive bus lines was "to provide a

The gas-powered rail bus was an early attempt by the New Haven Railroad to compete with the automobile. New York, New Haven & Hartford Railroad

coordinated service with the rail company's trains, reducing the number of station stops, and permitting the discontinuance of some uneconomical train service." Within a few years, the company was operating more than 150 buses over more than one thousand route miles.[64]

Automobility also impacted the New Haven's steamboat services. By 1916, as highway improvements spread through the region, trucks became a viable alternative to shipping freight by steamer for trips up to fifty miles in length. As a result, freight tonnage on the New Haven system, which had always been more important than the revenue from passenger service, dropped nearly 50 percent between 1917 and 1921 and continued to fall throughout the 1920s, though not as precipitously. In addition, in the period between the two World Wars, many manufacturers moved out of New England for points south and west, so that all modes were competing for a smaller amount of total freight tonnage. As a result, long-running steamboat service from New York City was abandoned piecemeal: to Bridgeport and New Haven in 1920, to Hartford the following year, and on the outer sound to New London and Norwich in 1934. A strike by steamboat workers in July 1937 finally put an end to all steamboat service on Long Island Sound.

As steamer service to New York City came to an end in the 1930s, the New England Transportation Company added a fleet of gasoline-powered trucks to its operations in an effort to compete for freight traffic. Two express freight trains with motor-truck feeders served many major cities in the New Haven's territory, including New York and Boston, under

In another attempt to compete with the internal combustion engine, the New Haven Railroad considered establishing its own airline, in partnership with Trans World Airlines, to be called TWA New England. However, ticket pricing proved too expensive, and the service was never begun.
New York, New Haven & Hartford Railroad

the motto "Accept Today—Deliver Tomorrow." To attract new long-distance rail passengers, the New Haven also introduced the Yankee Clipper in 1930, its fastest-ever train service from New York to Boston, which traveled the distance between the two cities in a speedy four hours and forty-five minutes.[65]

Last of all, the Connecticut Company, operator of the New Haven's street railways in cities around Connecticut, announced in 1931 that it planned to substitute motor buses for trolley service on its interurban lines, where thanks to the automobile, large-capacity trolley cars were no longer required. Over the decade, as the popularity of the automobile continued to rise, some intracity trolley lines that had become unprofitable were abandoned, while others were replaced with gasoline-powered motor buses, as once well-used trolley tracks were paved over in city after city around the state. By 1941, those routes still remaining in the Connecticut Company's Hartford Division were completely converted to motor bus service, though some electric trolleys continued to run on the streets of New Haven until 1948.[66]

Yet despite all these attempts to adapt to the new world of automobility, the debt accumulated during the Morgan and Mellen expansion still encumbered the New Haven's balance sheet. It was only through a combination of good management, belt tightening, and federal loans authorized by the Emergency Transportation Act of 1933 that the New Haven was able to remain afloat during the early years of the Great Depression, even as the corporation's gross revenues declined from $142 million in 1929 to $71 million in 1935. Still, the inevitable could not be postponed forever. Unable to cover the interest on its bonded debt, and with no further outside loans forthcoming, the New Haven Railroad finally filed for bankruptcy on October 23, 1935.

What followed was a prolonged corporate reorganization that required twelve years, eleven ICC reports, fourteen circuit court decisions, and eight U.S. Supreme Court decisions to untangle the financial affairs of the New Haven and its subsidiaries. At the heart of the road's financial rehabilitation was the elimination of $200 million in bonded debt, an amount not coincidently similar to that squandered by Morgan and Mellen on their steamboat and trolley purchases a generation earlier. As the ICC noted, "It is apparent that the losses resulting from the New Haven's investment in other companies are more than sufficient to explain the profit-and-loss deficit existing as of October 23, 1935."[67] Indeed, what was remarkable was that the New Haven managed to remain solvent for as long as it did following the financial mischief created by Morgan and Mellen. But in the end, even with a combination of competitive initiatives, good management, and outside financial assistance, the once mighty New Haven, try as it might, could not outrun its own history.

Chapter Two **Connecticut Takes to the Sky**

In addition to its impact on ground transportation, the internal combustion engine allowed humankind to turn its ancient dream of flight into reality. Overall, the history of aviation in Connecticut mirrors the history of aviation in general and follows a similar timeline, from colonial-era hot-air balloons and post-Civil War dirigibles to early-twentieth-century heavier-than-air flying machines and the coming of the jet age in the 1960s. However, the history of aviation in Connecticut also contains the controversial case of Gustave Whitehead, a German immigrant living in Bridgeport, who some claim achieved heavier-than-air flight in an aircraft of his own design two years before the Wright brothers. In the decades between two world wars, experimentation by daredevil pilots evolved into a national aviation industry and Connecticut became home to one of America's most influential aviation companies, Pratt & Whitney Aircraft. After World War II, as the role of the national government in aviation affairs expanded, a federal-state partnership was established similar to that already existing in highway construction. With federal and state assistance, Connecticut developed an infrastructure of state and municipal airfields to accommodate the aviation needs of the state. By the 1960s, state-owned Bradley International Airport—the second largest airport in New England—emerged as the mainstay of modern aviation in Connecticut.

Progress through Experimentation

Aviation in Connecticut began with foolhardy experiments in ballooning, dirigibility, and powered flight (including the controversial work of Gustave Whitehead) and by the 1920s had produced the state's first airports and commercial air services.

LIGHTER-THAN-AIR FLIGHT: BALLOONS AND DIRIGIBLES

Mankind's fascination with flight in the modern era—a fascination that would lead to the achievements of the Wright brothers early in the twentieth century—had its roots in the scientific experiments of the Enlightenment, particularly in the work of English scientist Joseph

Priestley in the seventeenth century. Priestley discovered that the air around us was composed of different gasses, including hydrogen, which by itself was much lighter than common air. With this discovery came the realization that if an object could be filled with hydrogen so that its total weight was less than that of the weight of air it displaced, it would rise up from the surface of the earth and into the atmosphere. This knowledge resulted in the first manned balloon flights in and around Paris in 1783, which used spherical balloons made of silk or taffeta fabric, coated with a form of liquefied rubber to seal the outer surface of the balloon.[1]

Two years after the first balloon ascension in Paris, Josiah Meigs, a former senior tutor at Yale College and the editor of the *New Haven Gazette*, initiated the balloon era in Connecticut by flying an unmanned cylindrical balloon eleven feet long and eight feet wide, and made of paper, above the New Haven green. A record of the flight survives in the diary of Ezra Stiles, president of Yale College. According to Stiles, on the evening of April 24, 1785, Meigs's balloon reached a height of some three hundred feet, while during a second try the following noontime rose only to a height "nearly equal the Top of the Brick Steeple [Church on the Green]" before being taken downwind on a southerly breeze a distance of fifty or sixty rods to land near the house of a Mr. Pierpont.[2] During a third attempt on May 4, a new spherical-shaped balloon eleven feet in diameter and "decorated with the figure of an Angel flying . . . took fire in its ascent, and being converted into a pyramid of flame at its greatest height, exhibited a grand and pleasing object to the Spectators, who had only to regret that the same spectacle was not shown in the night."[3]

A first tentative step toward manned balloon flight occurred in Connecticut in the summer of 1800, when a man named John Graham advertised in the *Connecticut Courant* for ascensions in a balloon tethered to the ground, which he erected on a hill near Hartford's south green. The balloon was attached to a mechanical winch that allowed Graham to raise and lower up to eight passengers "with slow and steady or more rapid movements as they may order; so that persons of a timid cast will enter with assurance and be much delighted; others may progress 500 yards per minute." The charge was nine pence per passenger. The scheme—certainly one of the first commercial aviation ventures in the new nation—had been patented a year earlier by a Massachusetts man named Moses McFarland and was operated by Graham under "a deed of exclusive right for the county of Hartford." Though the Graham-McFarland balloon ascension was presented in the spirit of good fun, much like an early carnival ride, it was also advertised as having a possible health benefit. By ascending in a balloon, "healthy persons may experience pleasure and delight," while those feeling less well "may regain their health by a sudden change of air and atmosphere, and a sudden revulsion of the blood and humors."[4]

Free, untethered balloon flights in Connecticut were infrequent before the Civil War.[5] However, the use of balloon flights during the Civil War to survey and photograph the placement of troops and fortifications on the battlefield popularized the sport of ballooning across America in the postwar decades. One famous balloonist of the late nineteenth century was a native of Plymouth, Connecticut, named Silas Brooks. Brooks was a musician who began his career in the 1840s working for Connecticut's preeminent huckster, P. T. Barnum. After touring with a band of "authentic Druid musicians" that Brooks himself had created on Barnum's instruction,[6] Brooks formed his own circus troupe in Cleveland, Ohio, in the 1850s that included an aeronaut who lifted off in an untethered balloon flight at each performance. One day, with the regular balloonist ill, Brooks took his place and discovered his true calling. During a subsequent circus career that lasted forty years, Brooks made 187 balloon ascensions and became an aeronaut of national repute.[7]

One notable ascension made by Brooks occurred on the Fourth of July, 1884, at Cherry Hill Park in Collinsville, Connecticut. That day, Brooks attracted spectators to his show by filling his balloon with hydrogen gas manufactured on site in "one of the greatest experiments ever witnessed." The hydrogen gas was made in large retorts from a combination of five thousand gallons of water, twenty-four hundred pounds of sulfuric acid, and two thousand pounds of wrought-iron turnings. As an added attraction, Brooks took with him in the balloon a small dog, which he then tossed overboard—having first attached the dog to a small parachute.[8]

The main disadvantage of balloon flight, its susceptibility to wind and weather, was obvious from the first, and men looked for ways to control the flight of a lighter-than-air balloon in windy conditions. Their solution was the dirigible, a balloon-like ship with or without a rigid inner frame that utilized a power source of some kind, along with a rudder, by which a pilot could navigate through the air to achieve directed flight. While dirigible experiments were being conducted in France in the 1870s, Bridgeport inventor Charles F. Ritchel designed Connecticut's first dirigible flying machine, a crude, hand-cranked dirigible made out of a rubberized gasbag manufactured by Goodyear Rubber of Naugatuck. Ritchel's dirigible was described in the *Hartford Daily Courant* as follows:

A black silk cylinder, some twelve feet in diameter and twenty-four in length. The cylinder will hold nearly 3000 feet of gas. Suspended from the gasbag by means of cords and rods is a car composed of slender brass rods which extend the whole length of the cylinder, tapering to a point at either end. The platform upon which the operator sits is attached to the center of the car. Two cranks, attached to a wheel, front the seat. The wheel connects to an upright shaft, and to this at the lower end is attached a fan closely resembling the screw of a propeller. The fan, which is constructed of thin brass plates, is level with the bottom of the platform. Another brass fan is affixed to the front end of the car, and this is so constructed that it can be turned in any direction by the occupant simply moving his feet, while at the same time he can work the center fan with his hands. When the occupant prepared for his flight, the silk cylinder is filled with hydrogen gas. This will sustain all but a fraction of the weight to be carried, and the rest is lifted by the central fan, which presses upon the air with a movement similar to that of a propeller wheel in the water. A man of ordinary strength can revolve the handles at a rate of about 100 per minute, which will give the fan about 3,500 revolutions.[9]

Having first flight-tested his patented "Flying Machine" inside one of the surviving exhibition halls of the 1876 Centennial Exposition in Philadelphia, Ritchel brought his flying machine to Hartford to conduct the first outdoor flight of a dirigible in America on June 12, 1878. The pilot on that historic occasion was a young, lightweight man named Mark Quinland, who took to the air from a field behind Colt's Armory before a crowd of spectators who paid fifteen cents each to view the event. Cranking away as fast as he could, Quinland lifted himself into the air, sailed above the Armory Building and out over the Connecticut River, circling back to the park to land without incident. A second flight was attempted the following day, but a strong wind overcame the pilot's ability to maneuver the craft and drove the dirigible off course to a landing in Newington, thus proving the need for a power source greater than that provided by hand cranking. Ritchel also flew his dirigible in Boston and later built and sold five of his flying machines, all the while making plans for a larger version of his design to be powered by a crew of eleven aeronauts, hand-cranking in unison, for long-distance travel. Although

Charles F. Ritchel's successful dirigible flight in Hartford made national headline news. Harper's Weekly, *1874*

Ritchel's experiments made no lasting contribution to the future technology of the dirigible, the success of his flight in Hartford demonstrated that it was possible for a man to take off in a lighter-than-air craft, control the path of flight, and return to his point of departure. It was an aeronautical first that was widely reported and gave encouragement to aviation enthusiasts everywhere.[10]

Early experiments in balloons and dirigibles also led to Connecticut's first excursion into the business of building aircraft when in 1913 a group of businessmen incorporated the Connecticut Aeroplane Company in New Haven. Though the company had originally intended to build heavier-than-air aircraft, its directors, including former Connecticut governor Rollin S. Woodruff, partnered instead with Thomas S. Baldwin, a pioneer in the construction of lighter-than-air aircraft, and redirected the company's focus to the building of dirigibles. To that end, the company purchased a factory building in New Haven along with a former army airfield in Maryland and changed its name to the Connecticut Aircraft Company—the first company in the nation devoted exclusively to the construction of balloons and dirigibles. When Congress appropriated one million dollars for aeronautics in 1915, the navy awarded its first dirigible contract to the Connecticut Aircraft Company. The aim of the government contract was to stimulate the manufacture of dirigibles in America and to train naval officers in the science of aeronautics. The company's first dirigibles measured 175 feet in length and 65 feet in height, had a two-ply, nonrigid rubberized envelope, and were powered by a 140 horsepower, eight-cylinder gasoline engine that could keep a crew of eight airmen aloft for several hours while moving through the air at a speed of thirty miles per hour.[11]

In March 1917, Congress appropriated another five million dollars for aeronautics, including funds for a fleet of sixteen smaller navy dirigibles, approximately half the size of the original model. While the Goodyear Tire & Rubber Company of Akron, Ohio, built most of the fleet, other contractors were used as well, including the Connecticut Aircraft Company, which manufactured two of the sixteen blimps. By summer of that same year, the fleet of blimps, each carrying a two-man crew and staying aloft for ten hours at a time, was commissioned to guard the country's Atlantic coastline during World War I.[12]

The fortunes of the Connecticut Aircraft Company improved during the war, as it built 185 observation and supply balloons for the United States Army. The observation balloons, twenty-five feet in diameter and eighty-two feet high, were able to carry a pilot and one observer to a height of three to four thousand feet. Because of the danger from enemy gunfire, the airmen had to also be trained as parachute jumpers. However, once the war ended, the company was unable to find any customers, and floundered. In 1921, the Connecticut Aircraft Company was taken over by the Aircraft Construction Transportation Company of Delaware, which hoped to use the company's factory in New Haven to build a line of large zeppelin-like airships that it would then put into commercial service between New York and Chicago. But the airships never left the drawing board, and the new company dissolved in March 1926, ending Connecticut's early foray into the aviation industry.[13]

On August 18, 1901, the following account appeared in the *Bridgeport Sunday Herald*:

> He stationed his two assistants behind the machine with instructions to hold on to the ropes and not let the machine get away. Then he took his position in the great bird. He opened the throttle of the ground propeller and shot along the green sod at a rapid rate . . . "We can't hold her!" shrieked one of the rope men. "Let go, then" shouted Whitehead back. They let go, and as they did so the machine darted up through the air like a bird released from a cage. Whitehead was greatly excited and his hands flew from one part of the machinery to another. The newspaperman and the two assistants stood still for a moment watching the airship in amazement. Then they rushed down the slightly sloping grade after the airship. She was flying now about fifty feet above the ground and made a noise very much like the "chung, chung, chung," of an elevator going down the shaft. Whitehead had grown calmer now and seemed to be enjoying the exhilaration of the novelty. He was headed straight for a clump of chestnut sprouts that grew on a high knoll. He was now about forty feet in the air and would have been high enough to escape the sprouts had they not been on a high ridge. He saw the danger ahead, and within two hundred yards of the sprouts made several attempts to manipulate the machinery so he could steer around, but the ship kept steadily on her course, head on for the trees. To strike them meant wrecking the airship and very likely death or broken bones for the aeronaut. Here it was that Whitehead showed how to use a common sense principle which he had noticed the birds made use of thousands of times when he had been studying them in their flight or points to make his airship a success. He simply shifted his weight more to one side than the other. This careened the ship to one side. She turned her nose away from the clump of sprouts when within fifty yards of them as prettily as a yacht on the sea avoids a bar. The ability to control the airship in this manner appeared to give Whitehead confidence, for he was seen to take time to look at the landscape about him. He looked back and waved his hand exclaiming: "I've got it at last!"[14]

The account was also later reported in the *Boston Transcript*, the *New York Herald*, the *American Inventor*, *Scientific American Magazine*, and *Aeronautical World*, and the event it portrayed has sparked a historic debate that has lasted more than a century: did in fact a German immigrant by the name of Gustave Whitehead design, build, and fly a heavier-than-air craft over Bridgeport, Connecticut, nearly two years before the historic first flight of the Wright brothers?

Most historians believe not. At best, they say, the question cannot be definitively answered, for Whitehead kept no records of his experimental trials, involved no impartial observers in his claimed flights, and made no photographs of his craft in the air to document any of his flights—all of which the Wright brothers did. Still, more than a century later, there remains a small cadre of Whitehead supporters led by Australian historian John Brown, whose 2016 book *Gustave Whitehead and the Wright Brothers: Who Flew First?* provides an extensive and detailed discussion of the facts of the case. Brown's investigation concludes that the claim that Whitehead made "manned, powered, controlled and sustained airplane flights prior to December 1903 rises to a standard of proof exceeding *beyond reasonable doubt* [supported by testimony from at least two independent witnesses] and in many cases, rises to the standard of *clear and convincing evidence* [comprising multiple sources and witnesses]." As Brown is careful to note, he reached this conclusion on the basis of the Rules of Evidence as used in a court of law, and not on the traditional criteria of historical interpretation.[15] Nonetheless, in 2013 Brown convinced aviation's oldest reference work, *Jane's All the World's Aircraft,* to take note of his research and declare in the publication that although "the Wrights were right, Whitehead was ahead."[16] As a result of Brown's work, Connecticut governor Dannel Malloy and the Connecticut legislature that same year declared a Powered Flight Day in honor of "the first powered flight by Gustave Whitehead, rather than the Wright Brothers."[17]

Gustave Whitehead, born Gustave Weiss Kopf in Leutershausen, Germany (near Nuremberg), was twenty-one years old when he arrived in America in 1895. He began his aeronautical activities in Boston, working for the Boston Aeronautical Society, where he built one or two unsuccessful gliders. Later, in Pittsburgh, he is said to have built a steam-powered aircraft, which he flew a half mile at a height of twenty feet before crashing into a brick wall, though no reliable evidence exists to support this claim. In 1900, Whitehead arrived in Bridgeport, with his wife and two-year-old daughter, and took up residence on Pine Street. It was here that Whitehead built airplane no. 21, whose supposed flight was reported in the *Sunday Herald* of August 18, 1901.[18]

It is claimed that Whitehead made two straight-line flights with plane no. 21 that year, the first covering half a mile, the second a mile

Gustave Whitehead circa 1890.
Source unknown

and a half. The following year, Whitehead built another craft, airplane no. 22, of a similar design but with a watertight hull, which he claimed to have flown a distance of seven miles in a circular path before landing, unharmed, in the waters of Long Island Sound.[19] As compared to the first flights of the Wright brothers at Kitty Hawk, North Carolina, in 1903, which traveled a mere nine hundred feet and were less than a minute in duration, Whitehead's accomplishments, if true, would have been considered phenomenal in their day. If we presume such an accomplishment, Whitehead's complete disregard for substantiating his work in any way—which Brown attributes to Whitehead's need to earn money elsewhere so as to support his wife and child—must truly baffle even his staunchest supporters.

In addition to a lack of documentation, Whitehead made no effort to duplicate or build on the claimed success of planes nos. 21 and 22. Unlike the Wright brothers, who used their initial success to improve the performance of subsequent designs, Whitehead moved from one new challenge to another: first, to the construction of a large monoplane glider, for which he and Stanley Yale Beach, the editor of *Scientific American Magazine*, received a joint patent in 1908, then to an attempt to convert the glider into an airplane by adding an engine and propeller, an experiment that failed due to the weight and low power of the engine. Whitehead then turned to the design of bi-wing and tri-wing gliders of the type proposed by aviation pioneer Octave Chanute, though none of Whitehead's gliders got off the ground. Lastly, from 1911 to

Gustave Whitehead and his daughter with Plane 22, 1902. Courtesy of the Library of Congress

1913, Whitehead turned to the problem of vertical-lift aircraft, building two prototype helicopters; neither proved successful. Whitehead died in Fairfield, Connecticut, in October 1927 (a few months after Lindbergh's solo flight across the Atlantic), penniless and unrecognized. He is buried in a pauper's grave at Bridgeport's Lakeview Cemetery.[20]

Historians of the Wright brothers point out correctly that the debate over who flew first is seductive but also in the end irrelevant. They note, for example, that the revelation that Whitehead or someone else (perhaps Augustus Herring) might have made a controlled flight before the Wright brothers "would have little effect on history," for no one else built on their accomplishments, whatever they might have been, in a way that helped to make heavier-than-air flight a reality. The true contribution of the Wright brothers—contained within the kernel of their first flights at Kitty Hawk—was the scientific development of aerodynamic control in three-dimensional space (roll, pitch, and yaw) along with the piloting skills it took to apply this knowledge effectively in flight. As one source proclaims:

> By 1908, the Wrights had developed a practical airplane capable of carrying two people and flying for an extended period of time (as long as the gasoline lasted) . . . [and] in 1909, they began to teach these skills to

students. These two events—not their first tentative flights in 1903—mark the beginning of modern aviation. Within a few years, aviators were flying successfully in every part of the globe . . . [using] variations of the Wright control system . . . [and] the basic flying skills the Wrights had developed. This remains true even today.[21]

Modern aviation derives directly from the work of the Wright brothers, their ingenuity, their systematic experimentation, and their persistence. No one else, including the supporters of Gustave Whitehead, can make that claim.

DAREDEVIL DAYS OF CONNECTICUT AVIATION

Following the success of the Wright brothers—at Kitty Hawk in 1903 and more publicly in Paris in 1908, where Wilbur astonished crowds with dozens of well-executed flights in the brothers' latest bi-wing aeroplane—aviation entered a phase of development that focused on air meets and exhibitions around the country and the world undertaken by young daredevil pilots. The purpose of such exhibitions was twofold: first, to familiarize the public with the technological miracle of flight, and second, to give pilots who were willing to risk their lives the opportunity to test the limits of that technology in real-world circumstances. This period of aviation history, from the 1910s through the 1920s, is commonly referred to as the barnstorming days of early aviation, and it arrived in Connecticut on the Fourth of July weekend of 1910.

The work of Gustave Whitehead notwithstanding, the first heavier-than-air flight in Connecticut, indeed in all of New England, was made above New Britain by Charles Keeney Hamilton during an Aviation Day celebration held at Walnut Hill Park on July 2, 1910, before an estimated crowd of fifty thousand spectators. Hamilton's success, following hours of delay caused by mechanical difficulties, brought the excitement and the reality of modern aviation to Connecticut. The following account from the *New Britain Daily Herald* describes the exhilaration in the crowd caused by Hamilton's accomplishment:

> Fighting, doggedly persistent against perverse fate, Charles K. Hamilton, the greatest of living aviators, achieved a success out of what appeared to be blighting failure, before the finest crowd of people of social political prominence that has been gathered in one city in Connecticut in a decade at least, at Walnut Hill park Saturday afternoon . . . It was an afternoon such as weaker natures would have succumbed to. But not so Hamilton. He

fought against fate hour after hour and was rewarded at last. He repaired his engine and then followed a flight over the city constituting a sight that young men will not have forgotten when they are bowed with years and old men will carry the recollection to their graves . . . high over his home city he flew, over factory chimneys and busy stores, while the people ran into the street and roared their applause. Crowds of people not possessing the Hamilton pertinacity, who had left the park and were at the station crowding into trains to leave the city, were overtaken and thrilled. Then they realized that they had not waited in vain . . . After eighteen minutes of flight, the aviator, sometimes working on seven cylinders, sometimes on but six, returned to the aviation field where the assembled thousands awaited him . . . "I am ready to die now," said one old lady. "I never expected to see this in my lifetime. I do not believe there is anything now left for the hand of man to create or the mind to conceive . . ." For all time it will be written in the history of New England that the first successful flight in a heavier-than-air machine took place in New Britain, Connecticut, and a New Britain boy had achieved the feat.[22]

Charles Keeney Hamilton was born in New Britain on May 30, 1885, and at eighteen years of age left home for a career as a daredevil aeronaut. Hamilton first toured fairs and carnivals in the Southwest as a hot-air balloonist and parachutist, then flew experimental gliders towed into the air behind automobiles and speedboats in New York City, and later made some of the earliest dirigible flights in Japan. In 1909, under the tutelage of ace pilot and Wright brothers' competitor Glenn Curtiss, he extended his skills to heavier-than-air flight and became an expert aviator. As a member of the Curtiss Exhibition Team, Hamilton traveled the country and thrilled crowds everywhere with his daring "Hamilton dive," a one-thousand-foot, near-vertical drop that he made to within a few feet of the ground before leveling off in front of a grandstand of cheering spectators. In June 1910, Hamilton achieved national recognition for the first sunrise-to-sunset round-trip flight between New York and Philadelphia. It was soon after this achievement that Hamilton returned to New Britain, already a hometown hero, to make the first heavier-than-air flight in New England.[23]

Hamilton's historic flight was followed by the exploits of other aeronauts anxious to show off their flying skills and air machines, and in so doing advance the new science of aerodynamics. For example, Frank Coffyn in his Wright biplane demonstrated his flying ability above a crowd of forty thousand onlookers on the opening day of the Connecticut Fair held at Charter Oak Park in Hartford in the fall of 1910, where his abilities were highly praised: "The aviator had no difficulty in lifting his machine from the ground, and after he had once guided it upwards to a height of from seventy-five to 100 feet, the biplane soared round and round with all the ease and grace of a great bird. To those who looked upward at the man-bird from the ground, flying seemed as easy as walking or riding a bicycle. There was absolutely no flaw to mar the exhibition, and from beginning to end, it was as good a demonstration of the art of flying as any one could ask for."[24]

But perhaps the most noteworthy of all daredevil events occurred in Connecticut the following year when Charles Keeney Hamilton again found himself in New Britain, though under less than favorable circumstances. While recovering from a bout of tuberculosis at a local sanitarium, Hamilton met fellow aviator Nels Nelson, also of New Britain, and the two men decided to hold a public exhibition of their flying skills in the form of an aerial duel, by which they could both earn some much-needed money. The two-day event was held at the Berlin Fairgrounds on July 26–27, 1912. As part of the duel, each man attempted to outperform the other in a specific series of aerial contests: bomb dropping, altitude climbing, accurate landing, and quick takeoff, as well as several air speed races. To the overall winner would go the prize money collected from an entrance fee of 25¢ a person. Some five thousand people attended the first day's events, but when the points were tallied hometown favorite Hamilton lagged behind Nelson by a wide margin. After news of the lopsided results spread across town, attendance on the second day rose to eight thousand. Now, however, it was Hamilton who outperformed Nelson, and in the end, to the satisfaction of all, the Hamilton-Nelson duel was declared a draw and the prize money was divided evenly between the two men. Sadly, it was the last time that Charles Keeney Hamilton performed as an aviator, for he succumbed to tuberculosis two years later at the young age of twenty-eight. Only at the end of Nels Nelson's life (in 1961) did he divulge the fact that his aerial duel with Hamilton was fixed from the start. He and Hamilton had agreed beforehand which events each would win, so as to ensure that the contest would draw a goodly crowd yet end in an equitable draw.[25]

The Great War of 1914–18 gave tremendous impetus to the cause of aviation. Airplanes were well used in the war as a means of

reconnaissance and aerial photography and—once aircraft designer Anthony Fokker had invented a device that synchronized the firing of machine gun bullets from the cockpit with the revolution of a plane's propeller—as an offensive weapon as well. As a result of the Great War, the airplane went from being a mechanical toy to an important military weapon, and as such found a permanent place in our technological culture. Though it would still take decades for the transport implications of long-distance air service to be fully felt, after the Great War the future of aviation was forever linked to the effectiveness of the airplane as a military weapon.

Commercial air service first came to Connecticut in 1922 thanks to Harris Whittemore Jr., an ex-airman from Naugatuck who after the war retained more than a casual interest in aviation. When an itinerant flyer landed in an open field in Bethany, Whittemore, employed in his family's iron manufacturing business, saw it as a business opportunity. Having persuaded the pilot to stay, Whittemore purchased three war surplus airplanes, along with the field in Bethany; there, at the state's first airfield, which he named Bethany Airport, Whittemore inaugurated the state's first commercial air service, known as the Bee Line. As a charter service for hire, the Bee Line did a fair amount of business over the next few years but struggled to earn a profit.[26]

The opportunity for success that Whittemore had hoped for came in 1925, when Congress passed the federal Air Mail Act. As it had with other modes of transportation, from post rider to stagecoach to railroad and motor truck, the federal government signaled the acceptance of the airplane as a new mode of transport by paying its operators to carry the U.S. mail. In the Air Mail Act, Congress authorized the Post Office to contract with private airlines to provide safe and reliable airmail delivery along government-selected routes. This gave fledgling airline operators like Whittemore—as it had stagecoach operators a century earlier—the financial impetus they needed to succeed.

Whittemore's Bee Line was reincorporated in 1924 as Colonial Air Lines, and along with Eastern Air Transport of Boston it bid on the lucrative Newark to Hartford to Boston airmail route, with an understanding that regardless of who was awarded the federal contract, the two companies would merge into one. Therefore, in 1926 the resulting company, Colonial Air Transport, became Connecticut's first scheduled air carrier on the route from New York to Boston, though it made only one Connecticut stop (in Hartford) and carried only one "passenger" (the U.S. mail).[27]

In addition to the efforts of individual daredevil pilots and the federal government to promote air transportation, cities and states soon became involved trying to accommodate the latest in transportation technology. As early as 1911, Connecticut enacted its first aviation law. Sponsored by A. Holland Forbes, an avid flyer and founder of the Aero Club of Connecticut, the law required the examination and licensing of all Connecticut balloon and airplane pilots, and the registration and numbering of their aircraft. It was the first such law in the nation and soon became a model for other states (including Massachusetts) and for federal aviation law as well. To oversee its enforcement, Forbes was appointed the state's first Commissioner of Aviation, and was given the first pilot's license issued under the new law. At first, enforcement of the state's aviation statutes was assigned to the Office of the Secretary of State, but in 1921 that responsibility was transferred to the Commissioner of Motor Vehicles.[28]

Since the business of aviation was seen as a means of stimulating local economies, some Connecticut cities took on the responsibility of providing landing areas near to their business centers to accommodate the newest means of transport (existing technology was still slow enough and small enough not to require large tracts of land). In 1920, as a result of an accident that had recently killed two army pilots in his city, Mayor Newton C. Brainard appointed a five-member commission to locate and develop an adequate municipal landing field for Hartford. The commission chose a publicly owned parcel of land in the city's south meadows, and Hartford Municipal Airport (Brainard Field), the first publicly owned airfield in the state (and the nation) opened on June 11, 1921. To publicize the event and attract pilots to the new airfield, an impressive air meet was held on opening day. The show, which attracted thousands of spectators, included events such as a Hartford to Springfield seaplane race, various classes of speed racing around a forty-five-mile triangular course, and one event entitled "bursting toy balloons" in which the contestant, his plane having reached an altitude of five hundred feet, had to burst three balloons released at one-minute intervals from the ground. The meet was so successful that for several years it remained an annual event. By 1925, aeronauts were entertaining spectators by skywriting, parachute jumping, and creating a one-thousand-foot-high, one-mile-long screen of dense white tetrachloride smoke.[29]

As other municipalities followed Hartford's lead, ten more airfields were added to the statewide total by 1928, including Municipal (Tweed) Airport in New Haven. The following year a State Airport Commission was created to acquire Trumbull Field in Groton, Connecticut's first state-owned airport. The state airfield became home to the Forty-Third Air Division of the Connecticut National Guard, until then stationed at Brainard Field.[30]

With some three hundred aircraft and six hundred pilots now registered in the state, Connecticut also reorganized its aviation bureaucracy, creating a separate Department of Aeronautics located in a new office building at Brainard Field, along with an Office of the Flight Surgeon that was responsible for conducting periodic medical examinations of all pilots. And Connecticut's aviation statute was thoroughly revised, becoming in the process "probably the most complete one operative in this country and is more thoroughly enforced than that of any other state."[31]

While Connecticut took significant steps in the 1920s to promote and regulate the business of aviation, it was the transatlantic solo flight of Charles Lindbergh from New York to Paris in May 1927 that gave the biggest boost to the public's desire for manned flight. Soon after his return, Lindbergh undertook a goodwill flying tour of eighty American cities to promote the possibilities of commercial aviation for everyman. The tour began in Connecticut, where Lindbergh landed at Hartford Municipal Airport at 2:00 p.m. on July 20, 1927. As Lindbergh waved from the cockpit of the *Spirit of St. Louis,* he could hear the blast of noise from factory whistles and automobile horns from all over the city even above the roar of the airplane's engine. Among the crowd there to greet the famous aviator was Governor John H. Trumbull, Hartford's acting mayor Houghton Buckley, and other city officials. Lindbergh spoke briefly about the coming age of commercial aviation. When asked if such service was to be made available to anyone who wanted to make a trip by air, Lindbergh replied prophetically. "You have a wonderful air mail service throughout the states," he said. "That service will be improved as time goes on [and] passenger service will follow the air mail."[32] After a reception at the airport, an entourage made its way to Colt Park, where a parade through the city began. Bushels of confetti cut from cloth and paper of all colors floated down on Lindbergh as he made his way along the parade route.

Because of professional aviators, such as Lindbergh, and the hundreds of daring stunt flyers that barnstormed the country, the American public came to accept the airplane—as it had the automobile—as yet another technological fact of life in the twentieth century. Before long, the airplane and the commercial air services it made possible would blur the boundaries between states and nations in the air in much the same way that the automobile had already blurred boundaries between city and country on the ground. Though on the land cities were spilling over into suburbs, in the air the world began to shrink into one global community. Together the automobile and the airplane marked a quantum leap in personal mobility for people everywhere, and a new age for transportation.

Central to the air age was the evolution of an internal combustion engine that could power ever larger aircraft ever farther, ever faster. Yet despite the advances that had been made by the 1920s, the future of commercial aviation at this point in time was hardly guaranteed. It would take the daring, not of a barnstorming pilot like Hamilton but of a new kind of entrepreneur with a vision for aviation's future and the managerial skills to transform that vision into a reality to make that future happen. That man was Frederick B. Rentschler, and his vision focused on a powerful, comparatively lightweight, *air*-cooled radial engine that he believed could power the different types of military and commercial aircraft the industry needed. Like Albert Pope with the ordinary bicycle, Rentschler would move to Connecticut from elsewhere and use the skilled workforce of the Hartford region to produce a series of aircraft engines that would once again make Connecticut's capitol region the home of a national revolution in transportation technology.

From Experimentation to Commercial Aviation

From 1925 to 1956, Connecticut became home to one of the aviation industry's premier engine manufacturers, Pratt & Whitney Aircraft, and the tremendous growth of the company became intertwined with the growth of commercial aviation and the role of the airplane as a military weapon.

RENTSCHLER ESTABLISHES PRATT & WHITNEY AIRCRAFT

Frederick B. Rentschler was born in Hamilton, Ohio, in 1887 into a well-to-do business family. In 1909, Rentschler graduated from Princeton College and for the next eight years worked in the family's several manufacturing companies honing his business skills. When America entered the Great War in 1917, Rentschler joined the Army Air Service as a lieutenant and was assigned to supervise the production of airplane engines at the Wright-Martin Corporation in New Brunswick, New Jersey. After the war, Rentschler continued with the company, now known as Wright Aeronautical, where as company president he assembled a talented team of managers and engineers to manufacture the *liquid*-cooled engines for which the Wright Company soon became famous.[33]

Accomplishments aside, however, Rentschler was not content. As he later remembered, those above him at the time "were almost all investment bankers, none of whom had an appreciation of what we were trying to do." In truth, Rentschler's displeasure was a reflection of his own inner vision in conflict with that of the Wright group. Whereas the Wright Company believed strongly in the liquid-cooled engines they manufactured, Rentschler was driven by the opportunity he saw to develop a new breed of airplane engine built around an air-cooled radial (circular) design. Rentschler was convinced that the future of aviation lay not in the airplane per se but in the vehicle's power plant. "It seemed very definite to me that the best airplane could only be designed around the best engine." Therefore, the objective of any aeronautical company should be "to have the world's dominant power plant." Rentschler was also aware of the Naval Limitations Treaty that the nation had endorsed in 1921,

Frederick B. Rentschler, the founder of Pratt & Whitney Aircraft Company, in 1925. Courtesy of P&W Aircraft Company

which restricted the total ship tonnage of naval powers such as the United States. As a result of the treaty, and with two battleships already under construction, the navy redesigned the rest of its postwar fleet to include several aircraft carriers, which created an immediate need for two hundred airplanes, a need that Rentschler saw as a business opportunity. It was this instinct that he could not continue in a company that did not see beyond the status quo that led Rentschler to leave the Wright Company in 1924 to pursue his own vision of aviation's future.[34]

Thanks to his business connections, Rentschler was put in touch with the Niles-Bement-Ponds Company, a manufacturer of heavy machinery whose main plant was located in his hometown of Hamilton, Ohio, and whose company president was a friend of the Rentschler family. It seemed that the Niles Company had spare working capital it was looking to invest. This led Rentschler to Hartford, where the company had factory space available in its Pratt & Whitney tool division. As if to highlight the continuity between the ordinary bicycle, the internal combustion engine, and the modern airplane, the floor space in question was located in a building formerly occupied by the Pope Manufacturing Corporation.[35]

The following summer, Rentschler assembled a team of six engineers, moved to Hartford, and signed a contract with the Pratt & Whitney Company that allowed him to use its factory space and its capital to build his visionary aircraft engine. The goal of the new company, incorporated as Pratt & Whitney Aircraft, was to produce a new kind of aviation engine rated at a minimum of four hundred horsepower using an air-cooled radial design that Rentschler hoped to sell to the U.S. Navy. By Christmas Eve of 1925, the first prototype had been assembled and was ready to be tested. At the suggestion of his wife, who associated the droning of the engine with the world of insects, Rentschler named the final product the Wasp. As test results accumulated over the following months, the Wasp's output soon astounded everyone, including naval officials who were "swept off their feet" by the engine's performance.

The Wasp not only outflew all competitors, but its particular combination of horsepower, weight, speed, and clean running characteristics "had never been previously approached in an aviation engine." In the fall of 1926, the navy signed a contract with Pratt & Whitney Aircraft for two hundred Wasp engines. Within two years, the U.S. Army adopted the Wasp as its engine of choice as well.[36]

Of course, achieving success and maintaining success were two different things. Here again, Rentschler chose to follow his instincts. While some in the industry thought the future of aviation lay in smaller flivver aircraft (vehicles for personal travel that would take over the skies much as the automobile had overtaken travel on the ground), Rentschler was keenly aware of the Air Mail Act of 1925 and the need to supply fledgling airlines looking to enter into

The first Wasp engine. The radial, air-cooled Wasp design provided the prototype for P&W engines through the 1940s.
Courtesy of P&W Aircraft Company

contracts with the U.S. Post Office with a power source reliable enough for repeated, long-distance operation. Also, he believed that to be financially successful such airlines would need to carry passengers as well as mail, so that as the demand for air travel grew, airplanes themselves would need to become larger, not smaller, which meant that the engines that powered them would have to become ever more powerful, their technology ever more dependable. To emphasize his belief, Rentschler adopted as the company logo an eagle with wings unfurled surrounded by the words "Pratt & Whitney: Dependable Engines."

No sooner had the Wasp engine entered production than Rentschler and his team set their sights on an even larger radial engine called the Hornet that would produce a minimum of 525 horsepower. Together, the Wasp and Hornet engines manufactured by Pratt & Whitney Aircraft soon revolutionized the aviation market, both military and commercial, in America as well as overseas, and established P&W as a premier manufacturer of aviation engines. By 1929, P&W engines had set the standard for the development of commercial aviation and were already being used by 90 percent of all commercial air transport in the United States. One indication of the impact the dependable performance of the

Wasp engine had on the industry as a whole came in 1932, when Wiley Post made the first solo flight around the world using the same engine in seven days and eighteen hours. In setting this record, Post traveled a distance of 15,600 miles in eleven hops, while the Wasp engine that powered his aircraft required only routine maintenance along the way. By contrast, a U.S. Army pilot made a round-the-world trip in 1924 using the then popular V-12 liquid-cooled Liberty engine, and his aircraft had required seven complete engine changes en route![37]

With the success of the Wasp and Hornet engines, orders continued to roll in from around the world and the number of workers employed by P&W quickly grew to more than a thousand employees, in the process outgrowing the company's production facility in Hartford. In 1929, with the production of both engines in full swing, Rentschler invested two million dollars in a massive new 400,000 square-foot plant in East Hartford. The 1,100 acre site, a former tobacco farm on Silver Lane, also included the company's own airfield, which came to be known locally as Rentschler Field. The success of Pratt & Whitney Aircraft created a thriving support industry for aviation manufacturing throughout Connecticut, with up to half of all engine work subcontracted to smaller firms as a way of mitigating the employment highs and lows created by the natural ebb and flow of market orders.[38]

As P&W grew in size, Rentschler soon merged his company with aviation companies in other sectors of the industry to form an aviation holding company called United Aircraft & Transport. The new company included Boeing Aircraft and Chance Vought Aircraft (builders of airframes), the Hamilton Standard Propeller Corporation, as well as the Sikorsky Aviation Corporation, whose famous seaplanes (powered by Wasp engines) were being used by Pan American Airways to provide international clipper service in the 1930s. The mergers created a vertical monopoly in the emerging aviation industry, with Pratt & Whitney engines at the center of things, literally and figuratively. Before long, the success of Pratt & Whitney had rubbed off on its new partners as well. By 1930, Boeing Aircraft secured the first transcontinental airmail contract from Chicago to Los Angeles, and produced the Boeing 247, a twin-Wasp-powered, twelve-passenger, all-metal airplane with retractable landing gear that is considered the first modern airliner.[39]

While the creation of a holding company that brought together companies that manufactured aviation equipment with those that provided

P&W Plant in East Hartford. As the aviation industry expanded, so too did P&W, until it became the largest employer in Connecticut.
Courtesy of P&W Aircraft Company

airline services did help to focus the aviation market on larger, more comfortable aircraft to serve both passengers and mail (as Rentschler hoped it would), the monopolistic business practices of United Aircraft & Transport soon met with disapproval from the federal government. After a sensational Senate investigation of possible collusion over airmail contracts, Congress put an end to the aviation trust in the Air Mail Act of 1934. As a result, the United Aircraft & Transport Corporation was splintered into three component parts by federal edict. All airline services were grouped under a new United Airlines Corporation, while manufacturing activities west of the Mississippi River came under a reorganized Boeing Aircraft Corporation of Seattle. East of the Mississippi, manufacturing operations that included Pratt & Whitney Aircraft and Sikorsky Aviation came under a new United Aircraft Corporation headquartered in East Hartford.[40]

By 1938, the aviation industry as envisioned by Rentschler was well established but still of small size relative to other American industries. For example, in that year the aviation industry had in total some 36,000 employees, less than the number employed by the American knit hosiery industry, and while aviation assets totaled $25,000,000, the amount was less than the assets of most large American breweries. But as nations abroad began to arm themselves for a second world war in as many generations, the fortunes and scope of the aviation industry in general and Pratt & Whitney in particular transformed dramatically. A 1940 executive order from President Roosevelt for fifty thousand new airplanes each year changed the industry literally overnight and provided an opportunity for Pratt & Whitney Aircraft to play a role in the coming Allied victory that cannot be overstated.[41]

To fulfill its unprecedented rash of engine orders, Pratt & Whitney not only expanded its Connecticut operation (to 24,000 employees during the war years) but was aided by several of the nation's major auto manufacturers, including Ford, Buick, and Chevrolet, who were licensed by Pratt & Whitney to supplement its wartime production and whose combined workforces were ordered to tool up for the exacting tolerances used in aircraft engine production. In the case of the Ford Motor Company, Pratt & Whitney even constructed a new plant in Kansas City, Missouri, that replicated its entire East Hartford manufacturing process, minimizing disruptions by training individual workers whenever possible to operate only single-purpose, single-operation machinery. By 1943, the company's workforce, including licensees, had swollen to forty thousand persons nationwide, with 60 percent of that number located in East Hartford and other satellite plants in Connecticut. By the end of the war, Pratt & Whitney and its licensees had built 363,619 aircraft engines that provided more than half of all the horsepower used by the combined U.S. air forces. Those engines were used in seventy different kinds of aircraft, including powerful fighter planes such as the Vought Corsair and the Grumman Hellcat. To prevent charges of profiteering, Rentschler early on limited his company's after-tax profits to a maximum of 3 percent, a voluntary gesture that was later required of the entire defense industry in the Renegotiation Act of 1942.[42]

Allied air supremacy during World War II was a result not only of the hard work of the men and women throughout the defense industry but also of the technological strides that were made in engine design during wartime production. Through innovative design advances, for example, the basic Wasp engine underwent several transformations, first as the Double Wasp and later as the Wasp Major, which made the Pratt & Whitney engine ever more powerful as the war progressed. The power output of the Wasp engine series nearly tripled from 1,200 horsepower at the beginning of the war to 3,500 horsepower by war's end. By then, the Wasp Major had become the highest-rated aviation engine in the world, producing nine times the power of the original Wasp design of twenty years previous.[43]

Increasing an engine's power brought its own problems, mainly by creating more heat, which in turn damaged valves, rings, and other engine parts and also resulted in the spontaneous ignition of unburned fuel, called engine knock; while a startling annoyance in an automobile, engine knock could be a fatal flaw in an aircraft engine. Efforts to minimize the problem of excess heat and engine knock in aviation engines resulted in two innovations: water-injection technology, which helped designers to control an engine's tendency to overheat, and the accidental discovery by the Shell Oil Company of the polymerization process, which allowed manufacturers of aviation fuel to mass-produce high, one-hundred octane gasoline at low cost for military use. It not only eliminated the danger of engine knock but at the same time increased an engine's power output by more than one third. The polymerization process (unknown in Germany), and the relationship between an engine's performance and the quality of the fuel it used, provide an important example of the systems aspect of all transportation engineering, which in this instance was a crucial contribution to Allied air supremacy, and therefore to the Allied victory in World War II.[44]

THE COMING OF THE JET AGE

For Pratt & Whitney Aircraft the war ended on August 14, 1945, as abruptly as it had begun, with an order by President Harry S. Truman to cancel more than $400,000,000 in current engine contracts. As a result, Pratt & Whitney plants closed for two weeks and 26,000 Connecticut workers were furloughed while the company shifted gears into a peacetime production program. Because of its vital contribution to the war effort, Pratt & Whitney had become in one sense a victim of its own success. During the war, as German and British scientists experimented with the possibilities of jet propulsion, Pratt & Whitney focused on what they did best: the manufacture of high-quality piston engines, which put the company at a disadvantage in jet propulsion once the war ended.[45]

Unlike the four-stroke cycle of a piston engine, jet propulsion involved the continuous burning of a compressed air and fuel mixture in the engine's combustion chamber. The thrust produced by the exhaust escaping from such continuous combustion had the potential to move a plane forward at incredible speeds, the only downside being increased consumption of fuel per unit of power produced. Meanwhile, in light of the advances made during the war, the piston engine, even one as powerful as the Wasp Major, was approaching its design limits. Clearly the future of aviation lay in jet propulsion, and Rentschler was not about to relinquish the legacy of innovation and dependability he had worked so hard to achieve since 1925. As with his original Wasp design, Rentschler was clear as to his postwar intentions: "Our job is not to catch the others, but to be first. There is no such thing as a second best air force. There is the best, or nothing."[46]

With the encouragement of several government contracts, Rentschler decided to pursue a jet propulsion program whose aim was to produce a turbo jet engine of extremely high power within five years. The program included many technological challenges, including learning to work with sheet metal as opposed to more traditional castings and forgings. Only a sheet metal design could incorporate the alloys required to withstand the heat and high pressure of a jet engine environment. The company chose to focus on an axial design, in which the intake air moved straight through to the engine's compressor, resulting in a slimmer design with less drag and greater power output. While its jet propulsion research program was underway, Pratt & Whitney secured its financial position through the production of piston engines, which continued to dominate the commercial aviation market in the postwar years.[47]

The first test flight of Pratt & Whitney's new J-57 jet engine took place in 1951, and with the J-57 Rentschler knew he had reached his objective. The J-57 produced more power than other jet engines (ten thousand pounds of thrust as compared to five to six thousand pounds then produced by engines of other companies), *and* it did so while consuming less fuel than other engine designers thought possible. As a test pilot of the J-57 commented, "That monster's got a lot of pizzazz." When completed the following year, the J-57 was able to power a jet fighter to fly faster than the speed of sound.[48]

However, no sooner had Rentschler redirected Pratt & Whitney Aircraft into the jet age by establishing the J-57 as the industry standard than he began a difficult three-year battle with cancer, which he ultimately lost in 1956. With Rentschler's death, Connecticut and the aviation industry lost a true visionary. By the time of his death, Rentschler had used his talent and vision to lead aviation through not one but two monumental transformations; the first surrounding his design for the original Wasp engine in 1925, which led to the creation of commercial airline service and an Allied victory in World War II, and the second with his commitment to jet propulsion twenty-five years later, which made worldwide commercial airline service a common mode of transportation. Meanwhile, as a result of his originality as an entrepreneur and engine designer, Frederick Rentschler established Pratt & Whitney Aircraft as a global leader in the aviation industry and one of the largest employers in the state's booming postwar economy.

Another Federal-State Partnership

As commercial airline service became an established mode of transportation worldwide, another transportation partnership was formed between the federal government and the state of Connecticut similar to the one created for highway building.

THE FEDERAL ROLE IN AVIATION

In addition to the incentive provided by the Air Mail Act of 1925, the federal role in the development of commercial aviation was formalized by the Air Commerce Act of 1926, which institutionalized federal involvement in aviation within the U.S. Department of Commerce and directed its secretary to establish a national system of airways, to license pilots, certify aircraft, and install radio beacons as navigational aids. While the standardization that followed improved air safety dramatically, the economics of the Great Depression deterred the industry from expanding fully. In 1938, with economic conditions on the upswing, Congress transferred the federal government's aeronautical responsibilities to a new Civilian Aviation Authority (CAA) intended to administer air travel and safety as a public agency independent of the executive branch. In addition, a subsidiary of the CAA, the Civilian Aviation Board (CAB), was created to select airline routes, regulate fares, monitor airline mergers, and award airmail contracts. Through the administration of the Civilian Aviation Board, eighteen existing airlines were assigned permanent rights to the routes they were then flying, an arrangement that helped to stabilize the industry for decades as air travel went from a rare occurrence to being commonplace.

Also in 1938, Congress for the first time designated federal funding for airport improvements. Like the first federal-aid highway program of 1916, federal aviation funding was hesitantly received; yet it established an important precedent for the federal support of airport construction and improvement that (like its highway counterpart in the 1920s) expanded during the postwar period.

The first program of federal aid to airports of the postwar era was enacted in the Federal Airport Act of 1946, which set aside a total of $234,000,000 over the coming decade to help cities and states build and improve their airports. The funds were allocated partly (25%) on the basis of need, and partly (75%) on the basis of formulas that took into account the land area and population served by the airport, thereby ensuring that most congressional districts received at least some level of federal funding. As with highway funding, federal airport aid required a one-to-one dollar match from local government.

Once the federal program was established, multiyear funding continued with the Federal Aviation Act of 1958. The new act also created a Federal Aviation Agency whose main function was to control the nation's air traffic (civilian and military) as the number of airplanes and the route miles they traveled increased, as well as to establish safety standards for pilots and their continually evolving aircraft. The Aviation Act of 1958 increased the level of federal funding to about $100,000,000 a year and extended the life of the airport aid program through 1963. Meanwhile, local airports prepared for the coming of the jet age with longer runways and improved navigational aids.

A MAJOR AIRPORT COMES TO CONNECTICUT

Connecticut's modern airport system had its origins in World War II. In 1941, when the federal government considered establishing a military airbase in Connecticut, the state purchased 1,700 acres of tobacco farmland in Windsor Locks, north of Hartford, and then leased the site to the federal government for military use. The army airbase constructed on the land was named in memory of Second Lieutenant Eugene M. Bradley, a twenty-four-year-old newlywed pilot who was killed when his plane crashed during a routine training exercise in August 1941. Under military stewardship during the war, Bradley Field served as a training base for air combat units, as a staging area for overseas deployments, and near the end of the war as a camp for German prisoners of war. Bradley Field was deactivated in 1945, and returned to state ownership the following year.[49]

Because the airfield was located inland and therefore not troubled by coastal fog, Bradley Field after the war was viewed by the state as a possible site for a major commercial airport midway between New York and Boston. Plans for its conversion to commercial use began in the late 1940s as the first of many master plans for the site was prepared. In 1950, the construction of a terminal building and control tower began, funded jointly by the Federal Aviation Agency and a two-million-dollar bond issued by the state of Connecticut. When completed two years later, Murphy Terminal contained all the passenger and administrative facilities necessary to operate the new airport. Commercial aviation service began soon after with regional flights provided by Eastern, United, Northeast, and American airlines. The airfield's importance increased in 1957 with the scheduling of the state's first transcontinental air service operated by Trans World Airlines between Bradley Field and Los Angeles, with a stopover in New York City.[50]

As the volume of traffic moving through the airfield increased (to 500,000 passengers and 17,000,000 tons of cargo per year by the end of the 1950s), the first plans were made to upgrade the facility. To accommodate jet-powered aircraft, the main runway was extended to a length of nine thousand feet, additional acreage was set aside for parking lots, and an expressway connection was built to nearby Interstate 91 (Route 20). These improvements were intended to signal that Connecticut and its largest airfield were ready for the jet age. To mark the occasion, an F-100 fighter plane flew just above ground level to cut through a celebratory

Lt. Eugene M. Bradley. Namesake of Connecticut's major aviation center, Bradley died during a training exercise at the site when it was a military base during World War II.
Courtesy of the New England Air Museum

Bradley Air Field in the 1950s, after the opening of the Murphy Terminal in 1952. Courtesy of the Hartford Courant

ribbon stretched across the new extended runway. Scheduled jet service at the now renamed Bradley Airport began in February 1961 with an American Airlines flight to San Francisco and Los Angeles via Cleveland. The aircraft used to provide the service was a Boeing 720, powered by the latest aviation technology: four turbojet engines manufactured by Connecticut's own Pratt & Whitney Aircraft Corporation.[51]

Chapter Three **Parkways, Expressways, and Interstates, Part 1**

I n the mid-1930s, with auto and truck traffic clogging the lower post road between Greenwich and New Haven, Connecticut built the Merritt Parkway to help alleviate the congestion and reduce traffic accidents. As the state's first controlled-access highway, the Merritt Parkway represented a new mode of travel: a high-speed superhighway for the age of automobility. No sooner was the parkway completed than plans were made to extend it across the state as part of the first high-speed automobile route between New York and Boston. In the 1940s, the federal government made plans to build three expressways through Connecticut as part of a forty-thousand-mile nationwide system of controlled-access interstate highways. Disagreement over how best to finance the federal system—together with the Korean War—delayed construction for more than a decade and left states unprepared to accommodate the postwar boom in motor vehicle ownership and long-distance highway travel. By the 1950s, with traffic congestion along the lower post road in Connecticut at levels not seen since before the construction of the Merritt Parkway, the Connecticut Highway Department built a second expressway parallel to the post road, the 129-mile-long Connecticut Turnpike, which like similar projects in other states was financed through the collection of tolls.

The Merritt Parkway

As a solution to persistent traffic congestion on the lower post road, the Connecticut Highway Department in the 1930s built its first controlled-access highway, the Merritt Parkway.

A NEW KIND OF HIGHWAY

By the 1920s, traffic congestion on the lower post road in Fairfield County—the most heavily traveled link in the state's entire trunk line system—was reaching unacceptable levels. The problem occurred in Connecticut, but it was hardly a local problem. Studies showed that nearly half of the vehicles using this stretch of roadway originated in New York State and were headed for points beyond Fairfield County, something that would hardly surprise anyone who was familiar with the long history of that particular highway. But now, in addition to congestion, serious traffic accidents were also on the rise. The length of the lower post road in Fairfield County amounted to about 4 percent of the state's total trunk line system, yet this heavily traveled link was responsible for 20 percent of all traffic deaths and injuries in the state. Clearly, something had to be done.[1]

Beginning about 1923, the Connecticut Highway Department (CHD) began a multiyear program specifically aimed at improving the traffic-handling capacity of the Boston Post Road between Greenwich and New Haven. Where feasible, the roadway was widened to four travel lanes; curves were straightened; pavement damaged by heavy truck traffic was replaced; traffic signals were installed and coordinated to help regulate the flow of traffic; and in a few places, the roadway itself was moved to a new location so as to avoid congested town centers. Still, State Highway Commissioner MacDonald knew these improvements alone would not be enough.[2]

As post road improvements got under way, MacDonald, in a speech to the Bridgeport Chamber of Congress, proposed building a new "superhighway" inland away from existing centers of population and commerce, so as to siphon through traffic away from the commercially congested post road.[3] MacDonald's proposal was one of the first mentions by the Highway Department of what would become the Merritt Parkway, and his concept of a superhighway represented in effect a new kind of roadway for Connecticut. What MacDonald envisioned was a wide swath of concrete strewn across the landscape like a cement ribbon. With no at-grade intersections, access along the entire length of the highway would be controlled so that drivers could enter and exit only at designated interchanges, and in between could travel at high speeds undisturbed by interrupting traffic. Such a controlled-access roadway was in fact so different from the typical full-access highway as to be considered a new mode of transportation. Providing much the same kind of line-haul transport made popular in the previous century by steam railroads, the controlled-access superhighway was sometimes referred to by highway engineers as a cement railroad for the age of automobility.

*The Merritt
Parkway meanders
over the natural
landscape
through Westport,
Connecticut.
Connecticut
Highway
Department*

The concept of a controlled-access highway originated in landscape design, specifically in the separated roadways used by landscape architect Frederick Law Olmsted in his design of New York's Central Park to segregate horse and carriage traffic from pedestrians walking through the park. Seen as a progressive idea by City Beautiful supporters, the concept was first applied to automotive travel with the construction of the Bronx River Parkway in New York early in the century. Afterward, New York Park Commissioner Robert Moses promoted the concept in a big way in the highways that he would build throughout the greater New York region. Indeed, by the 1920s, one such Moses superhighway, the Hutchinson River Parkway, was already under construction through Westchester County to a point a few miles from the Connecticut border. MacDonald was convinced that such a superhighway, in this case a park-like roadway for auto traffic only, was just what Connecticut needed to reduce traffic congestion in Fairfield County, while at the same time providing Connecticut residents with a high-speed automotive connection to New York City via the Hutchinson River Parkway.

Getting such a superhighway built, however, presented super problems of its own. With an estimated price tag of twenty million dollars, the thirty-eight-mile-long Merritt Parkway—named for Fairfield County Republican congressman Schuyler Merritt—would be the largest highway project undertaken, not only in Connecticut but also in the entire country to that time. Funding for the highway began modestly in 1925, when the legislature allocated fifteen thousand dollars for the Highway Department to survey an inland route for the parkway. The project, however, stalled for several years. Legislative representatives of both parties from upstate communities were reluctant to spend such a large sum on a traffic problem in a single downstate county. But with the onset of the Great Depression, resistance to the parkway lessened as the project became—as much as a traffic improvement—a way to provide much-needed employment for the state's construction industry. In 1931, the legislature passed three bills directed at turning the Merritt Parkway into a reality. One bill directed the CHD to lay out the highway as a trunk line route, while another allocated one million dollars for initial right-of-way purchases. A third act created a nine-member Merritt Parkway Commission to "supervise the expenditure of all moneys that may be appropriated by the county of Fairfield for the development of the highway and the adjacent land."[4]

The Merritt Parkway Commission was intended to function much the way similar commissions and districts had been used in the past to build expensive bridge crossings. In addition, the governor made sure that members appointed to the commission were all concerned citizens of Fairfield County, whose involvement he hoped would minimize local resistance to the project. However, no sooner was the Merritt Parkway Commission created in law than Commissioner MacDonald called its authority into question. Even though he was an ex officio member of the commission, MacDonald saw the group as a threat to the power of his own highway fiefdom and quickly sought an opinion on the legality of the commission from the state's Republican attorney general. Contrary to the intent of the legislature to create a commission that would oversee construction of the parkway, the attorney general produced a tortuous interpretation of a phrase in the bill that called the commission into existence "when the Merritt highway shall be constructed"[5] and ruled that the phrase meant the Parkway Commission could not begin its work until *after* the parkway had been completed! The attorney general also concluded that while the Parkway Commission might consult with MacDonald and his department about the highway, MacDonald was under no obligation to follow the dictates of commission members.

With MacDonald's supreme authority over the design and construction of the parkway restored, attention turned to how best to finance the frightfully expensive project. First thoughts turned to securing funds from various New Deal programs, and indeed in 1934 Connecticut received two grants from the Federal Emergency Relief fund totaling $438,000 to help finance the parkway.[6] When Schuyler Merritt went to Washington to lobby for more substantial federal relief, it appeared that Connecticut might receive a $6.75 million grant from the Public Works Administration as well as an $8.25 million loan from the Reconstruction Finance Corporation to cover the bulk of the parkway's cost. However, when push came to shove, Connecticut's appeal for federal funding was denied.[7]

Instead, in 1935, the state of Connecticut authorized Fairfield County to issue bonds to cover the cost of building the parkway, with principal and interest to be repaid, not through the collection of tolls, as one might expect, but directly by an annual payment to the county of one million dollars from the Highway Department's ongoing budget. By the time the last of the county bonds were retired in 1952, the cost of the Merritt Parkway had totaled $21,225,334.[8]

As preparations for construction got under way, the Merritt Parkway Commission tried for several years to wrest control of the parkway from MacDonald through legislative action, but to no avail. When the commission finally became empowered with the completion of the first section of the parkway in the summer of 1938, its authority was directed toward relatively mundane matters: publishing a promotional map of the parkway, and regulating the use of parkway land for picnicking. In July 1943, the commission decreed that despite the normal ban on truck traffic, trucks carrying war materiel could use the parkway, a privilege it rescinded as soon as the war was over. The commission was still in existence in May 1946 when it reported on the accident rate along the parkway, as compared with that on the old post road. It seemed that from 1940 to 1945 the post road had more than three times the number of accidents as the parkway and nearly five times as many fatalities, confirming for the public what engineers already knew: controlled-access highways provided safer travel conditions at higher speeds than traditional roadways.[9]

LAND ACQUISITION, DESIGN, AND CONSTRUCTION
With the attorney general's ruling behind him and with financing options being heavily debated, MacDonald kept the project moving by creating a special unit within the CHD to design the superhighway, headed by chief

engineer Warren Creamer. Unable to gather adequate mapping for the parkway from local sources, Creamer used aerial photography for the first time to determine the route of the highway—which at MacDonald's insistence was kept an in-house secret for several years. (The first map of the parkway's general location did not appear in newspapers until the spring of 1935.) Meanwhile, Commissioner MacDonald hired Leroy "Jack" Kemp, a former Republican state representative and a realtor from Darien, to act as a special purchasing agent for land acquisition. Using property details prepared by the department's Bureau of Boundaries and Rights-of-Way, Kemp was expected to negotiate a quick cash purchase for each parcel required, so as to avoid the time-consuming court hearings that accompanied more traditional land condemnation proceedings.[10] Given the magnitude of the project and the cost involved, the direct negotiation approach to buying land was a situation ripe for abuse, and Kemp did not disappoint.

Knowing which parcels of land were needed for the highway, Kemp hired two broker friends to approach unsuspecting owners and offer their services as agents for the sellers. In return, Kemp's real estate partners agreed to kick back half of their brokerage fees to Kemp. With the route of the parkway under tight wraps, and therefore little chance that outside realtors might interfere with Kemp's scheme, cash purchases of land proceeded at a steady clip.[11]

To inflate broker fees, Kemp typically offered to purchase a parcel of land for two to five and even more than ten times the parcel's assessed value. For example, Kemp purchased one fifteen-acre parcel in Greenwich valued at $7,500 for $93,000. In Westport, Kemp sold twenty-five acres of land that he himself owned, and which was assessed by the town for $13,618, for $183,000, but only after having the land reevaluated by an "independent" appraiser that Kemp had personally chosen for the job. Kemp was also careful to share his largesse with well-connected Republicans in Fairfield County. In one instance, Republican state representative Stanley Mead received $100,000 for a twenty-eight-acre parcel of land assessed at $14,050. Later, when a parcel of land was purchased from the Greenwich Water Company, Kemp recorded a payment of $3,700 to Clarence G. Willard, secretary of the Republican State Committee, for "friendly services and influence in expediting the sale."[12]

To make matters worse, MacDonald chose to purchase a three-hundred-foot right-of-way for the project—twice the width required by the parkway itself—so that he could build a parkway 150 feet wide on half of the right-of-way while reserving the other half for possible future expansion. As the parkway's chief engineer noted, "It was easily discovered by us that in the obtainment of the right-of-way we could pass that way but once."[13] It is estimated that as a result of MacDonald's decision to double the rights-of-way needed for the project, and Kemp's insider land fraud scheme, the state paid upward of six million dollars for parkway land that should have cost closer to one million.

In its design, the Merritt Parkway was a combination of the latest in road-building techniques and more practical cost-cutting measures. From Greenwich to Milford, the parkway had a total of twenty-one interchanges and seventy-two bridges along its route. The basic design consisted of two twenty-six-foot cement roadways (each with two travel lanes) separated by a twenty-two-foot median strip. However, to minimize the cost of bridge construction, the median strip was "pinched" to a mere sixteen feet as the roadway approached each overpass or underpass, thereby shortening the length of each bridge span (and its cost) by nearly 30 percent from what it would have been had the full median been maintained throughout.[14]

Because of its east-west orientation, the alignment of the parkway cut across the north-south hills and valleys of the Connecticut landscape, which provided engineers with little opportunity to fit the roadway snugly into the rolling topography of Fairfield County. As a result, extensive earthen cuts and fills were required. Even with engineers taking care to lay out the roadway so as to minimize the volume of cuts and fills, the resulting alignment created excessive grades in places, some as steep as 7 percent, and required forty-six curved sections, some as sharp as seven degrees. Although engineers made sure to bank the roadway through its curved sections, at the posted speed limit of fifty miles per hour the parkway's curves, while contributing to its scenic value, provided a challenge for speedy drivers.[15]

In one instance, the parkway's design was also influenced by local politics. When the residents of the Greenfield Hills area of Westport learned that the CHD was required to build interchanges only with other state highways, they convinced their town selectmen not to seek a local road interchange in their part of town, so as to keep unwanted traffic out of their affluent community. The result was a 7.5-mile section of parkway between Route 57 in Westport and Route 58 in Fairfield with no entrance or exit. To this day, that portion of the Merritt Parkway remains the longest stretch of controlled-access highway in the state without local access.[16]

Despite the parkway's natural beauty, which was enhanced by more than one million dollars of postconstruction landscaping, the overpass bridges became its most striking visual feature. Their design presented little technical difficulty—most were simple steel arch spans—yet each was given a unique facade to provide ongoing visual interest for the motorist. George Dunkelberger, an architect forced by the Depression to work as a draftsman for the CHD, designed all bridge facades along the parkway. By using concrete—in contrast with the more expensive stone facing used on the Hutchinson River Parkway—Dunkelberger was able to give each bridge a unique appearance. On the features of the facades and adjacent abutments, Dunkelberger used architectural styles that varied from Classical Revival and Richardsonian Romanesque to the then popular Art Deco. Dunkelberger also provided tubing inside each bridge structure to carry away the rainwater, so that it would not run across the concrete facades and stain them. On some structures Dunkelberger even colored the concrete using a palette of earth tones to better blend the bridges and their abutments into the natural landscape. As yet another way to vary the appearance of the bridges, Dunkelberger even left the inner steel structure of several spans unfaced and exposed to view.[17]

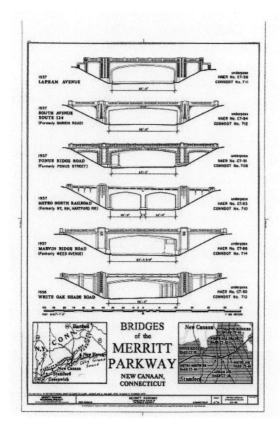

Different bridge designs were a major feature of the Merritt Parkway.
Connecticut Highway Department

Ground was broken for the Merritt Parkway in July 1934, with construction on the first section of the project, from Greenwich to Norwalk, beginning at both ends simultaneously. The first section of the parkway, to New

Canaan Avenue (Route 7) in Norwalk, was completed on June 29, 1938, when Governor Wilbur L. Cross and a host of other dignitaries officially opened the "most modern stretch of highway in the state" to great fanfare. All along the route, parkway bridges "were jammed with spectators as a long motorcade drove slowly over the parkway's fresh concrete" from Norwalk to Greenwich, "stopping in each of the four towns along the route for ceremonies, photographs and speeches."[18] The remaining twenty miles of the parkway, from Norwalk to Milford, were opened in sections over the next two years, until the thirty-eight mile parkway was completed in September 1940.[19]

POLITICS AND SCANDAL

Jack Kemp was able to sustain his land fraud scheme for the time it took to acquire much of the right-of-way for the Merritt Parkway. But in the end, he did not escape scot-free. To process the acquisitions, Kemp had to submit a payment voucher for each sale to the Highway Department for review, first by project engineer Warren Creamer and then by Commissioner MacDonald, who would sign the voucher and forward it to the state treasurer for payment. In the spring of 1937, Creamer became suspicious of the voucher Kemp submitted for payment of $3,700 to the secretary of the Republican State Committee for "friendly services and influence" in expediting a particular sale, and refused to give his approval. But MacDonald overruled Creamer's objection and processed the voucher as usual.[20]

By then, rumors of Kemp's questionable activity were spreading and had reached the ears of Governor Wilbur L. Cross and Robert A. Hurley, commissioner of the newly created Connecticut Department of Public Works; both were progressive Democrats. Governor Cross had established the Connecticut Department of Public Works as part of an effort to reform state government and to force department heads to report directly to the governor instead of acting as independent leaders of their own bureaucracies, as was the norm. Acting as if the authority of the Public Works Department included all state highways, Commissioner Hurley with the backing of Governor Cross executed an internecine coup and, over MacDonald's disbelief, took control of the Connecticut Highway Department. In a turnabout considered fair play, the legality of Hurley's action was confirmed by a ruling of the current attorney general (a Democrat) who read the law giving the Department of Public

Works control of "all state buildings and property" to include highways, an interpretation that was as far-fetched as the reading by a previous Republican attorney general of the statute creating the Merritt Parkway Commission.[21]

Ultimately, Connecticut's rotten borough, status quo minority challenged Hurley and his progressive agenda, and MacDonald won back his position through court action. In *Connecticut Rural Road Improvement Association v. Robert A. Hurley* in February 1938, the State Supreme Court of Errors ruled that the law "entitled An Act establishing a Department of Public Works, manifests no legislative intent to deprive the highway commissioner of jurisdiction over the layout, construction, reconstruction and improvement of state and state-aid highways and bridges, or to limit or impair that jurisdiction or his powers and duties relating thereto by transferring them to the department or the commissioner of public works."[22]

By then, however, the damage had been done. With direct access to Highway Department files, Hurley began a review of departmental affairs, in particular those relating to the Merritt Parkway, and before long information about Kemp's questionable land transactions began to appear on the front pages of newspapers around the state. With the scandal exposed, independent inquiries were initiated by both the state attorney general and the state's attorney for Fairfield County. As a result—and to the embarrassment of the many Republicans who had benefited from Kemp's scheme—a special grand jury was convened on the matter in January 1938.[23]

While Kemp tried to cover his tracks by altering records, his accomplices quickly sold him out and pled guilty in return for a minimal fine of five hundred dollars each for their involvement in Kemp's scheme. In the end, the grand jury indicted Jack Kemp for fraud, a crime for which he was subsequently tried, convicted, and sentenced to serve from three to seven years in prison. Although MacDonald was not indicted for any criminal conduct per se, the grand jury did recommend that the commissioner be removed from his position for his grave mismanagement of the parkway project. With the grand jury's report in hand, Governor Cross asked for MacDonald's resignation as head of the Connecticut Highway Department, which he received on April 30, 1938, just weeks before the first section of the Merritt Parkway opened to traffic.[24]

Probe into Parkway Land Sales Widened By Attorney General

M'LAUGHLIN ORDERS EXHAUSTIVE STUDY OF PROPERTY DEEDS

Investigators to Trace 'Rapid Fire' Purchases of Land Later Sold to State.

U. S. STUDIES TAX ANGLE

Internal Revenue Agents Scan Prices; Cross Rejects Macdonald Ouster.

TURNS DOWN PHILLIPS

Supreme Court to Hear Arguments Jan. 7 on Highway Control Fight.

BY STAFF REPORTER

HARTFORD, Dec. 29.—Attorney General Charles J. McLaughlin disclosed late today that his inquiry into Merritt Parkway land purchases will include a special study of all transactions involving land which had changed hands a short time before the state's purchase.

The attorney general said that his study to date has revealed "numerous" instances where Fairfield county real estate changed hands a relatively short time before the same land was purchased for the right of way for the parkway.

Seeks to Trace 'Tips'

"We will attempt to establish whether the parkway route was known to real estate dealers or speculators in advance and whether they took advantage of such knowledge to acquire property with a view to reselling it to the state at substantially higher prices." Mr. McLaughlin said.

He declined at this time to disclose what transactions are being scrutinized with this aim in view, but did declare that the several ... which Dr. Alvin

way sales, a separate inquiry by the U. S. Internal Revenue bureau was reported to be under way.

The Federal government's interest in the transactions develops from income tax returns. Departmental agents were reported today to be making a check-up of tax returns against parkway transactions already reported from official sources. The sales have totaled $6,500,000 in the last five years, and the government is checking to see if Uncle Sam got his share in income taxes.

Thomas S. Smith, collector of internal revenue for Connecticut, declined to discuss this phase of the situation at his office here.

Phillips' Demand Rejected

While Mr. McLaughlin, State Highway Commissioner John A. Macdonald and State Comptroller Charles C. Swartz pushed forward with work on separate reports for Governor Cross on the parkway land purchases, the governor summarily rejected a demand by Congressman Alfred N. Phillips, Jr. of Stamford that he remove Macdonald from office.

In a press conference, at which he said he would reply later to Congressman Phillips' wire, the governor commended State's Attorney Lorin W. Willis of Fairfield county for joining in the inquiry; said the investigations now being made "may possibly lead to a grand jury investigation" of the parkway purchases; and declared that in any event the parkway disclosures will make necessary "reconstruction" of the State Highway department at the next session of the Legislature.

Gov. Cross, commending State's Attorney Willis for his "alertness to

to Gov. Cross within two weeks.

More Must Be Spent

In addition to the expenditures revealed by Post-Telegram investigation, it is expected that about $500,000 more must be spent to acquire some 40 parcels of land in Fairfield and Trumbull. Condemnation proceedings against owners of these lands have been undertaken.

Post-Telegram figures for the total expenditures to date are based on official reports by highway Commissioner Macdonald and the preliminary reports by Comptroller Swartz.

$2,143,550 To Greenwich

Greenwich property was the most expensive, a total of $2,143,550.18, being spent in that town for land acquisitions for the parkway project.

These figures, published for the first time, now disclose that the second highest expenditure for land

Tabulation of Figures

Here are the figures:

Greenwich	$2,143,550.18
Stamford	760,037.73
New Canaan	720,774.43
Fairfield-Trumbull	* 167,166.34
Trumbull-Stratford	* 464,062.72
Westport	317,945.50
Fairfield	319,273.80
Norwalk	158,411.05
Stratford	67,651.11
Fairfield-Norwalk	* 300,603.74
New Canaan-Wilton	* 531,168.19
Total	**$5,950,663.89**

*—Highway department originally divided parkway into projects, some projects covering more than one town and land acquisitions are so listed in official records.

Robert A. Hurley has legal jurisdiction over the State's highways.

The date for the hearing was assigned in Supreme court today and an early verdict on the question who controls the Highway department is expected soon.

Col. Ernest L. Averill will appear for the Connecticut Rural Roads Improvement association which started suit to restore control of the department to Commissioner Macdonald.

The Supreme court will decide the question whether State highways are "real assets" within the meaning of the Public Works act under which Commissioner Hurley, acting under an opinion of former Attorney General Edward J. Daly and assumed jurisdiction over the highways.

Text of Phillips' Demand for Ouster

DARIEN, Dec. 29.—Congressman Alfred N. Phillips, Jr. made public today the following telegram to Gov. Wilbur L. Cross asking him to oust Highway Commissioner John A Macdonald:

"In the light of the shocking Merritt Parkway disclosures, as a citizen and taxpayer, I hereby call upon you to procure the resignation of your appointee, Highway Commissioner Macdonald, felt by many to be the cornerstone of the Republican machine in the State of Connecticut.

"In replacing your appointee, said Macdonald, I respectfully request that you appoint a Connecticut man, not a stranger from another State whose salary is paid by Connecticut taxpayers."

In an attempt to mend political fences, Governor Cross did invite MacDonald to accompany him during the opening-day ceremonies, but the gesture did little to assuage the public shame that came with MacDonald's loss of power. Indeed, the whole political fiasco ended tragically for both men. Just a few weeks after opening day, MacDonald died unexpectedly on July 8, 1938, while that fall Governor Cross lost his bid for reelection to Republican candidate Raymond E. Baldwin, in no small part because of the Merritt Parkway scandal.[25]

THE WILBUR CROSS EXTENSION

As first proposed, the Merritt Parkway was to terminate on the lower post road in Stratford at the Washington Street crossing of the Housatonic River. When local businessmen opposed the idea for fear of the traffic congestion it would cause, plans were made to build a bridge to carry the parkway across the Housatonic River, so as to bring the superhighway to an end on a less crowded portion of the existing post road in Milford. This was intended to be only a temporary situation, since prior to the opening of the first section of the parkway, Commissioner MacDonald had announced a $100 million long-range plan to extend the route of the Merritt Parkway across the entire state of Connecticut—complete with a loop road around Hartford—as part of the first multistate controlled-access superhighway between New York and Boston.[26]

The span across the Housatonic River was built in 1940 at a cost of one million dollars and named the Sikorsky Bridge in honor of helicopter pioneer Igor Sikorsky, whose factory was nearby. To keep the cost to a minimum, the bridge was designed with an open steel deck instead of a more traditional deck of poured concrete. Though perfectly safe, the

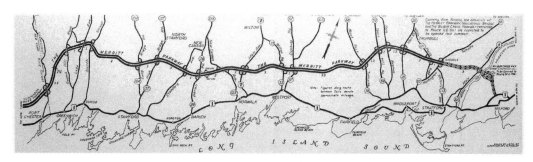

Route of the Merritt Parkway, with terminus on Route 1 in Milford.
Connecticut Highway Department

resulting side-to-side swaying and swishing sound of rubber tires moving at high speeds across the open steel grid unnerved drivers using the bridge for decades. The unusual design, however, did indeed save the CHD money: first on the cost of the bridge deck itself, and second on the cost of the steel substructure needed to support the lighter, open-grid deck.[27]

The change in terminus for the Merritt Parkway and the subsequent plan for a cross-state expressway were part of a realization by engineers that traffic congestion at the point of reentry on the post road was only part of the problem. A superhighway like the Merritt Parkway, a new kind of high-speed transport, needed to be part of a full network of similar superhighways. As an extension of the Hutchinson River Parkway traveling north from New York City, the Merritt Parkway was part of something larger than itself. It was but one piece in a new kind of transportation facility, a controlled-access highway that would connect the region's two most populous cities, New York and Boston.

The next piece in this continuous cross-state expressway was a twenty-nine-mile-long extension of the Merritt Parkway that ran from the

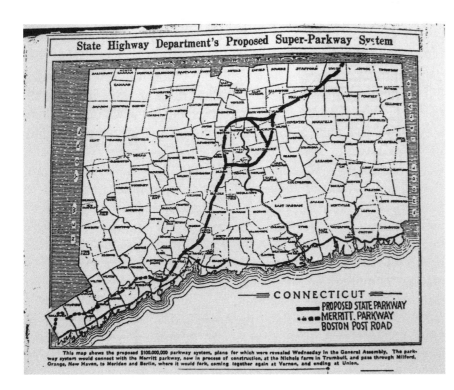

The cross-state parkway, first proposed in 1936, was an extension of the Merritt Parkway to Boston. Courtesy of the Hartford Courant

Sikorsky Bridge in Stratford to the Berlin Turnpike (U.S. Route 15) in Meriden. This stretch of the cross-state expressway was to be known as the Wilbur Cross Parkway in honor of Governor Cross. Though conceived as a parkway, similar to its sister road, the Merritt, the Wilbur Cross Parkway traversed a landscape that was more urban than its predecessor, and as a result the design of the second parkway was more utilitarian than aesthetic. The roadway itself was built slightly smaller, with four twelve-foot lanes separated by a (nonpinched) twenty-foot median, and although Dunkelberger designed the bridges for this parkway as well, the facades were done in the plainer International style; as a result, the bridges of the Wilbur Cross Parkway are noticeably less eye-catching than those of the Merritt Parkway.[28]

Instead, the most interesting feature of the Wilbur Cross extension proved to be the West Rock Tunnel, the only expressway tunnel in all of New England. As the route of the parkway approached New Haven, it had to traverse a high rock ridge known locally as West Rock. When it proved to be impractical to veer around the ridge to the north (too indirect) or to the south (too populated), it was decided to bore twin tunnels, 1,200-feet long, directly through the mountain, each tube large enough to carry two lanes of traffic.

Although construction of the Wilbur Cross Parkway began soon after the Merritt Parkway was completed in 1940, work was soon suspended due to the war and did not resume until the war was over in 1945. Construction of the West Rock Tunnel itself did not begin until January 1948. Since the grade of the roadway through the tunnel was slightly uphill from west to east, drilling began at the west portal so that water would not accumulate against the work face. Work on both tubes progressed simultaneously. However, to better control the risk of cave-ins from dynamiting, the type of work being done in each bore of the tunnel was deliberately varied. While the crew in one bore drilled the rock, loaded the dynamite, and blasted the rock away, the crew in the other bore of the tunnel was busy removing the muck from the last round of blasting, and installing the steel frame that would support the interior walls of the tunnel. After each shift, the two crews alternated tasks.[29]

After nearly a year of drilling, the tunnel broke through to the eastern face on November 8, 1948. To celebrate, the contractor hosted a party for Governor Baldwin and three hundred invited guests at Ceriani's Café, a well-known nightspot in New Haven, while the miners enjoyed their own celebration at the more aptly named Hog House near the job site. The entire Wilbur Cross Parkway including West Rock Tunnel was completed from the Sikorsky Bridge to the Berlin Turnpike (U.S. Route 15) in Meriden by the end of 1949.[30]

Unlike the Merritt Parkway, paid for with Highway Department funds appropriated from dedicated gas tax and motor vehicle revenues, the legislature chose to raise the revenue needed to construct the Wilbur Cross Parkway by installing toll stations on the already completed Merritt Parkway. The first toll station was erected in Greenwich in June 1939. With traffic along the new parkway already at a high volume, the ten-cent toll produced $61,000 in revenue in its first month alone. In the face of such success, the state soon added two additional toll stations, one in Wallingford and another in Milford, thereby increasing the parkway's revenue stream. By the time the Wilbur Cross Parkway was completed in 1949, the toll revenue collected had been sufficient to cover the entire cost of construction, which amounted to $17.5 million, including West Rock Tunnel.[31]

While the Wilbur Cross Parkway was under construction, improvements were also being made farther along the route of the cross-state expressway as it continued toward the Massachusetts state line in Union. With all pretense of a parkway-like road now abandoned for a more practical approach, this third section of the route from Meriden to Union was referred to as the Wilbur Cross *Highway*. The first improvements along this section included the widening of the existing Berlin Turnpike into a four-lane divided highway with at-grade intersections; the construction of the Charter Oak Bridge across the Connecticut River; and a short section of expressway (known locally as the South Meadows Expressway) connecting the Berlin Turnpike to the river bridge, all of which were completed by 1942. Therefore, by the time the Wilbur Cross Parkway opened in 1949, the state's first high-speed expressway route was operational as far eastward as Silver Lane in East Hartford.

Federal Policy Shapes an Era

In the 1940s, federal highway engineers formulated a plan to build a national system of controlled-access expressways to connect the nation's largest cities, while politicians missed a historic opportunity to coordinate the new highway program with other urban renewal efforts.

Building on the idea of conducting scientific planning studies to help determine future highway needs, as it had done in Connecticut in 1926, the federal Bureau of Public Roads began to promote highway planning as a national standard by allowing state highway departments to use 1.5 percent of their federal highway allotment each year specifically for planning purposes. Such efforts typically began with an inventory of existing conditions, traffic volumes, and financial resources. By collecting such data on an annual basis, highway departments amassed large amounts of information from which they could extract past trends and forecast values for some future year. This progressive methodology of collecting and analyzing data also made it possible for engineers to study certain important aspects of road construction, for example the durability of different types and thicknesses of pavement over time under different traffic conditions, and to improve their construction techniques accordingly. However, the analysis of survey data for experimental purposes must not be confused with planning. Highway planning required a crucial third step beyond the collection of data and the identification of trends. By definition, it also included the projection of those trends into the future, so that conditions *that did not yet exist* could be analyzed and highway needs in some future year predetermined.

In Connecticut, the incorporation of an ongoing planning function into the responsibilities of the state's Highway Department began on October 1, 1942, with the creation of a Bureau of Highway Planning Studies within the department. The function of the bureau was to create a program for future highway development in the state, in particular the construction of additional controlled-access expressways, and to study individual projects in light of estimated future needs. With the creation of a Bureau of Planning within the Connecticut Highway Department and similar bureaus in other states, the federal Bureau of Public Roads had created a method to standardize highway policy among states. In the world of progressive scientific management, planning had become policy.[32]

The possibility of a national system of interstate superhighways was first taken seriously in 1935, when President Franklin Delano Roosevelt—in the tradition of the first transcontinental railroad—asked Commissioner Thomas H. MacDonald (not to be confused with the highway commissioner of Connecticut) and the Bureau of Public Roads to investigate the feasibility of building a handful of controlled-access superhighways from the Atlantic seaboard to the Pacific. Over the next decade, as a result of planning studies done by the bureau with input from state highway departments across the nation, Roosevelt's simple idea for a few transcontinental expressways evolved into a grander proposal for a forty-thousand-mile network of controlled-access highways to connect all American cities with populations of fifty thousand persons or more.[33]

During that process, the Bureau of Public Roads defined the nature of such a system and how it might be financed, in several important ways. First, and importantly, the interstate system was envisioned from the start not as a series of individual highways built to serve specific travel needs (such as the Merritt Parkway in Connecticut) but rather as a complete highway *system* designed as a whole to serve a single national purpose: to bring high-speed automobility within the reach of all Americans. It was as if, in the previous century, the Union Pacific and the Central Pacific railroads had undertaken to build not just the first two-thousand-mile transcontinental railroad from Council Bluffs, Iowa, to Sacramento, California, but instead a forty-thousand-mile railroad network for the entire nation in one fell swoop.

Second, as with any highway system many segments of the network would carry significantly less traffic than other segments and therefore, the bureau concluded, could not generate enough revenue to cover the cost of their construction through the collection of tolls. This led to a firm decision to build all interstate expressways as non-toll, free roads, and as a result the terms "freeway" and "expressway" became synonymous with such controlled-access highways.

Last of all was the idea of how best to serve the numerous cities around the country to be connected by such interstate highways. As early as the 1920s, regional planning advocates such as Lewis Mumford were suggesting that such large highways should avoid direct contact with urban centers and be built instead around them, with an offshoot highway to connect the city to the high-speed through-road, an idea Mumford termed the "townless highway."[34] In other words, since broad, multilane highways such as the interstates were not by their nature compatible with dense, overcrowded urban areas whose internal traffic moved at much slower speeds, they should be routed around, and not through such areas. In the Mumford tradition, plans for the first Connecticut cross-state expressway unveiled in the 1930s showed the route splitting and diverting around Hartford to the north and south rather than going directly through the center of the city.

Unfortunately, Mumford's idea of a townless highway made little sense to Thomas MacDonald and his fellow engineers at the Bureau of Public Roads. In 1936, when the idea of building superhighways across the country was still in its infancy, MacDonald went to Germany to inspect the network of autobahn highways being built there, the first portions of which had just been completed. While MacDonald agreed that the roads were "wonderful examples of the best modern road building," he did not consider them an appropriate model for America. The *Reichsautobahnen*, he noted, was essentially a network of rural highways that served relatively small amounts of traffic, which led some to speculate that Hitler was building such roads, not for economic reasons, as he had stated, but for military purposes, as in fact he was.[35]

On his return, MacDonald shared his observations with the American Society of Civil Engineers. "The system of German roads," he said, "is being built in advance of, and to promote the development of, highway transportation. In the United States, the situation is just the reverse [and] the building of superhighways must be limited to areas where the present and prospective traffic will justify it . . . From the developments abroad and in the United States, one can conclude that superhighways will be created, but only in the vicinity of metropolitan areas, for relieving traffic congestion within those areas."[36]

In true progressive fashion, MacDonald confirmed his intuition by conducting an origin and destination study of the traffic moving along U.S. Route 1 between Baltimore and Washington, D.C. From the data collected, MacDonald identified what he termed the "root fallacy" behind the concept of loop or bypass roads around urban centers: "On main highways at the approaches to any city, especially the larger ones, a very large part of the traffic originates in or is destined for the city itself. *It cannot be bypassed.*"[37] Therefore, since studies showed that the large majority of urban traffic began and ended in the heart of the city's central business district, MacDonald and the bureau rejected Mumford's idea of a townless highway in favor of building their controlled-access expressways directly into and through city centers, where traffic was most congested. Unlike the Germans, MacDonald would put his superhighways where the traffic already was, and truly wanted to be.

From the mid-1930s to the mid-1940s, the Bureau of Public Roads continued to plan for a trunk line system of interstate superhighways that would bring high-speed automobility to all Americans. Further, it was decided that those highways would be built directly into and through the nation's largest cities, and that they should *not* be financed through the collection of tolls. All of this planning activity culminated in the passage of the Federal-Aid Highway Act of 1944. With this landmark piece of legislation, Congress authorized the designation of a National Interstate Highway System, not to exceed forty thousand miles in length. However, because the federal legislators were at odds about how to pay for such a system, the law contained no provision for financing this bold national undertaking.

With a National Interstate Highway System authorized but unfunded, MacDonald and state highwaymen spent the next few years discussing how best to allocate the forty thousand authorized miles to specific routes. The process was completed in 1947, and a national map of officially designated interstate routes was officially adopted.[38] In Connecticut, the system included three interstate highways: I-84 across the middle of the state from Danbury to Union; I-91, directly north from New Haven to Springfield, Massachusetts; and I-95, along the shoreline from Greenwich to Rhode Island, for a total of 297 miles. So while federal funding continued to flow to states for the improvement of their existing federal-aid primary and secondary systems, Connecticut engineers and other highwaymen, fully aware of the interstate routes to be built in their respective states, considered how best to utilize existing highway funding to address their postwar traffic problems in the absence of full funding for the interstate system.

It should be noted that while the template for building a nationwide system of interstate highways was being forged in Washington in the 1940s, it was widely recognized that such a program would be but one part in the postwar revitalization of America's cities. And many federal engineers, including MacDonald, were well aware that their highway plans represented only one segment of the nation's total transportation network. Acknowledging the possibility that automobility alone might not be the best solution to postwar transportation needs, especially in urban areas, MacDonald noted that superhighways should be located so as to "best and most conveniently serve to promote their use in proper coordination with other transportation means."[39] He saw coordination with housing and city planning authorities; railroad, bus, and truck interests; airport officials; and others as necessary to ensure the success of his program, especially when building through dense urban centers. But how

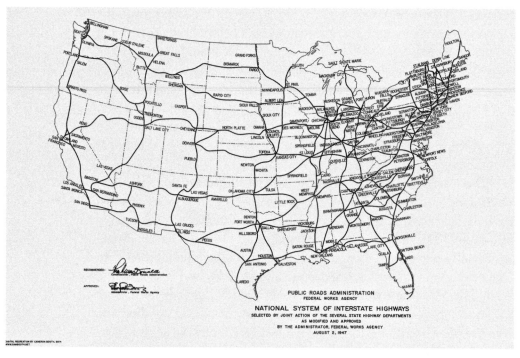

The interstate highway network as first designated in 1947 included three routes in Connecticut: I-84, I-91, and I-95.
Public Roads Administration

could MacDonald make that happen when his congressional mandate was limited to highways alone?

MacDonald was also conscious of the failure of city planning to counteract the movement of people and businesses out of the cities, and the "dynamic forces that have made decentralization of the original city inevitable."[40] Instead, he saw the construction of express highways through city centers, in coordination with other urban programs, as a possible way to reverse or at least slow this decentralizing trend, which he saw as draining the economic vitality of cities everywhere. So in 1947, while he continued to work with state highway agencies to finalize specific interstate routes, MacDonald brought his idea of inter-agency coordination to Major General Philip B. Fleming, administrator of the Federal Works Agency and at the time MacDonald's immediate boss. Together they considered the idea that MacDonald's highway building program might be used to spearhead the much-needed renewal of city centers, with the Bureau of Public Roads removing substandard housing to make room for superhighways while coordinating its efforts with other federal agencies responsible for building courthouses, office buildings, and affordable housing in downtown areas, all in an interdependent fashion that would help revitalize the economic base of America's largest cities.[41]

It was a grandiose idea that unfortunately was by its very nature unsuited to the progressive tendency to divide and subdivide and reduce urban problems to their separate parts rather than integrate them into a holistic approach. For example, at the same time that MacDonald and Fleming were discussing their plans for a coordinated federal effort in the revitalization of cities, Congress was busy debating a stand-alone housing bill designed to fund a national program of slum clearance and urban redevelopment by local public housing agencies. Therefore, when Fleming brought MacDonald's plan for a multiagency, coordinated approach to the problems of the city to President Truman, the president rejected the proposal outright, thinking it wiser "to hold to the provisions [of the pending legislation] . . . for the present," lest by complicating the matter political support for the housing bill might be lost.[42]

With Truman's backing, the Federal Housing Act of 1949 was enacted by Congress. With that, MacDonald's plan for combining the two great government programs intended to remake American cities in the postwar years—interstate highways and slum clearance—was dismissed for political expediency and the two programs went their separate bureaucratic ways. In hindsight, a historic opportunity was missed. Even though Truman did leave the door open for a possible reconciliation of the two programs at some point in the near future, that possibility soon vanished as the president's (and the nation's) attention turned to the Korean War.

Connecticut Takes Matters into Its Own Hands

With the question of funding for the interstate highway program unresolved, Connecticut and other states built their own expressway projects, many along designated interstate routes, to meet the increasing traffic demands of the postwar years.

With its three interstates routes officially designated but no funding available to turn those plans into reality, the Connecticut Highway Department undertook several initiatives of its own to address the expected increase in highway traffic following the war. First, improvements were begun on the remainder of the Wilbur Cross Highway from East Hartford through Manchester, Bolton Notch, and across northeastern Connecticut to the Massachusetts border in Union, paid for out of regular federal and state highway funds. This portion of the controlled-access route was completed between 1949 and 1954. In Massachusetts, the route was extended by that state to the town of Sturbridge, where it joined with the Massachusetts Turnpike then under construction to Boston, thereby completing Connecticut's first cross-state expressway, and with the completion of the Massachusetts Turnpike, the region's first high-speed automotive route between New York and Boston.

Second, the Highway Department used existing federal and state funding to build short segments of express highways in or near the center of the state's most congested urban areas. It was expected that such projects would ease postwar congestion while at the same time providing a head start on future expressway projects of which they were a part. From the mid-1940s to the mid-1950s, short segments of express highways were built in New London (1943), Hartford (1945), Old Saybrook (1948), Waterbury (1948), Middletown (1950), East Hartford (1952), West Haven (1954), and Darien (1954).

Third, following the federal example, Connecticut highway engineers expanded on MacDonald's plan for a single cross-state expressway and put together their own plans for a system of *intra*state expressways. On March 18, 1953, Highway Commissioner G. Albert Hill unveiled the department's first long-range expressway plan to the Connecticut Society of Civil Engineers. The map Commissioner Hill displayed included not only the cross-state route from New York to Boston and the three expressway routes designated as federal interstate highways, but additional Connecticut expressways the department expected to build in trunk line corridors around the state. These included four north-south expressways in the corridors of routes 7, 8, 5, and 52; two east-west expressways along routes 6 and 44; and three diagonal expressways from the Hartford area toward the shoreline along routes 2, 9, and 15. Contrary to the proposal for the first cross-state expressway put forth by Governor Cross, but in conformance with the federal idea of building expressways directly into city centers, Hill's plan did not include a circumferential expressway around the city of Hartford.[43]

East-West Expressway, Hartford. This photograph illustrates the impact of a major expressway going through an urban center. Connecticut Highway Department

Forty years after the legislature had adopted Connecticut's first trunk line system of full-access state highways, Commissioner Hill proposed a network of trunk line superhighways to be built in the state. In total, Hill's system included about six hundred miles of controlled-access expressways, evenly divided between interstate expressways already designated as part of the federal system (297 miles) and intrastate expressways initiated by Connecticut engineers (303 miles).[44]

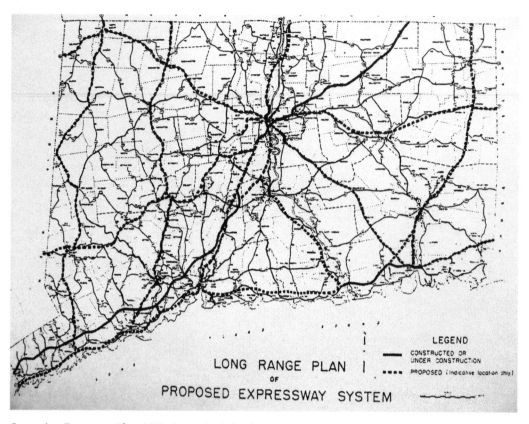

LONG RANGE PLAN
OF
PROPOSED EXPRESSWAY SYSTEM

LEGEND
CONSTRUCTED OR
UNDER CONSTRUCTION
PROPOSED (indicative location only)

Connecticut Expressway Plan, 1953. Connecticut's first long-range expressway plan shows expressways in most major travel corridors in the state.
Connecticut Highway Department

That there was a growing need for such expressways seemed undeniable, especially in Connecticut's most heavily used travel corridor, the post road between Greenwich and New Haven. By the mid-1950s, traffic on the lower post road in Fairfield County had returned to about the level it had been before the opening of the Merritt Parkway. In addition, truck traffic along Route 1 had increased substantially and presented a problem similar to that presented by automobiles a generation earlier. Studies indicated that by the 1950s, heavy trucks made up 17 percent of the total volume of traffic using the post road; light trucks, an additional 15 percent. Together this amounted to one third of all traffic on the existing post road. Taking into account the additional length of roadway these commercial vehicles required due to their longer lengths and stopping distances, this translated into an equivalent of 44 percent of total traffic volume when compared to automobiles. To compound the problem, all of the heavier trucks originated outside of Connecticut and nearly three-quarters of them were destined for places beyond Fairfield County. Most light truck traffic, on the other hand, was local in nature.[45]

As early as 1951, in anticipation of the interstate expressway (I-95) to be built through Connecticut, the Highway Department began to study possible locations for a second controlled-access expressway through Fairfield County to help solve the problem of excessive truck traffic along the lower post road. As opposed to the inland routing of the Merritt Parkway, however, consensus for the new expressway focused on a shoreline route, which it was thought would better serve businesses along the post road and best match the alignment being considered by the state of New York for the New York State Thruway.

In the months following Hill's unveiling of Connecticut's first statewide expressway system, however, the shoreline expressway project underwent a major transformation. Originally planned to end somewhere in the vicinity of New Haven, the project was not only extended across eastern Connecticut to the Rhode Island line, but rerouted inland to the northeast near Waterford to terminate at the state line in Killingly, doubling its length to an estimated 129 miles. The turn away from the shoreline to an inland routing was made as a result of an idea being promoted by Walter C. McKain Jr., a professor of sociology at the University of Connecticut, who advised Connecticut legislators that benefits to nonusers should also be considered in planning superhighways such as the shoreline expressway. According to McKain, "State outlays on highways should be planned not only to meet current deficiencies, but also to take account of future state and local land use programs, the economic requirements of specific areas and possibly, the use of highway location as an instrument for stimulating economic development." McKain believed strongly that "the creation of a thruway to Rhode Island would immediately be a boom to the area east of the Connecticut River for the attraction of much needed industry, and both commercial and recreational traffic." Testifying on behalf of the new inland route, McKain declared, "This bill will start Connecticut on another industrial expansion."[46]

In the spring of 1953, the argument put forth by McKain and his supporters in favor of nonuser highway benefits such as job growth and increased property values won the day in the legislature over the more traditional view that highways should be built only "after their need is demonstrated."[47] Therefore, in May 1953 the legislature authorized construction of Connecticut's second cross-state expressway project, the 129-mile controlled-access highway officially named the Greenwich-Killingly Expressway but soon labeled by McKain and his supporters as Connecticut's "Ribbon of Hope."

To fund the project, the legislature created an Expressway Bond Committee to sell the bonds necessary to build the highway, and then pay off the debt with toll revenue collected from the cars, trucks, and buses using the expressway. Though the move was contrary to federal policy concerning the interstate system, it was consistent with a new local toll road movement that had begun with the opening of the Pennsylvania Turnpike in 1940 and more recently had included the New Jersey Turnpike completed in 1952. The success of both projects in raising revenue sparked a toll road movement that quickly spread to New York, Massachusetts, Maine, and other states who, like Connecticut, were also looking for a way to address their postwar expressway needs by building toll road turnpikes while awaiting funds for the interstate program.

In addition to authorizing the Bond Committee to build the Greenwich-Killingly Expressway as a toll road, the legislature also created an Expressway Reserve Fund into which all toll revenue would be deposited. Tolls were to be set by the highway commissioner, sufficient to pay for the construction of the Greenwich-Killingly Expressway. In addition, the commissioner was allowed to "fix and collect further tolls" to be deposited in a separate "additional expressway construction fund" and used for the planning and construction "of such additional expressways as may be hereafter authorized" by the General Assembly. Clearly, if federal funding for the interstate system did not materialize, Connecticut was prepared to use toll revenues to construct its own statewide expressway system as proposed by Commissioner Hill.[48]

Construction of the Greenwich-Killingly Expressway (commonly referred to as the Connecticut Turnpike) began in January 1955 in Norwalk, West Haven, and Old Saybrook and continued outward from these three locations one section at a time as rights-of-way were acquired. There were, in all, fifty separate road-building contracts plus an additional forty contracts for ancillary items such as toll areas, fencing, and lighting. Yet the expressway opened to traffic a mere three years later and was immediately touted within the state as "the most significant public works project of the post-war era." The turnpike's connection to the New York Thruway, however, including bridges over the Mianus and Byram rivers, took an additional ten months to complete and did not open until October 1958.

It is difficult today to grasp the magnitude of the engineering challenge posed by such a massive project, but a smattering of statistics suggests the true accomplishment that the construction of the Connecticut Turnpike represented: total length, 129 miles; Connecticut towns traversed, 28; land purchased, 4,690 acres from 4,688 property owners; bridges built, 274, including 8 high-level crossings over navigable rivers; on-off interchanges, 100; toll plazas, 8; gas and food service areas, 4; maintenance garages to service the route, 15. And when all was said and done, the Connecticut Turnpike cost an unprecedented $350 million, or about $2.7 million per mile.[49]

Many hoped that the Connecticut Turnpike would open the more rural areas of eastern Connecticut to economic development.
Connecticut Highway Department

The Federal Promise Is Fulfilled

With passage of the Federal Aid Highway Act of 1956, Congress created a Highway Trust Fund by which to finance construction of the National System of Interstate and Defense Highways through the collection of federal taxes on gasoline and other petroleum products, putting an end to the toll road movement in Connecticut.

While the Connecticut Turnpike was under construction, the multistate toll road movement came to an abrupt halt with the passage of the Federal-Aid Highway Act of 1956 (FAHA 56) one of the most significant pieces of legislation enacted in the nation's history. Under political pressure from President Dwight D. Eisenhower and after several years of additional study, Congress finally reached agreement on how to pay for the interstate highway system.

FAHA 56 contained several key provisions that refocused state highway programs on a single goal: completion of the interstate highway system, which in recognition of the potential military relevance of such superhighways in the Cold War era, was now officially known as the National System of Interstate and Defense Highways. First, the act added an additional 1,500 miles to the already approved 40,000-mile system for a total of 41,500 miles, and proposed a target completion date of 1972. Second, the act created a Highway Trust Fund to finance the program. Fed by revenues from federal taxes on the sale of gasoline, tires, and other petroleum-based products, the Highway Trust Fund was to be dedicated solely to the construction of federal-aid highways, including the federal share of not only the new interstate highway program but also the existing federal-aid primary and secondary highway programs. Equally important, the act increased the federal share of the interstate program from the originally proposed 60 percent to a whopping 90 percent, leaving the states to fund only 10 percent of the total cost of interstate construction. (Meanwhile, other federal-aid highway programs remained at the more traditional 50–60 percent funding level.) While Connecticut (and other states) were ready to commit themselves to toll revenue as the main source of funding for new expressways, the federal government held to its stance against toll roads and chose to use gas tax revenue to fund its network of interstate express highways.

In recognition of the fact that many states, including Connecticut, had already built toll roads as part of their postwar highway programs, FAHA 56 made it possible for such existing toll roads to be included as part of the interstate system, so long as a non-toll highway existed nearby to provide similar service toll-free. Since the new toll expressways were typically built in major trunk line corridors within individual states, a traditional full-access U.S. highway route usually ran parallel to the new toll expressway, as U.S. Route 1 (the Boston Post Road) did alongside the Connecticut Turnpike. Therefore, the existing Connecticut Turnpike was quickly incorporated into the interstate system as I–95 as far east as Waterford, Connecticut, the point at which it turned inland, thereby leaving only the remaining portion of the shoreline route from Waterford to the Rhode Island border in Stonington still to be constructed as part of the approved interstate system.[50]

Passage of FAHA 56 impacted Connecticut's highway program in several ways. First, following the federal example, Connecticut returned to the traditional gas tax revenue model to cover its share of the interstate and other federal-aid highway programs. Second, as interstate funding began to flow, Connecticut had to accelerate its construction program (and therefore its matching funds as well) to be able to fully utilize the level of federal funding suddenly available after 1956. For example, whereas federal funds allocated to Connecticut before 1957 totaled about one to two million dollars per year, by 1957 the amount had increased to ten million dollars, and by 1960 would triple to thirty million dollars per year. As a result, in 1959 the state legislature enacted an accelerated bonding program of $522 million, which included state matching funds for both the interstate and federal-aid primary and secondary programs for the next four years.[51] (State funding allocations were based on the estimated cost of the entire interstate system, which in the 1950s was thought to be twenty-five *billion* dollars. As construction progressed, this cost estimate increased to upwards of forty billion dollars, and the gasoline tax and other auto-related user fees were typically increased to raise the additional federal and state funds to keep highway trust funds solvent.)

Enacting a program of such magnitude, even one with as much bipartisan support as the interstate system, brought with it some criticism, in particular of the program's impact on the urban centers through which these interstate expressways would pass. To help engineers and others discuss that impact, a first-of-its-kind conference on the new superhighway program was held in Hartford in September 1957. Entitled "The New Highways: Challenge to the Metropolitan Region," the four-day symposium was hosted by the Connecticut General Life Insurance Company and attended by six hundred "nationally recognized leaders in transportation, business, finance, education and government." Despite being commonly known as the Hartford Conference, the gathering was held on the insurance company's new Bloomfield campus—a suburban business complex complete with "its own medical suite, general store, beauty parlor, bowling alley [and] cafeteria"—the suburban campus itself a sign of the very exodus from the city center that had prompted the conference.[52]

One of the opening speakers was Bertram D. Tallamy, head of the Federal Highway Administration in Washington, D.C., and the man who was directly responsible for administering the federal-aid highway program. Tallamy admonished his audience that since at least half of the money allocated for interstate highways would be spent in and around urban areas, "the system of new highways must be carefully conceived and integrated with other practical programs for city development," but he was confident that this could be done "through the cooperative effort of both public and private agencies . . . working with the state highway departments." State highway officials in turn stressed the need to complete the interstate system on schedule and without delay. And the president of the American Association of State Highway Officials was quick to note, in the arrogant tone associated with scientific managers convinced of the certainty of their progressive planning techniques, that state highway officials did not need "some expert assistance from outsiders," especially those who dealt "in the realm of untried theories." If an urban area did not already have a plan of transportation and land use development in place, he continued, "it is doubtful that time can be afforded . . . to develop such plans."[53]

Not surprisingly, highwaymen in attendance were not pleased by the comments of the conference's final speaker, Lewis Mumford, an internationally known planner and social scientist who was highly critical of the impact interstate highways would have in urban areas, and who suggested that interstate construction be suspended for two years so that the nation's cities could develop comprehensive land use plans and, where necessary, relocate the planned superhighways to better advantage. Clearly, Mumford declared, for planning purposes emphasis should be on the region and not solely on urban renewal.[54] While the conference ended on a positive note, stressing the need for a regional agency to coordinate plans for city and suburb, at the same time critics like Mumford succeeded in portraying federal and state highwaymen and their superhighways as the "bad guys" in the effort to revitalize the nation's urban core.

As the 1960s began and Connecticut readied itself to play its part in what has been called (and rightly so) "the greatest public works project in the history of the world," unbeknown to highway engineers and the public alike the nation was about to enter one of the most turbulent and tumultuous periods in its history. The interstate highway program was about to collide head-on with an unprecedented boom in population and automobiles that would bring a shocking new awareness to the public consciousness, namely the impact that such large-scale growth and technological progress was having on the natural ecology of the land. As a result, new national and state laws were passed in an effort to mitigate that impact, and the federal-state megagovernment took on added responsibility for regulating the natural as well as the man-made environment. Afterward, with the collective view of humankind's place in the natural world altered forever, nothing would be as simple as it once was, including the new multimodal world of publicly financed transportation.

Chapter Four Parkways, Expressways, and Interstates, Part 2

ith the creation of the national Highway Trust Fund and an acceleration of financing by the state, highway funding in Connecticut increased dramatically after 1956, and the construction of controlled-access highways proceeded at a rapid pace around the state. In the coming years, Connecticut would build more than six hundred miles of express highways, almost equally divided between those expressways on the interstate system and those on the Connecticut system. By the 1960s, however, the disruption of neighborhoods and the displacement of people and businesses that accompanied highway construction—along with the increase in air pollution and traffic congestion that followed it— aroused persistent public protest against the government's highways-only policy and strong opposition to continued expressway construction at the expense of mass transportation. Meanwhile, as part of a growing awareness of humankind's interdependent relationship with the natural environment, Americans everywhere began to question not only the government's highways-only policy but also the nation's long-held belief in the efficacy of technology, progress, and unlimited growth.

Regions: Re-envisioning the Land

An unprecedented boom in population after the war, together with accelerated expressway construction, brought people, businesses, and retail stores to suburbia in substantial numbers and in the process created a new entity on the land: the region.

BABY BOOM HITS THE LANDSCAPE

In the decades following World War II, Connecticut experienced a boom in population that was unprecedented in the state's history. Coupled with the mobility provided by the automobile and the new superhighway, the baby boom had a substantial impact on the distribution of the state's population and on the appearance of the Connecticut landscape. From 1940 through 1970, the population of the state nearly doubled, increasing from 1,700,000 to 3,000,000 souls in the span of a single generation. At its peak in the 1950s and 1960s, this baby boom added more than 500,000 persons to the state's population every ten years, a million total during those two decades—or nearly one thousand persons week after week, year after year, for twenty years running. Though the state had seen a significant population boom earlier in the century during the industrialization of the 1910s and 1920s, in absolute size the population explosion of the 1950s and 1960s was twice that of the earlier boom. At the peak of industrialization, as the population of the state neared the one million mark, the decennial increase was on the order of 250,000 persons, compared to the 500,000 seen in each decade of the later boom. While it took three hundred years for the population of Connecticut to reach the one million mark (in 1910), it took only forty years to reach two million (in 1950) and only twenty more to top three million (in 1970).[1]

The postwar baby boom was different in another important respect. Whereas the boom leading up to the Roaring Twenties was composed largely of European immigrants looking for work in Connecticut at busy factories, the second boom was due largely to the increased birthrate of the state's native-born population, together with some migration into the state from overseas or elsewhere in the region. And this time the attraction was not factory jobs, which by then had already begun to move out of the state, but instead the possibility of a family home situated in the bucolic landscape that lay just beyond each of the state's crowded urban centers. In the postwar period, such a middle-class suburban home became the American idyll. As a measure of the magnitude of this rush to the suburbs, of the 500,000 persons being added each decade to the state's population at the height of the baby boom, only 12 percent wound up living in a Connecticut city, leaving 88 percent to settle outside an urban center in one of the state's blooming suburbs. By contrast, during the boom of the 1920s the percentages were nearly reversed: industrialization brought 78 percent of the state's new residents into one of its dozen or so urban centers, with only 22 percent finding their way to suburban settings made accessible by the early automobile and the state's first paved highway system. While the move to the suburbs certainly can be said to have begun in the early auto age, it accelerated to unprecedented proportions during the postwar baby boom.[2]

And of course the postwar baby boom involved much more than just people. In addition to the automobiles and superhighways so essential to the suburban lifestyle, the burgeoning population required other public services as well: public schools, police stations, firehouses, colleges, and shopping centers.

In the area of retail sales, a new phenomenon appeared on the landscape: the shopping mall. Before the postwar boom, retail sales took place in stores, large and small, concentrated in urban neighborhoods and city centers along with the population they served. In Hartford, for example, the department store G. Fox and Company operated one of the largest retail spaces in the state, a nine-story, two-building complex on Main Street that contained one million square feet of retail floor space. As the postwar population moved to the suburbs, where there had been nothing but open space, everything they required—highways, all manner of support services, even the retail stores where they worked and shopped—moved with them, including concentrations of retail commerce that varied from omnipresent strip malls containing a dozen or more stores, to mega malls with hundreds of stores designed to serve the needs of multiple suburban communities. These mega malls represented a new element on the landscape: vast amounts of retail space arranged in temperature-controlled settings at places easily accessible by superhighways and therefore surrounded by huge parking lots and ramp garages. In the years from 1947 to 1975, developers in Connecticut built some two-dozen malls of all sizes around the state, containing in total more than 1,300 separate retail stores with a total of eleven million square feet of retail space. Included in this number were five mega malls, *each* on average containing one million square feet of floor space, or the equivalent of a G. Fox-sized store at each of five locations around the state outside an existing urban area.

As for automobiles, 625,000 were added to Connecticut highways in the 1960s alone, with increases nearly as large in each of the two following decades as baby boomers came of driving age, bringing the total number of cars in the state to nearly two million by 1980. Whereas during the move to the suburbs in the 1920s the state contained one automobile for every fifteen residents, by 1980 not only had the number of people in the state skyrocketed, but such was the increase in car ownership that the ratio of cars to population had risen by a factor of ten, to one car for every 1.5 residents.

Statistics notwithstanding, it is still daunting to imagine the amount of physical change that took place during this postwar baby boom. It

Connecticut Shopping Centers, 1947 to 1975

SHOPPING CENTER	TOWN	TYPE	SIZE IN SQ. FT.	# OF STORES	ANCHORS	YEAR OPENED
Ridgeway Shopping Center	Stamford	3 levels open	330 000	33	Stop & Shop	1947
Waterbury Plaza	Waterbury	1 level open	295 000	32	Stop & Shop	1954
Hamden Plaza	Hamden	1 level open	320 000	40	Shaws	1955
Hamden Mart	Hamden	1 level open	342 000	24	Walmart	1960
Westfield Connecticut Post	Milford	3 levels enclosed	1 077 000	150	Filene's Sears	1960
Colonial Plaza Shopping Center	Waterbury	1 level open	247 000	48	Railroad Stores	1960
Bristol Shopping Center	Bristol	1 Level open	296 000	39	Super Stop & Shop	1962
Westfield Shoppingtown	Trumbull	2 levels enclosed	1 152 000	191	Macy's	1964
Mountain View Plaza	Naugatuck	1 level open	253 000	23	Super Stop & Shop	1965
Chapel Square Mall	New Haven	2 levels enclosed	405 000	65	none	1965
Orange Promenade	Orange	1 level ooen	244 000	20	Burlington Coat Factory	1966
New London Mall	New London	1 level open	268 000	23	Marshalls	1968
Norwichtown Mall	Norwich	1 level enclosed	241 000	18	Super Stop & Shop	1968
Old Saybrook Shopping Center	Old Saybrook	1 level open	288 000	40	Stop & shop	1969
Manchester Parkade	Manchester	1 level open	365 000	33	Super Stpop & Shop	1970
The Dock	Stratford	1 level open	310 000	15	Super Stop & Shop	1970
Enfield Commons	Enfield	1 level open	265 000	12	Bob's Stores	1971
Stateline Plaza	Enfield	1 level open	458 000	9	Home Depot	1971
Westfield Shoppingtown	Enfield	1 level enclosed	843 000	81	Sears, Filenes	1971
Westfield Shoppingtown	Meriden	2 levels enclosed	907 000	154	Filene's, Sears	1971
Papaco Shopping Center	Bloomfield	1 level open	255 000	35	Stop & Shop	1972
Simsbury Commons	Simsbury	1 level open	256 000	20	Super Stop & Shop	1972
Westfarms	Farmington	2 levels enclosed	1 291 000	164	Nordstrom, Filenes	1974
East Brook Mall	Willimantic	1 level enclosed	250 000	43	JC Penny	1975
TOTALS			10 958 000	1 312		

seemed that wherever one looked, large areas of orchards and farmland were being bulldozed to make room for endless tracts of suburban homes with two-car garages, new schools, public parks, mega malls, and other support services required by the state's burgeoning population. For the baby boom generation, change was the status quo; it was everywhere. And to make the most of it, one had to have what every mother, father, and sixteen-year-old in the family coveted most: an automobile.

And what of the Connecticut cities left behind? There, too, the whirlwinds of change were reaping their own rewards. With impetus provided by the Federal Housing Acts of 1949 and 1954, a national program of slum clearance and urban renewal became a permanent presence in many American cities. Entire neighborhoods were demolished to eliminate blighted housing, and thousands of city residents (many poor, and persons of color) were relocated to other parts of the city to live in newly built blocks of high-rise apartments, or left to fend for themselves in the housing market. In New Haven, for example, the lively Oak Street neighborhood was razed to make way for Route 34, designed to provide direct expressway access to the downtown area. Meanwhile, in Hartford, the long-established Italian American neighborhood along Front and Market streets was torn down and replaced with that city's first major redevelopment project, Constitution Plaza, a "mixed-use complex of office towers, parking garages, a hotel, fountains and walkways." Both projects removed from the urban centers the very kind of person-to-person street interactions that made a neighborhood vibrant, without replacing them in kind. Instead, the cities received a face-lift that replaced old structures with new offices and commercial areas while separating the people from the new facilities, which in any event did not often provide the kind of services the displaced residents required.

As slum clearance got under way, Jane Jacobs, a mother and activist trying to preserve the Greenwich Village neighborhood in which she lived from a proposed Manhattan expressway, published a book that described in detail the fallacies behind the federal approach to urban renewal. First and foremost, Jacobs revealed, while we were quick to replace the old with the new at the heart of American cities, we knew little or nothing of how a vibrant city functioned. Filled with examples taken from cities around the country, Jacobs's book, *The Death and Life of Great American Cities,* was offered as a first attempt to understand "the intricate social

Slum clearance in Hartford (before). This 1947 photograph shows the old Italian American neighborhood looking north along Front and Market streets in Hartford before the construction of Constitution Plaza. Spanning a Century: The Buckeley Bridge 1908–2008. Courtesy of ConnDOT

Hartford Aerial View of Bulkeley Bridge in 1960

Slum clearance in Hartford (after). The same area looking west in 1960 during the construction of Constitution Plaza and I-91. Spanning a Century: The Buckeley Bridge 1908–2008. Courtesy of ConnDOT

and economic order under the seeming disorder of cities."[3] Instead of recreating the once thriving neighborhoods that were now demolished, urban renewal focused on separating residents from the central activities of the city, turning new housing away from the street to face instead inner green spaces, which were a barrier to street life, while isolating commerce in self-contained places in other parts of town, such as the Chapel Street Mall in New Haven and Constitution Plaza in Hartford.

To make matter worse, federal housing and urban renewal policies were blatantly racist. Low-cost, thirty-year mortgages from the Federal Housing Administration (FHA) made the large-scale movement of white residents to the suburbs possible, but FHA policy also encouraged the practice of redlining, denying the benefits of the program to those who lived in sections of the city the FHA considered undesirable. Whereas personal prejudice had always existed in the housing market, the FHA "exhorted segregation and enshrined it as public policy."[4] Redlining not only prevented black people from moving to the suburbs; it "destroyed the possibility of investment wherever black people lived."[5] As a result, housing for nonwhite Americans was more often than not restricted to redlined neighborhoods, increasing the number and density of urban ghettos. By 1970 in Connecticut, nearly three-quarters of the state's nonwhite population lived on 30 percent of the blocks of the state's six largest cities.

Perhaps the only bright spot in the federal urban renewal effort was its funding of urban transportation. Building on an initiative begun by President John F. Kennedy, Congress in 1964 created the Urban Mass Transportation Administration (UMTA) to provide federal funding in order to rescue existing, privately owned bus systems from extinction and to help purchase new equipment by providing up to two-thirds of its capital cost. Within several years, UMTA assistance was broadened to subsidize the operating costs of bus lines that could not raise sufficient revenue from the fare box. UMTA funding was a major reason for the preservation and expansion of public transit in Connecticut in the 1970s and continues to be to this day. However, even here the success of UMTA funding must be evaluated against the fact that by the mid-1960, federal programs for housing, urban renewal, and expressway construction had already made it possible for the people and commerce that most benefited from public transit to leave the city for the suburbs. One cannot help but wonder how much more effective all of these mighty federal efforts might have been had they been conceived and implemented not separately but with some forethought as to how one program might influence another.

The ineffectiveness of urban renewal in Connecticut was in retrospect a clear indication that for all Connecticut cities the century of urbanization that began after the Civil War, which made cities what we thought they should be—centers of population, commerce, and industry—was sputtering to a halt. In its place, a new pattern of regionalization was creating its own imprint on the landscape, one that redistributed the baby boom generation and much retail commerce to less crowded suburban communities, leaving behind those who could not afford more progressive living in the suburbs or who were otherwise excluded from moving outward.

REGIONAL PLANNING WITHOUT REGIONAL GOVERNANCE

By 1939, the textile industry in Connecticut, one of the oldest industries in the state, was on the decline. To promote the state's manufacturing interests and hopefully reverse the trend of established industries leaving New England for more attractive labor and tax conditions in sunnier climes, the state legislature established the Connecticut Development Commission (CDC). One way to promote industry, it was thought, was to increase cooperation among neighboring communities, and in 1947 the state followed up on earlier attempts to promote local planning and zoning by passing legislation that enabled local communities to join together to form multi-town regional planning agencies. The following year, several towns in the New Haven area did just that and formed the Regional Planning Authority of the South Central Region, Connecticut's first regional planning agency. But there the movement stalled, mainly for lack of incentive. The need to think regionally had not yet become apparent to many local communities, nor was it as yet required as a precondition for funding from federal or state programs.

With passage of the Federal Housing Act of 1954, region-wide planning went from being a nice idea to a prerequisite of federal policy and a requirement for the receipt of federal housing grants, which like highways included funding for regional planning efforts. With federal funds for slum clearance and public housing at stake, the Connecticut Development Commission took it upon itself to delineate regional planning areas for the entire state (some fifteen in all), and as federal funds for slum clearance began to flow through the CDC during the 1950s and 1960s, more and more Connecticut towns joined together to establish the regional planning agencies designated by the commission. As other federal programs were enacted as part of President Lyndon B. Johnson's "Great Society," similar planning efforts were required for criminal justice, urban renewal, and mass transit, and the need for towns throughout Connecticut to combine into regional planning agencies (along with the financial benefits of doing so) was reinforced many times over. As with transportation planning a generation before, federal programs had turned the progressive concept of regional planning, whose roots dated to the City Beautiful movement at the turn of the twentieth century, into standard policy for federal, state, and town governments.[6]

In an effort to provide a statewide framework for regional agencies around the state, the Connecticut Development Commission in 1960 undertook its own statewide planning initiative, known as the Connecticut Interregional Planning Program (CIPP). For a period of six years, CIPP gathered data on trends ranging from population and the economy to transportation, urban development, and open space lands; produced reports and staff papers on relevant topics; and shared the results of these studies and the trends they delineated with towns and regional agencies around the state.[7]

In the process, several key assumptions emerged, based on the projection of postwar growth trends (as anomalous as they were) far into the future: first, that the population of Connecticut would reach five million persons by the year 2000; and second, that while the growth of the state's manufacturing sector would taper off, total employment would more than double by 2000, providing jobs sufficient for the expanding population; third, that the number of automobiles owned by Connecticut residents would increase by 20–25 percent per decade to a total of 2.5 million by 2000; and fourth, that although Connecticut was projected to be a remarkably different place at century's end, CIPP planners identified several ways that this overall growth in people, jobs, and traffic could be absorbed and distributed on the landscape. For CIPP the complexities of regional planning were reduced to a problem of land allocation, that is, finding a way to "use the space of the state to take care of the growth while preserving the kind of atmosphere in which people like to live."[8]

In a final report released in 1966 called "Connecticut: Choices for Action," the Connecticut Interregional Planning Program presented four different land use patterns into which the projected growth might be directed. The first possibility (Trend Projection) was basically a do-nothing option in which the current trend of new growth sprawling outward from urban centers was allowed to continue as before. A second option (Plans Composite) aggregated all existing regional plans into one statewide land use pattern. Two additional options (Linear Concentration, and Multiple Urban Centers) redirected future growth into one of two additional patterns: one that concentrated growth into a dense linear pattern along the spine of the state from Greenwich to New Haven to Hartford and Springfield, with smaller linear concentrations in the Naugatuck, Thames, and Quinebaug river valleys; and a second pattern that clustered growth into multiple urban centers around the state, creating in effect large islands of urban density amid the greener, more open space around them.[9]

The goal of the CIPP was to establish parameters for a statewide Plan of Conservation and Development that might serve as a guide for everyone

Alternate growth patterns discussed during the CIPP study of the 1960s. Courtesy of the Hartford Courant

from state transportation planners and regional planning agencies to town planning and zoning boards and local developers. However, when the plan was presented to the legislature in 1966, state lawmakers were not eager to add another layer of planning controls to the state statutes. At this point, CIPP planners entered what might be called planning's "twilight zone," where the systematic work of planning meets the chaotic work of politics. How do you convince others to enact your plan? How do you ensure that the future you have planned is the future that actually happens?

Lewis Mumford, who was quick to support the need for "large scale planning at every level," addressed this issue in his anti-expressway presentation at the Hartford Conference in 1957. As to implementation, Mumford spoke of two ways to turn those plans into a political reality. On the state level, he recommended the creation of a State Development Authority "with power to zone all the land on the scale necessary, power to relocate population and industry and business and to re-order transport routes so as to have the fullest utilization of all the facilities of our civilization." On the local level, he added, "We need to invent a new form of federated municipal government capable of acting beyond metropolitan limits and capable of uniting the over-all regional authority with the local authorities . . . that will have to [live] within the larger regional pattern."[10]

The first idea, too reminiscent of the kind of centralized planning first popularized in the 1930s by communist nations, was dismissed by most Americans as being simply "un-American." However, the second idea, instituting some form of regional governance in Connecticut, was in fact considered in some detail during the decade following the conference. To begin with, in 1959 Connecticut abolished all county government in the state, which had existed since the unification of the Connecticut and New Haven colonies in the 1660s. Since that time, the responsibilities of county government, once an effective intermediary between town and state on matters of transportation and civil law, had been significantly reduced as many of those duties were absorbed by the state legislature.[11] Meanwhile, regional planning agencies were being formed around the state to act as intermediaries between the local communities and both federal and state governments in matters of population growth and land use. Unlike county government, however, the statutes governing regional agencies made their membership voluntary and their recommendations advisory. They had neither the power to raise funds to support regional projects, nor the power of eminent domain through which to implement land use decisions. However, it seemed timely to consider whether these regional agencies might not be converted into councils of governance, whose elected officials, given the powers of taxation and eminent domain, might become a new form of "county" government, one positioned to implement land use plans for each of the state's planning regions.

In 1965, therefore, the legislature created the Commission to Study the Necessity and Feasibility of Metropolitan Government. Specifically, the twenty-four-member commission was charged with determining the need in Connecticut to join "communities into a body politic coextensive with the territorial limits of constituent municipalities and exercising within said territorial limits all powers of government, including taxation and eminent domain,"[12] just the kind of agency, answerable directly to the voters, that might be effective in shaping and directing growth around the state.

Editors of the *Hartford Courant* took notice of the commission in a positive light, citing both some of the problems faced by Connecticut cities and towns as a result of the mass move to the suburbs, and equally important the role of automobility in creating a new regional order on the landscape: "If there is a single giant industry, as in East Hartford [Pratt & Whitney]," the editors noted,

> the tax money goes to the town in which the industry is located. But the children of its employees, brought here from all over the country, are educated in the schools of nearby towns. These towns may have to float bond issues to build schools to house these children—but still they must rely on their own real-estate tax exclusively for income. Town and city boundaries were created in a day of slow motion, when a trip from Hartford to Bloomfield or Glastonbury was an adventure. The mobility of society has changed all this. It is only in the political structure of government that this overwhelming fact is not recognized.[13]

In January 1967, the commission released a report of its findings that indeed set the course for future development in the state, though not in the way the editors of the *Hartford Courant* might have hoped. While the commission found a large measure of support in the Hartford, New Haven, and New London areas for advisory councils of elected local officials such as comprised existing regional planning agencies, it discovered little or no support for metropolitan government or regional councils with any added powers. Therefore, while conceding that certain local and state functions may be more effectively administered at the regional level, "the Commission has concluded that metropolitan government is neither necessary nor feasible in Connecticut."[14] Instead, the commission advocated "strengthening of the state's role by placing responsibilities for planning, personnel and budgeting in the executive branch."[15]

And that is exactly what happened. Following release of the commission's report, the legislature created the State Planning Council to advise the governor on such matters, as well as a legislative Committee on State Planning for its own use. Also, a new Department of Community Affairs was established to coordinate the local planning and zoning efforts of Connecticut cities and towns. As for the CDC and CIPP, their land use planning efforts were transferred to a new Office of State Planning created within the existing Department of Finance and Control. In the matter of regional development—a central issue of the modern era—Connecticut chose a strictly advisory role for its regional councils, sufficient to qualify for federal and state funding programs (including transportation) but unable to deliver true regional governance.

All of these planning efforts of the 1960s led ultimately to the drafting of a statewide Plan of Conservation and Development in 1973. Although the plan was drawn up at the request of the legislature, once it was completed the legislature could not muster the political will to enact the state's first comprehensive land use, water resources, and open space planning document into law. Instead, the plan was "endorsed" by an executive order of Governor Thomas Meskill in September 1974. But as Governor Meskill was quick to note, "This is not statewide zoning, and doesn't make anybody do anything or prevent anybody from doing anything." Instead, the state's only means of enforcing the plan was "in deciding which development programs it will help fund."[16]

FINALLY, A NEW CONSTITUTION (STILL THE MYTH PERSISTS)

By 1958, the imbalance between the populations of urban and rural communities in Connecticut was such that voters representing less than 10 percent of the state's population were able to elect a majority of members in the lower house of the state legislature. Although state senators were now elected by district, their districts had not been reapportioned since the turn of the century, and the imbalance in representation in the upper house of the legislature was almost as bad. While similar conditions existed in other states, such as Tennessee and Alabama, by the mid-twentieth century Connecticut's rotten borough system of town representation was so egregious as to be considered "a national scandal."

The situation was allowed to exist in part because federal courts long considered the apportionment of state political districts to be a *political* issue, not one that should be adjudicated in the courts. However, in a momentous 1962 decision in *Baker v. Carr*, the U.S. Supreme Court reversed that opinion by agreeing with the plaintiff that such imbalances did indeed violate the right of every voter to equal protection under the law in accordance with the Fourteenth Amendment, an argument that soon became a national battle cry for one person, one vote. This opened the door for all manner of reapportionment lawsuits, including one against the state of Connecticut brought by the League of Women Voters in 1964. In *Butterworth v. Dempsey*, the Court finally declared the Connecticut system of town representation unconstitutional and suggested the state rectify the matter or the federal courts would step in and do it for them.

The Supreme Court decision in *Butterworth v. Dempsey* led to a call for a constitutional convention, the first since the failed attempt of 1902, to try once again to address the matter, this time under much greater duress. As a result, a new state constitution was adopted the following year that divided the state into more or less equal districts for legislative voting purposes and made a provision for those districts to be rebalanced after each federal census. As a result, Connecticut was subdivided into eighty urban, seventy-seven suburban, and twenty-two rural voting districts, and the balance of power in the legislature shifted, as many expected it would, from Republican to Democratic.

Unfortunately, the adoption of a new state constitution did not destroy the myth that accompanied the state's town-based system of representation, a myth born of the Puritan ideal that the power of the town, conjoined as it was in colonial times with the power of the Congregational Church, was the source of the colony's authority over its citizens. It was an erroneous belief that had never been true and since the founding of the new nation in 1789 had been repeatedly rejected by the Connecticut Supreme Court of Errors. As we saw in *Buckeley v. Williams* in 1896 concerning reconstruction of the Hartford Bridge, the Supreme Court proclaimed unequivocally that Connecticut towns "have no inherent rights. They have always been the mere creatures of the Colony or the State, with such functions and such only as were conceded or recognized by law."

Yet the myth persisted well into the twentieth century, sabotaging an earlier attempt to modify the town-based policy at the constitutional convention of 1902, and helping to set the political stage for the Merritt Parkway scandal of the 1930s. Indeed, the state's penchant for town autonomy was evident even at the 1965 constitutional convention itself. Delegates of that convention who still believed that Connecticut towns had some exceptional birthright that originated with the Fundamental Orders and the Connecticut Charter of 1662 made their position known, though this time they could not keep the convention from doing what it had to do; representation in the new 1965 constitution was made to conform to the one person, one vote federal ruling. Nevertheless, the new constitution did include the provision that "the establishment of districts in the general assembly shall be consistent with federal constitutional standards." Introduced by delegate Albert Waugh, a professor at the University of Connecticut's rural campus in Storrs, the provision was suggested not, as one might think, in support of the one person, one vote ruling but rather, as Waugh himself testified, to allow for a "return to our traditional system of town representation" should that possibility ever become constitutionally permissible.[17]

It should also be noted that the reluctance of some to let go of the long-held, erroneous belief in town representation also influenced the outcome of the investigation into the feasibility of regional government in Connecticut by the legislative commission, whose members did their work in the two years immediately following the adoption of the new state constitution. Speaking to a meeting of the American Institute of Planners in Hartford in November 1966, Dr. Rita Kaunitz, chair of the commission's subcommittee on state and regional planning, noted, "We're not going to come out for metropolitan government." Her committee members, she said, believed "local government is worth preserving. We have come to like our wall-to-wall towns." Even though the commission emphasized in the title of their final report that local and regional problems are the state's biggest concern, the commission "cast aside metropolitan government as a framework for orderly growth in Connecticut," recommending instead that the role of the state in the planning process be strengthened.[18]

Town-based wishful thinking may also have influenced the state's one bold attempt to influence regional growth in Connecticut. In 1971, a group of Hartford businessmen led by Arthur J. Lumsden, president of the Greater Hartford Chamber of Commerce, in conjunction with private developers, created the Greater Hartford Process, Inc. "to design and implement . . . a vision of the region that could be used to guide its future growth." The 150-page planning document, released the following year, called for everything from community-based policing and universal healthcare to the protection of ecologically sensitive areas from damage by suburban sprawl, all forward-looking recommendations. A major element of the plan was the construction of new communities throughout the region to absorb population growth. To that end, Hartford Process proposed construction of a new community of 20,000 persons on 1,600 acres of land in Coventry, Connecticut, an existing suburban town of 8,500 people. It was proposed that the new town take twenty years to build, at an estimated cost of $200 million.[19]

However, as the developers were about to apply to the Coventry Planning and Zoning Commission for the variances they required, they suddenly withdrew the project, largely because of the downturn in the economic climate following the Arab oil embargo of 1973. But opposition was already mounting in Coventry, and one cannot help but wonder what the outcome might have been had the proposal come from a regional body whose members had been elected by the voters with the power of eminent domain. Instead, given that Hartford Process had no such political authority, some observers concluded that it "may have taken the state to make these kinds of changes, and the state wasn't so inclined."[20] All of which illustrates the truth behind the myth of town autonomy: when it comes to regional matters, towns (which is to say the people of Connecticut) abdicated control of their future only to strengthen the power of the state government over them. As we shall see, the myth of town autonomy did not die with the new constitution of 1965 but persists to this day and continues to make multi-town land use decisions difficult to implement.

Building the Connecticut Expressway System

With the passage of the Federal-Aid Highway Act of 1956 and the creation of a Highway Trust Fund, funding for the interstate system increased dramatically, and the construction of state and federal expressways accelerated as Connecticut built a network of more than six hundred miles of controlled-access expressways using a combination of federal funds, state gas taxes, and tolls.

BRIDGES AND FERRIES IN THE EXPRESSWAY ERA

Beginning in 1938 with the construction of the Aragoni Bridge in Middletown—named for the chairman of the legislative commission charged with building the structure—the state began replacing existing low-level drawbridges built to accommodate the traffic of the early auto age with high-level crossings that eliminated the need to interrupt the flow of high-speed highway traffic to allow for the passage of intermittent river traffic. In the 1940s, Connecticut built two important high-level crossings along the lower post road, one across the Thames River at New London in 1943, and another across the Connecticut River at Saybrook in 1948. Replacing the existing low-level drawbridges at each of these locations was an important first step in preparing the way for Connecticut's first interstate highway (I-95) proposed to be built along the lower post road from New Haven to Providence.

In much the way that the production of steel made possible the numerous bridges required by the railroad building spree of the nineteenth century, technological advances in construction materials and bridge design made possible the high-level crossings and numerous grade separations required by the spurt of superhighway construction in the 1950s and 1960s. As steelmaking techniques were refined, the beams, girders, and steel plates from which such bridges were constructed became stronger yet lighter, making longer spans technologically feasible. Also, modern engineering theory simplified the design of more complex bridge structures. Whereas previously bridge crossings were located so as to minimize the complexity and cost of their construction (with only secondary consideration given to the curvature and speed of the roadway), the new technologies made longer spans possible even in difficult locations, encouraging designers to better blend their bridge crossings into the general alignment and design features of the expressways they were designed to carry.

With passage of the Federal Aid Highway Act of 1956 and the acceleration of state highway building, bridge builders turned their attention to the greater Hartford area, which was the hub of several intersecting expressway routes, including I-84 and I-91 in Hartford, and state expressways 2 and 15 east of the river. Thus far, only the Charter Oak Bridge had been built, to accommodate the Route 15 crossing of the Connecticut River south of Hartford.

To construct the river bridges required by the additional highway crossings, in 1955 the legislature created the Greater Hartford Bridge Authority (GHBA), a nine-member board comprised of three representatives from Hartford, two from East Hartford, and one each from Windsor, South Windsor, Wethersfield, and Glastonbury. The Authority was to locate, build, and operate five new crossings of the Connecticut River in Hartford County: from Wethersfield cove to Maple Street in East Hartford (Putnam Bridge); at State Street in Hartford (Founders Bridge); from Wolcott Street in Windsor to South Windsor (Bissell Bridge); from Albany Avenue in Hartford to Route 5 in East Hartford (Buckeley Bridge); and from Tower Avenue in Hartford to Burnside Avenue in East Hartford. Only this last proposed crossing, located between the Bissell and Buckeley bridges, was never built. In addition to new construction, responsibility for the operation of the existing Buckeley and Charter Oak crossings was also transferred to the Greater Hartford Bridge Authority.[21]

As to financing, the GHBA had the power to issue bonds and set tolls sufficient to build and maintain each of these bridges. Construction of the four new bridges proceeded without incident. The Founders Bridge at State Street was the first to open in 1957, followed by the Putnam and Bissell bridges in 1959 and 1960 respectively. Tolls were collected at all new crossings and were installed on the existing Buckeley Bridge as well, despite much public protest.

The widening of the Buckeley Bridge to carry I-84 across the Connecticut River deserves special mention. As late as 1955, federal plans for the Hartford region indicated the location of the I-84 crossing of the Connecticut River to be south of the city in the vicinity of the existing Charter Oak Bridge. However, studies of a southern corridor for I-84 through the city of Hartford indicated that such a routing would be too disruptive and too expensive, and a decision was made to favor a more northerly route through Hartford, one that would make use of the existing Buckeley Bridge to cross the river. The existing bridge was widened to include the extra travel lanes required. To protect the aesthetic quality of the stone arch structure, the widening was done on the north side, where facing stones were carefully removed and their specific locations marked so that they could be exactingly replaced once the widening had been completed. The widened bridge opened to traffic in 1962 and marked the end of new bridge construction by the Greater Hartford Bridge Authority.

The following year, the legislature terminated the Authority, in part because of the public's dislike of the tolls imposed on the Buckeley crossing (which were subsequently removed), but more to the point because the Connecticut Highway Department was anxious to apply the toll revenue from the Hartford bridges to other expressway projects around the state, something the Authority was prohibited by law from doing. So in 1963, all assets, debts, and employees of the Greater Hartford Bridge Authority were transferred to the Connecticut Highway Department.

With the completion of the Bissell Bridge between Windsor and South Windsor, there was no longer any need for the ferry crossing serving that area. That left only two ferry crossings in the state, both on the Connecticut River: one at Rocky Hill, the other at Haddam, both operated by the Connecticut Highway Department since the 1920s. Over the years, the CHD made repeated efforts to shut down the two ferries as a cost-savings measure, only to be met with repeated opposition by the public; and so the last two river ferries in the state—the final remnant of a once essential mode of transport dating to the first days of the Connecticut colony—continue to operate (seasonally) to this day, more for historical reasons than out of a genuine transportation need.

The new Hartford crossings, of course, were only part of the construction needed to accommodate the massive interchanges that were required by the intersecting expressways on each side of the river. Such interchanges, each including numerous on-off ramps and crossover bridges, covered a large area of land. In Hartford, the interchange between I-84 and I-91 in the vicinity of the city's central business district proved particularly difficult to design, precisely because the land area needed to build the interchange properly was occupied by nearby commercial buildings. Therefore, to contain the impact of the interchange, the final design included a most unusual arrangement whereby westbound traffic exiting from I-84 and heading north onto I-91 had to leave the expressway, proceed through an at-grade intersection controlled by a traffic signal, and then enter I-91 via a local on-ramp.

On the other side of the river, the undeveloped meadowlands of East Hartford provided a logical (that is, empty) location for what the Highway Department referred to as the "East Hartford Complex Interchange."

East Hartford "Mixmaster." Interchanges for various superhighways consumed large tracts of land along the Connecticut River in Hartford and in the meadowlands of East Hartford. Spanning a Century: The Buckeley Bridge 1908–2008. Courtesy of ConnDOT

The East Hartford interchange was described by the engineers who designed it as "a maze of ramps, roadways and structures connecting all the north-south and east-west routes in East Hartford with the bridges over the Connecticut River to Hartford."[22] It took several years to complete, but once it was open to traffic, the driving public christened the interchange with a more descriptive name, referring to it sardonically as the "Mixmaster," thereby equating the highway complex with a popular brand of kitchen blender. The massive interchange complex was completed by the mid-1960s.

EXPRESSWAY CONSTRUCTION: AN OVERVIEW

With the accelerated bonding program authorized by the Connecticut legislature in 1959 and with the deadline for completion of the interstate system looming on the horizon in 1972, postwar expressway construction focused on completing the state's three main interstate routes—I-84, I-91, and I-95—as quickly as possible. Because Connecticut had already begun to work on urban portions of the system in the decade before the onset of interstate funding and had completed construction of the Connecticut

Turnpike as far eastward as Waterford, the state had a good head start toward meeting the federal deadline. By 1960, 150 miles (56%) of the state's interstate system were open to traffic; an additional 24 miles were under construction and the remaining mileage was being designed.[23]

Construction focused first on I-91 between Hartford and Springfield, which was completed north to Windsor Locks by 1958 and to the Massachusetts border the following year, including the noninterstate expressway connector to Bradley Airport (Route 20). Construction then proceeded south from Hartford, being completed as far as Meriden by 1965 and from Meriden to New Haven in January 1966, including the Oak Street connector (Route 34) to downtown New Haven. As for I-95, the final section of the shoreline expressway from Waterford to the Rhode Island line was finally built in 1964.[24]

The last of Connecticut's three interstate routes to be completed was I-84. Here construction proceeded eastward from Danbury and was completed to Newtown by December 1961. Thereafter, construction continued toward Hartford in piecemeal fashion until the final portion of

I-91 and Constitution Plaza. An office complex and an interstate highway replace a long-established neighborhood along Front Street in downtown Hartford.
Spanning a Century: The Buckeley Bridge 1908–2008. Courtesy of ConnDOT

the route (between Plainville and Farmington) was opened to traffic in 1969. With the completion of I-84, including the upgrading of the old Merritt Highway to interstate standards east of Hartford, the 297 miles of interstate highways that comprised the state's core interstate system were completed several years ahead of the 1972 deadline.[25]

While interstate construction was underway, the CHD also began construction of several state expressways around Connecticut. This work focused on building some of Connecticut's longest intrastate expressway routes along the corridors of three major state highways: Route 2 from East Hartford to Norwich, Route 8 from Bridgeport to Winsted, and Route 9 from Middletown to Old Saybrook. Expressway projects of smaller scope were also begun along Route 11 from Colchester to Salem, Route 7 in Norwalk, Route 25 in Bridgeport, and Route 72 in New Britain.[26]

It was only natural that a federally funded program as big as the interstate system would draw criticism as it progressed, especially with regard to its price tag. One newspaper article described the national construction project as "a vast program thrown together, imperfectly conceived and grossly mismanaged, and in due course becoming a veritable playground for extravagance, waste and corruption."[27] To counter such negative publicity, President Kennedy declared May 21–27, 1961, National Highway Week and encouraged individual states to promote the cause as well.

In Connecticut, the Highway Department invited the public to tour its district offices, speak directly to its engineers about their concerns, and view special exhibits on various expressway projects. In addition, May 22, 1961, was proclaimed Connecticut Highway Day, and a packet of free materials was distributed around the state that included a state highway map, a map of the Highway Department's latest long-range plan for expressways in Connecticut, and a "Report to Highway Users," prepared by the department to highlight the economic benefits anticipated as a result of superhighway construction. Since public opinion concerning highway construction in 1961 could still be considered favorable in the main, the event proved to be a public relations success.[28] But time does not stand still. During Highway Week, environmental activist Rachel Carson was putting the finishing touches on what would become one of the great works of scientific literature, *Silent Spring*. And in just a few years, as *Silent Spring* became a nationwide bestseller and the public became more aware of the true costs of unlimited growth and technological progress, highway engineers, so long respected for the work they did, would be as welcome at City Hall as a black sheep on one of Connecticut's many vanishing farms.

Discovering Limits

With expressway construction underway nationwide, the negative impact of auto-mobility on neighborhoods, air quality, and traffic congestion became apparent and widespread protest against the highways-only policy of federal and state governments brought significant reforms.

HIGHWAYS-ONLY POLICY DRAWS OPPOSITION

If sweeping changes to the physical landscape of rural and urban Connecticut were not enough, the baby boom decades were filled with a degree of social and political unrest not seen in America since the Great Depression. Beginning with the refusal of civil rights activist Rosa Parks to sit in the designated colored section of a public bus in Montgomery, Alabama, in 1955 to the resignation of President Richard M. Nixon in 1974 and the defeat of American troops in South Vietnam the following year, America experienced an extended period of turmoil and social confusion unlike any in its history. News of civil rights marches and sit-ins, four political assassinations, repeated protests in support of free speech on college campuses and against the war in Vietnam, antinuclear rallies, a series of historic space flights that ultimately landed American astronauts on the moon (not once but several times), the fatal shooting of four college students by the National Guard at Kent State University, together with ongoing revelations stemming from the Watergate scandal, saturated the daily headlines with a seemingly endless pageant of unnerving news.

Of all the social causes of the era, it was the environmental movement that most directly impacted the efforts of states to implement their long-range expressway plans. The public's ecological consciousness was first awakened by the 1962 publication of *Silent Spring,* a national best-seller. Rachel Carson's systematic study of the long-term effect of pesticides on avian reproduction brought what had been a postwar boom industry into sharp focus. While often misconstrued as an argument for choosing birds over people, what Ms. Carson in fact accomplished in *Silent Spring* "was to introduce to the general imagination the concept of ecology: the way the natural world fit together, the pieces so tightly and inextricably bound that you could not isolate cause and effect . . . So when we poisoned . . . [insects] with massive sprayings of DDT, we were, ultimately, poisoning ourselves." It was, to be sure, an uncommon perspective in 1962, particularly to those who believed strongly in the ethics of unrestricted growth. But it marked the beginning of an environmental awareness that would ultimately extend far beyond the single issue of pesticide spraying to all manner of growth-related hazards, such as smog, water pollution, garbage disposal, and the loss of open spaces, and to other, nonorganic technologies from the automobile to nuclear power.[29]

Ads such as this, for DDT, epitomize the belief in progress through technology so engrained in American society in the 1950s.
Life Magazine

The construction of superhighways through city centers first came under attack in the so-called Freeway Revolt that took place in San Francisco, California, between 1957 and 1966. Sparked by that state's plan to build a series of freeways through one of the country's most beautiful tourist cities, strong public protest led the San Francisco Board of Supervisors to declare their unanimous opposition to six of the city's most contested proposed freeways. Such political opposition presented the state highway agency with substantial difficulties, for without city approval "the state would not have the authority to close city streets or to alter them for access ramps or local service streets."[30]

With hundreds of millions of dollars in federal funding at stake, the state continued to pressure the city, through successive mayoral administrations, to find some way to accommodate at least one or two of the freeways through San Francisco that were considered an essential part of the statewide system. The issue came to a head in 1966 when city supervisors voted to reject construction of the Golden Gate Freeway through Golden Gate Park. As Mumford had predicted years earlier, the cornerstone of political opposition to this project was the damage that would be done to the Panhandle neighborhood adjacent to the park. As a state legislator representing the Panhandle district noted, "We seem to be caught in an insane bureaucratic vice, with $270 million being promised to destroy precisely those amenities that other departments of government are desperately trying to provide for our cities. This mindless cycle must be broken."[31] And so it was by the San Francisco Board of Supervisors, who defeated the state's proposal and ultimately voted to transfer more than $200 million of state gas tax revenue to the building of the Century Freeway in Los Angeles. Today San Francisco remains the one large city in the nation not crisscrossed by superhighways.

As expressway construction continued around the nation, the public became ever more conscious of the negative impacts of the government's highways-only policy, epitomized by the interstate program: from ever present traffic congestion within city centers to smog-choked skies above them. It should be noted, however, that throughout the expressway era, even as protests began to spread from state to state, highway engineers continued to believe that increasing traffic congestion was a sign not that there were too many superhighways, but that there were in fact too few to accommodate the public's insatiable demand for automobility.

To justify their call for more superhighway construction, engineers made widespread use of the latest in computer modeling techniques. By the 1960s, computer scientists could develop intricate machine models that simulated real-world traffic conditions, first by inputting zoning data on land use, population census information, and motor vehicle ownership and then by using a computer formula (or algorithm) that generated a specific number of trips for each kind of land use and forecasted the amount of traffic expected to flow through a particular travel corridor in some future year. By again using algorithms to assign that volume of traffic to a given highway network (existing or proposed), those sections of roadway that exceeded their recommended capacity were easily identified, as were the number of additional travel lanes needed to eliminate the future congestion. Yet despite their technical sophistication, the computer models used by highway engineers all had one fatal flaw. Given the government's policy of building only highways to the exclusion of other modes, the computer results were both predetermined and self-fulfilling: more people meant more cars, and more cars meant more expressways.

In Connecticut, the first study that utilized computer modeling techniques in developing expressway plans was conducted in the greater Hartford region in 1961. Known as the Hartford Area Traffic Study (HATS), its results were typical of the period. By using a target year of 1975, HATS projected that the region's core cities of Hartford, East Hartford, and West Hartford would contain (if highway planners had their way) on average one mile of expressway for every two square miles of land area, while the region as a whole would require no less than seven radial expressway routes and two circumferential belt routes around the

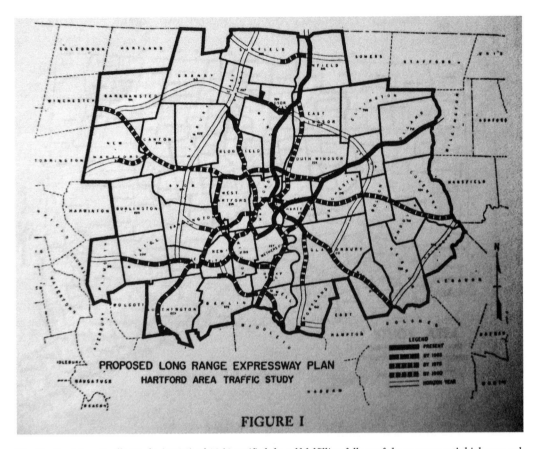

The Hartford Area Traffic Study (HATS) of 1961 typified the self-fulfilling fallacy of the government's highways-only policy: more people meant more cars and therefore more superhighways.
Connecticut Highway Department

city of Hartford, which would give the region "more miles of expressway per unit of area than any other section of the state."[32]

To highway engineers, constrained by a legal mandate to build expressways and *only* expressways, the HATS results seemed not only logical but also irrefutable. Taking this logic to extremes, one federal highway administrator as late as 1968 was led to believe that what was really needed to solve the nation's persistent problem of highway congestion was a *second* interstate program, to begin once the present program was completed; it was jokingly referred to in the press as "son of the interstate."[33] But to highway users, who could see and feel the negative impacts of expressway construction all around them, the HATS results seemed anything but logical. As their daily lives became more entangled in a web of concrete, traffic jams, and sooty air, commuters came to distrust the idea of more superhighways, no matter how sophisticated their justification, as the solution to their problems.

Though Connecticut was well on its way to completing its core interstate routes on schedule, it was far from finished with interstate construction. Congress twice added to the national system in the decades that followed, first in 1956 when 1,000 new miles were added, and again in 1968 when an additional 1,500 route miles increased the length of the national system to 42,500 miles. In addition to the 297 miles of routes allocated to Connecticut in 1947 (I-84, I-91, I-95), Connecticut received as a result of the system expansions an additional 80 miles of interstate routing after 1956, bringing the state total to 377 miles. The added mileage was designated as four new interstate routes: I-86, to run from Hartford to Providence in the corridor of state Route 6 (sixty-five miles total, forty-eight miles in Connecticut); I-291 and I-491, together forming a circumferential beltway around Hartford (thirty-one miles); and lastly I-484, a one-mile stretch of expressway through Bushnell Park connecting I-84 and I-91. Such was the changing climate of public opinion, however, that Connecticut engineers would spend more than twenty-five years trying to complete these new interstate segments, which amounted to 20 percent of the total Connecticut system. In the end, none would be built as originally envisioned.

The first of the new interstates to become the target of public protest was the portion of I-291 to be built through West Hartford. When a public hearing on the project was held at the local high school on September 25, 1969, an unexpected crowd of more than one thousand persons was met by a group of young guitarists on the school steps, singing a protest song they had composed called "The Spirit of I-291."[34] Most of those in attendance were adamantly opposed to the construction of the expressway since a large portion of the route traversed a reservoir and watershed land that supplied drinking water for the town. When the general location of the project had first been presented in 1960, no serious objections were raised. But as one speaker noted, much had happened in the interim: "The time which has elapsed since the original conception of this highway has provided for the beginning of a shift in public attitude regarding the desire for ultra convenience in automobile travel versus the desire for a quality environment."[35]

The outpouring of interest in the I-291 project was the result of the work of local activist Charlotte Kitowski, a West Hartford mother and registered nurse who headed a group called the Committee to Save the Reservoir.[36] The group obtained six thousand signatures on a petition promoting the issue, and their advocacy even spurred State Health Commissioner Franklin Foote to object to the project in writing based on the possibility of a chemical spill contaminating the local water supply. Following a long night of hearing testimony objecting to the project, state highway engineers left confused and dispirited, not knowing quite how to proceed. To make matters worse, a week later the West Hartford Town Council voted 7 to 2 to oppose the route through the reservoir, raising a possible legal obstacle to the construction of the project.

While the Connecticut Highway Department continued to work on the project (much as state engineers had in San Francisco), tinkering with the layout of the route in an attempt to minimize local objections, Ms. Kitowski and others continued to pressure the state to eliminate the project altogether. As the matter dragged on, the Connecticut State Senate on June 3, 1971, voted in favor of a bill to prevent the construction of I-291 through or over reservoir lands in West Hartford, a sign that political support for the project was wavering in the state. Yet the issue would not die. The following summer, representatives of West Hartford together with several citizen activists met with officials at the Department of the Interior in Washington, who expressed their surprise at the extent of the opposition and asked the state to restudy the route yet again. This led to a new public hearing on October 5, 1972, at which state engineers presented a somewhat revised plan, which they then submitted to the Federal Highway Administration for final approval. Finally, in September 1973, with the town of West Hartford threatening to take court action to block the project, Governor Thomas Meskill abruptly canceled all plans to build any portion of the I-291 route from West Hartford to Manchester, pending approval of the federal government for the state to use the $150 million of highway funds allocated to I-291 for other expressway projects.

That such an option was even possible signaled that something significant was happening at the national level as a result of the antihighway protests that were taking place in West Hartford and numerous cities across the nation. Indeed, while the tumultuous public activism associated with the 1960s had not solved many of the nation's social ills, it was producing significant reform in several different arenas, perhaps none more so than in the area of environmental protection and the negative impacts caused by the construction of superhighways such as I-291.

ENVIRONMENTAL PROTEST BRINGS REFORM

In retrospect, one can see how the evolution of expressway construction around the nation was fraught with potential problems, not the least of which was timing. Plans first developed in the 1940s were not funded until the 1950s, and their impacts were not made apparent until the social unrest of the 1960s, a generation after they were conceived. Of all the social movements of the day, the American freeway revolt made use of the democratic principle of protest and reform to the best advantage. As protests grew throughout the 1960s and beyond, so too did reforms to process. For example, as early as 1962, the Federal Highway Administration (FHWA) made comprehensive regional land use and transportation planning a requirement for the federal funding of housing and transportation projects. No longer would each project be considered in isolation but, in theory at least, only as part of some greater land use scheme compiled region by region within each state. In the case of highway construction, the FHWA also required two public hearings for each project, one when the general corridor for the highway was known, and another when the road was designed in enough detail to know whose land, houses, and commercial buildings would be taken. Their aim was to accommodate any change in public opinion in the time it took to take a project from the drawing board to construction.

Also, in 1969 Congress passed the National Environmental Policy Act (NEPA), landmark legislation that legitimized the public's concern for the environment by establishing a national environmental policy along with the means for federal agencies to implement that policy. As a result, engineers were required to consider alternative routes for each proposed highway and to evaluate each alternative with regard to its impact on the natural environment. Their results were compiled into an Environmental Impact Statement (EIS) for each project, and the information was presented and discussed at public hearings, after which the highway agency was required to respond in writing to any and all comments on the project. Passage of the NEPA also led President Nixon to create the Environmental Protection Agency, one of whose aims was to protect the natural environment by setting standards for air and water pollution and other potential environmental hazards.

The image of the whole Earth against the blackness of space came to symbolize the environmental consciousness that emerged in the 1960s and 1970s. Life Magazine

The earth as seen from Apollo 8 in space, showing the outlines of North and South America

The force of the new environmental legislation first became apparent in *Citizens to Preserve Overton Park v. Volpe,* a 1971 decision of the U.S. Supreme Court concerning the construction of a six-lane interstate (I-40) through a large public park near the center of Memphis, Tennessee. According to the new laws, the federal government could not approve any project that required the taking of public land "unless (1) there is no feasible and prudent alternative to the use of such land, and (2) such program includes all possible planning to minimize harm to such park." In the case of I-40, the federal highway agency had approved the project at its own discretion, without the necessary factual findings. While the Court recognized the reasons for the government's decision—the directness of the route and the reduction in costs and community disruption such a route represented—the Court noted that the very existence of the environmental laws indicated that "the protection of parkland was to be given paramount importance," which it had not been in this instance. Construction through the park was halted.[37]

Without question the new environmental regulations made the construction of all expressways more difficult. In recognition of that fact, the Federal-Aid Highway Act of 1973 contained a bold new provision that provided highway departments around the country with a way out when faced with a highly contested highway proposal. The new law allowed states to withdraw a contested interstate route from the system without losing either the mileage or funding allocated for the route. Instead, states were free to reassign the mileage and funding to other less controversial projects. It was because of this provision—and no doubt with an eye to the Overton Park decision as well—that Governor Meskill decided to withdraw I-291 from the interstate system.

In the midst of these reforms, Congress in 1966 took a major action toward redirecting the future of transportation in America by creating a federal Department of Transportation, a new cabinet-level agency designed to administer federal programs, not for just highways but for all modes of transportation under one bureaucratic roof. In what was seen as a definitive solution to centuries of disparate policies for different modes of travel, the new transportation agency symbolized the latest in policy thinking: the nation's transportation needs are best served by an integrated, multimodal system that utilizes each mode to the fullest to produce the most efficient system for the movement of people and goods within the national economy. It was a bold step, especially considering that a major component of the new multimodal system, the nation's railroads, was at the time still privately owned. But the shift in policy— from "every mode for itself" to "we're all in this together"—redefined the national approach to transportation. Given the power of federal funding, it should be no surprise that states followed the federal example; on October 1, 1969, Connecticut gathered together all existing state agencies, boards, and commissions concerned with particular modes of travel into one new state agency, the Connecticut Department of Transportation (ConnDOT).

While funding programs for individual modes such as highways and airports continued much as before, the federal-state transportation partnership, first created in the early auto era, was suddenly transformed into a new multimodal, mega monopoly more costly and therefore more powerful than anyone might have imagined just a few decades ago. However, what changed was more than just a shift in policy. The centuries-old relationship between government and transportation based on the regulation of transportation services provided by others was turned on its head. The reversal began with the advent of automobility and the decision of federal and state governments to provide the infrastructure this new mode of travel required with public money. The new policy was soon extended to include aviation, and with the creation of federal and state Departments of Transportation in the 1960s, the reversal was complete. Government would now use public tax dollars to provide the infrastructure for all modes of transportation—air, land, and water—and would administer this multimodal network, so essential to the nation's economic health, through a combination of scientific management, land use planning, and public participation. Over and above the many important aspects of Connecticut history in which (as we have seen) transportation has played a vital role, the reversal of the government's relationship to transportation that began in the 1920s and was completed in the 1960s is the most fundamental fact to be gleaned from the story of Connecticut transportation.

After centuries of technological invention, from the steam locomotive to the electric trolley to the gasoline-powered internal combustion engines that drove the automobile and the airplane, the future of Connecticut transportation was now the responsibility of a federal-state mega agency whose main purpose was to provide a total transportation system, with no mode favored and no mode ignored, able to accommodate economic growth and sustain our natural environment. After 350 years, transportation in Connecticut had reached both a cogent climax and a bold, new beginning. An ambitious task lay ahead, to be sure, but combining all transportation modes into one megagovernmental monopoly was a logical next step in the scientific management of Connecticut transportation.

Or was it?

Chapter Five A Public Monopoly

The First Fifty Years

ith the formation of the United States and Connecticut Departments of Transportation in the 1960s, all modes of transport came under the jurisdiction of a single administrative agency for the first time in the nation's history at both federal and state levels of government. Created in reaction to a long-standing but misguided policy that subsidized gasoline-powered automobility and aviation to the exclusion of other modes, the goal of the new mega monopoly over all transportation infrastructure was to produce a more balanced, multimodal transportation system for the postinterstate era that could accommodate growth yet reduce dependence on the automobile. The purpose of this chapter is to review the evolution of multimodal projects in Connecticut over the five decades since these two departments were formed; highlight the administrative and financial difficulties of operating a multimodal transportation monopoly; and document the recent efforts of Governor Dannel Malloy and Transportation Commissioner James Redeker to reinvigorate the state's transportation program.

ConnDOT: Becoming Multimodal

In the first phase of its fifty-year life thus far, the Connecticut Department of Transportation was preoccupied with bringing the state's rail system under public ownership, trying to complete Connecticut's interstate program, and dealing with unexpected changes in fiscal policy.

THE CHALLENGES OF BECOMING MULTIMODAL

The creation of a Connecticut Department of Transportation in 1969 was a reaction to the years of protest against the superhighway and in support of a sustainable natural environment. But realizing the department's mission—to reduce the state's dependency on automobility and redress the imbalance in the state's transportation system resulting from half a century of a highways-only policy of federal and state governments— was anything but straightforward. Today, after fifty years of operation, ConnDOT has made much headway in realizing its mission; yet achievements have been long in coming and in some areas still remain elusive. In retrospect, the agency's first fifty years can be viewed in roughly two phases, each about two and a half decades long. The first phase lasted from the creation of the department in 1969 to the completion of the interstate system and other superhighway construction in 1994 and should be thought of as a transitional period in which three main tasks were completed: the last of the state's superhighways were constructed; the final pieces of the department's multimodal system, the rail and bus operations of the New Haven Railroad, were transferred from private to public ownership; and several unanticipated changes in fiscal policy were made that had a significant impact on the funding of future transportation improvements.

In the 1990s, however, ConnDOT entered a postinterstate era dominated by a more fully multimodal view of transportation. In addition, the federal-state partnership now viewed the objective of transportation not simply as the movement of people and goods but in broader economic terms, where transportation was seen as a fundamental necessity for keeping jobs and economic activity growing. It was a shift in perspective that required important changes in how ConnDOT conducted its business. This second phase began in 1991 with passage of the Intermodal Surface Transportation Efficiency Act (ISTEA) and continues to this day as the state attempts to execute ConnDOT's first long-term, multimodal program of transportation improvements called "Let's Go Connecticut!" As we shall see, the main accomplishments in this second phase have been reforms to the management culture and organizational structure of ConnDOT, along with recognition, if not resolution, of the financial difficulties that threaten the state's transportation future.

It would take more than twenty years and much legislative activity in Washington and Hartford before the existing rail and bus industries controlled by the once powerful New York, New Haven and Hartford Railroad became publicly operated services owned and administered by the federal-state mega partnership that was ConnDOT. In essence, the nation's privately owned rail industry—under threat from the internal combustion engine since the 1920s—was allowed to fully fail before

ConnDOT headquarters in Newington. During the 1960s, many states as well as the national government placed all modes of transportation under one administrative roof in an effort to reduce America's dependence on the automobile.
Courtesy of ConnDOT

federal and state governments, acting in the public interest, intervened to save the nation's railroads and bus services from total ruin. How that happened is told in the following section.

Once all modes were assembled into a single federal-state mega agency, two stumbling blocks emerged to providing an effective multimodal system within Connecticut. First was the ongoing question of how, exactly, does a bureaucracy that is experienced in building only highways go about creating a more balanced, truly integrated multimodal transportation system? What does it mean to integrate different modes of transportation, to balance one against another? Should ConnDOT measure its success simply by its ability to maximize the amount of federal funds allocated to Connecticut for each mode, or should federal funding not be its primary concern? More to the point, how do engineers trained in a culture of highway building suddenly come to understand the business of rail transit, aviation, and water transport and reverse their ingrained fondness for highway solutions to all traffic problems? The dominant role of federal funding in the state's transportation partnership made such questions more difficult to answer. Without a major shift in federal policy away from superhighways (something that did not occur until the 1990s), ConnDOT was caught for more than two decades in a transitional phase of *becoming* rather than fully *being* multimodal; stuck, that is, between old policies and new goals, with its cadre of engineers doing the best they could to salvage, improve, and expand the state's rail transit system while at the same time continuing to build the expressway system that had created the imbalance in the first place.

Another obstacle to providing a multimodal transportation system was more prosaic: how do we pay for it all? Even if the bulk of transportation funds for all modes continued to come from the U.S. Congress, how was Connecticut to secure the revenue stream required to provide sufficient state matching funds, not just for highway building but for rail, bus, air, and water modes as well? It was a well-known fact that for highway plans to be executed in a timely manner they need to be funded from a secure revenue stream dedicated specifically to highway building, as they had been in Connecticut since the 1920s. But this question was now complicated by the rising cost of new social programs associated with the Great Society initiatives of the Johnson administration, with which transportation had to compete for funding, all within a balanced state budget. How was the state to pay for its obligations toward an increasing number of social programs as well as provide a steady, dedicated revenue stream for an expanded multimodal transportation program? The question vexed ConnDOT at its inception, as it still does today.

We will see how ConnDOT addressed these obstacles over its first fifty years of operation. While undergoing a cultural makeover that converted highway engineers into multimodal problem solvers, ConnDOT also executed projects that made Connecticut transportation more multimodal. Yet despite recent efforts by Governor Dannel Malloy and Transportation Commissioner James Redeker to encourage the General Assembly to adequately fund a bold new program that would ensure the future of the state's surface transportation infrastructure, lawmakers have remained reluctant to resolve the underlying causes of the ongoing state budget deficits that threaten ConnDOT's success.

Before we look too far ahead, let's return to the problem at hand in the 1960s: how was the state's extensive rail and bus system, managed by the New Haven Railroad, to be salvaged and placed under public ownership? That story begins in 1947 as the revitalized New Haven Railroad emerged from bankruptcy proceedings that resulted from the reckless overspending of J. P. Morgan and Charles Mellen at the turn of the twentieth century.

After emerging in 1947 from twelve years of court-ordered reorganization, a revitalized New Haven Railroad enjoyed several years of well-deserved prosperity. Indeed, the company earned a postwar high of nine million dollars in 1954, while carrying an overall debt burden well within normal limits for a corporation of its kind. However, revenues declined so sharply thereafter that a mere four years later the New Haven experienced a net operating *loss* of four million dollars, which increased to an *annual* loss of twenty million dollars by 1961. On July 7 of that year, the New Haven Railroad was forced to file for bankruptcy a second, and final time.[1]

The railroad's second bankruptcy was caused not by an excess of debt (as it was in 1935) but rather by a loss of operating revenue. This resulted from a combination of factors, not the least of which was unfair competition from the trucking and auto industries subsidized by the publicly built interstate highway system, including the Connecticut Turnpike, which ran parallel to the New Haven's main line into New York City. Overland competition from the sixteen-wheel tractor trailer was compounded in the air by the expansion of commercial airline passenger and freight service, and on the water by a decline in traditional bulk freight.

As a result, what was at stake this time around was significantly different from what had been at stake in the road's first bankruptcy in 1935. As the district court judge who handled the New Haven's second reorganization explained:

> The former reorganization, therefore dealt solely with the debt structure with a view to reducing the fixed charges to a level which could be met out of the profits from the Railroad's operations. *Today there are no net profits*. Then, the very existence of the Railroad was not threatened; *today it is*. Then, the reorganization was mainly concerned with the interests of various classes of bondholders and preferred and general creditors; the present reorganization is concerned not only with safeguarding the rights of similar groups, but it is also vitally concerned with the public interest *in preserving a transportation plant of major importance to the region in which it lies*.[2]

As might be imagined, the postwar triumph of the internal combustion engine took its toll on railroads other than the New Haven, including the Northeast's two largest railroads, the Pennsylvania and the New York

Central. In 1966, in an effort to create one financially stable road out of two nearly bankrupt ones (and at the same time keep the legacy of the New Haven alive), the Interstate Commerce Commission authorized the merger of these two regional roads into one Pennsylvania Central Railroad, on the condition that the new road include the floundering New Haven as part of its operation, a condition the new Penn Central reluctantly agreed to. Therefore, on January 1, 1969, the New Haven Railroad became part of the new Penn Central system and, after nearly a century of continuous operation, ceased to exist as an independent corporate entity. Unfortunately for the New Haven, the arrangement proved short-lived. In the face of unrelenting competition from the automobile, truck, bus, and airplane, the Penn Central Railroad itself succumbed to bankruptcy on June 21, 1970.[3]

With many of the nation's major rail systems facing similar difficulties, Congress at last intervened to protect the nation's interest in rail transportation. The effort began in 1970 with passage of the Railroad Passenger Service Act, by which Congress created a new public agency, Amtrak, funded entirely by public tax dollars to operate rail passenger service nationwide. Soon after, a national network of rail passenger service was assembled from the passenger lines of existing railroads and given over to Amtrak. In Connecticut, the new Amtrak system included two routes, a main shoreline route from New York to Boston via New Haven, New London, and Providence, and a connecting service that operated between New Haven, Hartford, and Springfield.

Another result of the bankruptcy of the Penn Central (and six other railroads in the Northeast and Midwest) was the Regional Rail Reorganization Act of 1973, by which Congress created the Consolidated Rail Corporation (Conrail) to operate a rail freight system comprised of the more profitable freight lines of the region's bankrupt railroads. Unlike Amtrak, Conrail from its inception was intended to be a profitable enterprise, not dependent on public subsidy. Conrail service in Connecticut included a shoreline route from New York to New London; a central valley route from New Haven to Springfield (with a spur line to Middletown); and a route to the west that ran from Devon, Connecticut, through Danbury to the Hudson River at Newburg, New York.[4] However (as had been the case with privately owned railroads), the restrictive regulations imposed by the Interstate Commerce Commission prevented Conrail from achieving profitability. To remedy the situation, Congress in 1980 passed the Staggers Act, which in effect deregulated the railroad freight industry; in the competitive environment that followed, Conrail eventually became the profitable railroad it was originally intended to be.

As important as the preservation of rail passenger and freight service was, the most cherished element of the New Haven system for Connecticut residents was the commuter rail service it provided from New Haven into New York City, then (as now) the most heavily used commuter rail service in the nation. In 1963, the state legislature created the Connecticut Transportation Authority to preserve this service. In conjunction with the Metropolitan Transportation Authority (its counterpart in New York State), the two agencies began to subsidize the operating cost of the commuter service with a combination of federal and state funds. This public subsidy ended in 1969 when the New Haven was included in the Penn Central merger, and for a brief time the commuter service returned to private operation under the Penn Central. Following that road's bankruptcy, the commuter service was once again placed into public hands, operated by the same two state authorities. This time around, however, the two agencies agreed to subsidize the cost of capital improvements as well as operating deficits.

In April 1976, responsibility for the commuter service was transferred to Conrail, which only added to that corporation's financial difficulties. This arrangement continued until after the passage of the Staggers Act in 1980, when Conrail was relieved of any and all commuter rail operations. For a third time, the partnership of the Connecticut Transportation Authority and the Metropolitan Transportation Authority assumed responsibility for the New Haven to New York commuter service. This time, looking for a long-term solution to the problem of commuter rail service in Connecticut, the Metropolitan Transportation Authority in New York created the Metro-North Commuter Railroad to operate three of that state's commuter rail lines, two of which were within New York State, the third being the New Haven line to Grand Central Terminal, which the Metro-North Commuter Railroad now operated on behalf of the CTA-MTA partnership. At last, the old New Haven commuter service had found a home. The Metro-North Commuter Railroad began its operations on January 1, 1983—thirteen years and three months after the formation of ConnDOT—and continues to this day as operator of Connecticut's sole commuter railroad into New York City.

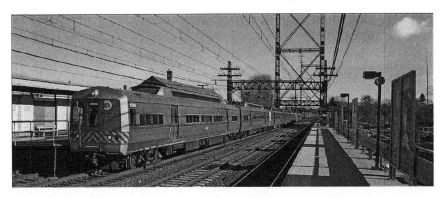

On January 1, 1983, New York's Metro-North Railroad began operation of the state's only commuter rail service for ConnDOT.
Courtesy of ConnDOT

As for the New Haven's trolley network, the last portions of which had been converted to motor bus operation by 1948, these services also made their way into public ownership over a period of years. Beginning in 1961, at a time when local bus service everywhere was feeling the pinch of competition from automobility, Connecticut passed a law allowing towns to rescue failing bus companies by joining together to form regional transit districts that could purchase, own, and operate local motor bus service.[5] With the creation of the Urban Mass Transportation Administration (UMTA) in Washington in 1964, federal funds became available to districts for the purchase of new buses and other capital expenses, with the federal government providing two-thirds of the total cost and Connecticut the remaining one third. By 1972, regional transit districts were functional in Hartford, Bridgeport, Westport, Shelton, and Middletown and received funding assistance from UMTA. Two years later, federal law made it possible for UMTA to subsidize operating costs as well as capital expenses in those districts where bus routes did not recover the full cost of their operation from fare box revenues. With the federal commitment to both capital and operating assistance in place (and matching state funds provided by ConnDOT), the number of transit districts in Connecticut grew during the 1970s, along with the total number of route miles of public bus service these districts provided.[6]

Meanwhile, the Connecticut Company, a former subsidiary of the New Haven Railroad, continued to operate motor bus service within the cities of Hartford, New Haven, and Stamford. By the 1970s, however, service in these larger cities was on the decline, and a labor strike in 1972 ultimately brought the Connecticut Company to its fiscal knees. In an effort to keep transit services operating in the three cities, ConnDOT provided an infusion of funds to the Connecticut Company that allowed it to remain under private ownership for four more years. Still, the handwriting was on the wall: bus transportation in all Connecticut cities would require ongoing public subsidy. So in 1976, ConnDOT purchased the Connecticut Company (with financial assistance from UMTA), changed its name to Connecticut Transit, and began to operate its own bus service in Hartford, New Haven, and Stamford. Today, Connecticut Transit, together with thirteen regional transit districts, provides local bus service in Connecticut, using state and federal funds to cover both capital expenses and operating losses. In addition, door-to-door transit services are also provided in many towns on demand for elderly and disabled passengers unable to use fixed route service.[7]

Beginning in 1974, the state expanded its commitment to public transit even further by initiating express bus commuter services from outlying suburban areas to employment centers in downtown Hartford, adding new routes over the years. Most recently, in 2017, commuter bus service was initiated between the newly completed University of Connecticut campus in downtown Hartford and UConn's main campus in Storrs. ConnDOT has made tremendous progress in preserving and expanding public bus transit of all types in Connecticut, but the achievement has taken decades and has required ongoing and ever increasing financial assistance from federal and state agencies.

INTERSTATE AND EXPRESSWAY CONSTRUCTION ENDS

While the state's rail system was being transferred piecemeal into public ownership, ConnDOT's Bureau of Highways continued to build portions of its interstate and intrastate expressway plan. However, public protest that resulted in the withdrawal of the I-291/491 projects by Governor Meskill in 1973 continued to plague the department in its effort to complete the two remaining interstate routes in Connecticut that were also designated as part of the system's expanded mileage: I-86, a long cross-state route from East Hartford to Providence, and I-484, a short connecting road through Bushnell Park in Hartford. As antihighway protest continued into the 1970s and after the Federal-Aid

Highway Act of 1973 made it possible for states to reassign controversial mileage to other projects, each of these two interstate routes, like I-291, was also either modified or withdrawn completely as ConnDOT was forced to reconfigure its interstate system in response to public pressure.

The construction of an interstate expressway from Hartford east to Providence was the largest remaining project, extending sixty-five miles from Hartford to Providence, forty-eight miles of which were within Connecticut. The public's new attitude toward expressways did not bode well for the large two-state project, estimated to cost nearly $600 million. This time a grassroots effort to stop the project was organized by Ms. Donna Parsons, a young mother and political activist who lived in eastern Connecticut and was concerned with possible damage to watersheds and aquifers in eastern Connecticut through which the interstate would pass.[8] Strong opposition developed in Rhode Island as well, where protest focused on a fifteen-mile portion of the route proposed to cross that state's Scituate Reservoir west of Providence. Wrangling over the project dragged on for years, but in 1982 Rhode Island officials finally decided not to build that portion of the road in their state. The following year, Connecticut officials also abandoned plans to construct the route as far as the Rhode Island border. Instead, they built only a small portion of the route eastward from I-84 in East Hartford to Manchester and redesignated it as I-384.[9]

The one remaining piece of the expanded system not yet built was a one-mile section of interstate called I-484, an extension of the old Whitehead Highway in Hartford intended to connect I-91 with I-84. However, the road had two major problems: not only was it planned to run underground through Bushnell Park in what engineers referred to as a cut-and-cover tunnel, but the project was also especially costly for so short a stretch of road, largely because of the need to tunnel through the park. After much public debate as to the project's merits, or lack thereof, I-484 was also withdrawn from the Connecticut interstate system to the relief of park supporters everywhere.

In the end, none of the four routes added to the interstate system in Connecticut as a result of system expansion (I-86, I-291, I-484, and I-491) was ever constructed as intended. Instead, the eighty miles associated with those four routes were applied to other expressway projects in the state, as follows:

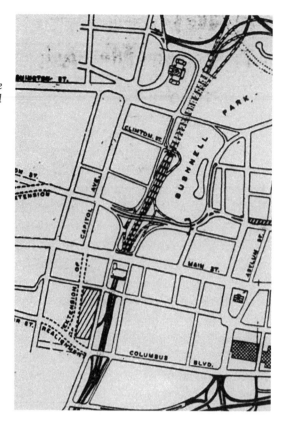

Proposed I-484 through Bushnell Park, Hartford. This short stretch of interstate highway was to be built underground through Bushnell Park but was ultimately withdrawn from the system due to controversy. Courtesy of ConnDOT

- I-691, a new interstate route constructed in central Connecticut from I-84 in Southington to I-91 in Meriden;
- I-395, a renamed portion of existing state expressway Route 52 in eastern Connecticut between I-95 in Waterford and Massachusetts, using mileage from the I-86 to Providence route after that plan was abandoned;
- I-384, the short piece of the abandoned I-86 route to Providence that was built from East Hartford to Manchester; and lastly,
- One quadrant of the original I-291 loop around Hartford (from I-91 in Windsor to I-84 in Manchester), which was reinstated and constructed as part of the state's interstate system.

In addition, one state expressway project, Route 10 from New Haven north through Hamden and Cheshire, was also abandoned in response to public opposition. In Cheshire, two alternate routes were proposed for the project: one to the east of the existing two-lane roadway that ran through the center of town, and another to the west. Cheshire was a rural farming town that became a suburban community in the 1960s but still retained much of its small-town character. At a public hearing on the project held in the high school auditorium in September 1974, ConnDOT planners were confronted with nonstop criticism from the seven hundred residents who attended. As the local newspaper reported, "Everyone who chose to make their voice heard spoke against the expressway." Like most public activism, the protest was emotionally grounded. As one resident put it, "You're being offered a blueprint for the destruction of this town." ConnDOT returned a few months later with a modified proposal to widen the existing highway while building a smaller bypass road through the town, but even the scaled-down proposal fell on deaf ears and ultimately the expressway as well as the widening and bypass were all but forgotten.[10] (Today ConnDOT operates hourly bus service along the route from Waterbury to New Haven.)

Construction of the state's reconfigured interstate system continued through the 1970s and 1980s, as did the building of state expressways around Connecticut. Some of the major state expressways completed during this time included Route 8 to Winsted, the extension of Routes 9 and 72 through central Connecticut, and the construction of Route 3 from Wethersfield to Glastonbury.

When all was said and done, ConnDOT had built a total of 634 miles of express superhighways in Connecticut, 347 miles (55%) as part of the federal interstate system, and 287 miles (45%) as part of the state expressway system. The last expressway to be completed was the reinstated portion of I-291 from Windsor to Manchester, which finally opened to traffic in September 1994, marking an end to six decades of superhighway construction in Connecticut that had begun with the Merritt Parkway. As one ConnDOT report noted at the time, "Although some additional roadways may be constructed in the future, the opening of I-291 northeast of Hartford marked the completion of the interstate system, and hence the end of massive highway building in the state."[11]

Much had happened during this transitional phase of ConnDOT's first fifty years, but more remained to be done before Connecticut could fully realize its multimodal future. As for the place of highways in the transportation hierarchy of the postinterstate era, ConnDOT was forced to admit that "for the first time in the Department's history, new roadway construction will *not* be the primary means of increasing system productivity."[12]

In addition to individual expressways, public protest also focused on the funding of highway projects, though here the impact was more symbolic than significant. In much the way that the superhighway became the symbol of all that was wrong with transportation in the new era of environmental awareness, the Highway Trust Fund, whose gas tax revenues paid for all highway construction, became the symbol of all that was wrong with transportation financing. As such, "busting" the trust fund (allowing gas tax revenues to be used for other than highway projects) became a battle cry of protesters. The goal was achieved initially in 1973, when the same Federal-Aid Highway Act that allowed states to withdraw controversial segments of highway from the interstate system also allowed those states to apply the amount of federal funds allocated for those highways to mass transit projects if they so desired. However, the transfer of gas tax revenues from highway projects to mass transit was not mandatory but at the discretion of the states. Since many suburban states, including Connecticut, chose to apply these funds not to mass transit projects but to other highway projects instead, this so-called busting of the Highway Trust Fund was not particularly effective. It was not until passage of the Surface Transportation Act of 1982 that a small amount of federal gas tax revenues was set aside specifically to fund mass transit projects across the country. With that law, which raised the federal gas tax from four to nine cents per gallon, one cent of the increase, even though deposited in the Highway Trust Fund, was specifically designated for mass transit projects. This amount was subsequently raised to 1.5 cents in 1990, 2 cents in 1993, and 2.85 cents in 1997. It was the specific dedication of gas tax revenue to mass transit beginning in 1982 that can be truly said to have "busted" the Highway Trust Fund.

Much happened to superhighway construction in Connecticut in the 1960s and 1970s as a result of public protest. The construction of individual highways was either modified or canceled; the environmental impact of highway projects became an important part of public discourse; federal laws were enacted to provide ongoing funding for mass transit through the Urban Mass Transportation Administration; and the Highway Trust Fund was busted so that gas tax revenues could be used for other than highway projects. Still, much remained to be done. In particular, the highways-only habits of ConnDOT engineers also had to be busted, and that would require much sustained effort. The certainty born of scientific management techniques, together with the arrogance that resulted from a sustained narrowness of focus (both inherited from the old Highway Department), were deeply engrained in the ConnDOT culture. For example, when the CHD held a public hearing on the proposed route of I-84 through Hartford, news accounts reported that "a few of the small gathering attending the meeting [were] intent on voicing strong opposition" but their voices, as well as their opinions, were subdued by the highway commissioner of the time who was in attendance at the meeting. Instead of listening to the public comments, he made "repeated statements . . . concerning the ten years already involved in planning the highway and the quality of those who planned [it]."[13] Such attitudes were difficult to undo and in the end required more than a decade of political reform under three Connecticut governors.

If that were not enough, ConnDOT in the 1980s suddenly faced two unexpected tragedies that consumed its attention for the remainder of its transitional phase and, in the end, brought a change of policy that made the financing of future transportation improvements more uncertain than ever before.

Tragedy Brings Change of Policy

In 1983, two tragic accidents on Interstate 95—a tollbooth crash in Stamford and the collapse of the Mianus River Bridge—illustrated the fiscal difficulties of funding transportation projects in a multimodal era.

HOW ARE WE GOING TO PAY FOR IT ALL?
In the decades following the baby boom, Connecticut began to experience a persistent financial dilemma, which first revealed itself in the increasing cost of public education. In 1950, Connecticut had educated 280,000 students at a cost of $62 million. By 1969, the number of students had more than doubled to 603,000, while the cost of their education rose to an estimated $350 million. Local school districts that had traditionally paid for education with revenue derived mainly from real estate property taxes found they could no longer do so and looked to the state for financial assistance.[14]

In the face of increasing costs for not only education but social programs such as healthcare and public welfare assistance derived from the Great Society initiatives of the Johnson administration, "lawmakers routinely balanced their books by carrying forward revenues earned in prior years, draining cash from various funds . . . and postponing funding for the state's share of guaranteed employee benefits."[15] As a result, in 1969 Governor Dempsey faced a budget shortfall of nearly 40 percent, which the legislature bridged by raising the sales tax (to 5%), increasing the corporate income tax (to 8%), and enacting a temporary two-year tax of 6 percent on net capital gains over one hundred dollars—the state's first modern tax on personal income.[16]

As the number and cost of Great Society social programs continued to grow, the problem persisted. In 1972, Governor Meskill faced a projected deficit of $250 million against a total budget of $1.2 billion. With the two-year temporary tax on capital gains about to expire, supporters of a state income tax who considered it a more progressive, more equitable way to raise new revenue, saw an opportunity to press their case. With Governor Meskill lukewarm about the idea, the legislature took matters into its own hands, and on July 1, 1971, enacted a graduated state income tax to raise the revenue necessary to balance the current budget. For income tax supporters, however, it was a short-lived victory. In the days following its passage, public protest against the income tax was so vociferous that the new law was rescinded in a special session of the legislature just six weeks later. With the income tax defeated, legislators balanced the budget that year with a variety of other tax increases, including a raise in the sales tax (to 6.5%), increased taxes on cigarettes, and a flat tax of 6 percent on dividends and capital gains, among other items.[17] Still, the underlying problem remained. How was the state to pay for the increasing cost of its social commitments, including education, healthcare, and state employee pension benefits, and still balance the state budget as required by law?

In 1974, Connecticut's budget dilemma collided head-on with the state's transportation program when the legislature dissolved the state's Transportation Fund (the long-standing Highway Fund renamed after the creation of ConnDOT to reflect the department's new multimodal mission). Suddenly, revenues that historically were dedicated to funding highway projects only were now deposited into the state's general fund. For the first time since Connecticut's original trunk line highway program had become self-supporting in the 1920s, funds previously dedicated solely to transportation use were now made available for nontransportation programs. For the first time in modern history, highway projects had to compete for funding with state-sponsored social programs and the state's legal requirement to balance its budget.

With monies designated for highways and other transportation projects now available to balance budget deficits created by nontransportation programs, the years that followed the dissolution of the Transportation Fund proved to be "a decade of underinvestment" for highway transportation, "particularly for routine maintenance and rehabilitation."[18] By 1980, the General Assembly was concerned enough about the impact of this underinvestment to direct ConnDOT to evaluate each state bridge and highway and to submit to the legislature a ten-year plan for road resurfacing and bridge repair. The evaluation, completed the following year, concluded that "63 percent of the state highway network and 61% of the state's more than 3400 bridges were in 'less than good condition' . . . and the possibility of emergency bridge closures and collapses cannot be discounted."[19]

Two years after this ominous warning—but before the legislature had taken action to remedy the situation—tragedy struck. On Tuesday, June 28, 1983, at 1:28 A.M. a one-hundred-foot section of the Connecticut Turnpike over the Mianus River in Greenwich collapsed. Despite the late night hour and light traffic conditions, two passenger cars and two tractor trailers were crossing the span when the steel and concrete bridge gave way and all four vehicles fell seventy-five feet into the water below. Three people were killed and three more were severely injured. Within days, a temporary two-lane span was erected to replace the damaged portion of the bridge, and investigators from the National Transportation Safety Board (NTSB) as well as ConnDOT began separate investigations to determine the cause of the collapse.[20]

Both investigations focused on the seven-inch-wide steel pins used to attach the roadway to the steel girders underneath. Portions of four broken pins were found in the debris from the collapse. While designs using such pins were no longer considered accepted practice (as they had been when the bridge was built in the 1950s), the outdated design did not in and of itself indicate that the bridge was unsafe. While the ConnDOT report pointed to the faulty design (and hence the bridge design company) as the cause of the collapse, a review of the accident by the NTSB determined that the collapse "was not related to design and was most probably caused by gradual, unchecked corrosion and forces due to ice formation." The NTSB concluded that while "effective inspection techniques were available to detect the deterioration," a lack of coordination between ConnDOT inspection units as well as a disregard for public complaints concerning unusual noises emanating from the bridge as traffic

A decade of underinvestment for routine highway maintenance in the 1970s led to the collapse of the Mianus River Bridge on I-95 in 1983.
Courtesy of ConnDOT

passed over it, led to the corrosion of the pins not being reported.[21] In the confusion immediately following the collapse, one of ConnDOT's bridge inspectors altered notes from his last inspection of the bridge to make it appear that he had warned his superiors about rust and other problems nine months before the bridge collapsed. He was charged with forgery, pleaded guilty, and was sentenced to a year of probation and 150 hours of community service.[22]

In the wake of the Mianus Bridge collapse, the legislature in February 1984 authorized a ten-year-long, $5.5 billion program to repair the state's major expressways and bridges, and to guarantee its timely completion created a new Special Transportation Fund (STF) into which all transportation revenues were once again deposited for transportation use only. If there was a silver lining to the Mianus Bridge tragedy, it was that the financial stability created by the Special Transportation Fund allowed the state to "reverse the deterioration of its transportation infrastructure" at a time when other states had yet to deal with the problem of aging highways. The creation of the STF made possible "one of the most extensive and ambitious transportation infrastructure renewal programs in the United States . . . because its established revenue stream provides a stable planning base."[23] However, by highlighting the budget difficulties that caused the cutback in transportation funding in the first place, the Mianus Bridge collapse underscored the pertinent question concerning transportation funding in a time of expanding state commitments to a wide variety of social programs: how are we going to pay for it all?

The surplus that accumulated in the STF during its first few years of operation (intended for future improvements) gave legislators the idea once again to use this dedicated transportation fund as a way to deal with some of the state's other budgetary needs. Since the STF could not by law be used directly for other than transportation items, lawmakers found a more insidious way to raid the fund. They began to use STF money to pay for "indirect" transportation costs such as pension benefits for ConnDOT employees, costs related to the operation of the Department of Motor Vehicles, including employee fringe benefits, and similar costs associated with the Highway Patrol section of the State Police, all items previously paid for out of the state's general fund. The payment of these "transportation" expenses took more than $150 million of tax money each year (which the public believed was being levied for transportation improvements) away from infrastructure repairs and rail subsidies.[24]

After a decade of spending under Governor William O'Neill in the 1980s, the budget shortfalls that had led to the dissolution of the state's first Transportation Fund in 1975 soon reappeared, only worse. When Lowell Weicker Jr. was inaugurated governor of Connecticut in 1991, he faced a fiscal shortfall of nearly one billion dollars in that year's budget, and a projected deficit of $2.4 billion the following year. When Weicker presented his budget to the legislature that February, it included a broad-based 6 percent income tax on the federally adjusted gross income of all Connecticut workers—along with a drop in the states sales tax (from 8% to 4.5%) and corporate tax rates (from 13.8% to 11.5%). Although he knew a political battle was sure to ensue, Weicker held strong to his income tax proposal.[25] That August, with no less painful way to close the budget gap in sight, the legislature enacted the proposed income tax. Finally, after a twenty-year lapse in the discussion, Connecticut joined more than forty states that relied on a state income tax to help pay for their increasing expenses. Today the state income tax (together with the sales and corporate taxes) remains a major component of the state's complicated tax structure.

CONNECTICUT BECOMES A TOLL-FREE STATE

In 1982, shoreline communities along the Connecticut Turnpike joined with their legislators to campaign for the removal of the thirty-five-cent tolls being collected at eight toll stations along the turnpike route. Because the highway bonds sold to build the turnpike by law had to be repaid from toll revenues, the issue was "quietly shelved" but hardly forgotten. The following year, when the legislature opened on January 5, more than twenty bills to eliminate turnpike tolls were filed by legislators. Even Governor O'Neill now favored their elimination so long as the tolls were removed "in an orderly fashion," but only after the turnpike bonds had been paid off.[26]

Two weeks later, on January 19, 1983, a fiery crash at the I-95 toll plaza in Stratford killed seven women and children and injured four others, when a semitrailer carrying a truckload of potatoes slammed into a line of stopped cars waiting to pay their toll. The crash produced an explosion that engulfed three cars in flames, charring the bodies of the victims beyond recognition. Miraculously, minutes before the explosion a tollbooth worker heard a three-year-old boy crying from within the wreckage and was able to pull him to safety. Sadly, the rescued boy's sister and brother were killed in the fire.[27]

Overnight the toll plaza accident turned what had been a reasonable debate over transportation financing into an emotionally done deal. Suddenly legislators and state officials viewed toll stations not as a source of revenue but as a safety hazard. Within months, the legislature decided to eliminate the hazard completely by removing all fourteen existing toll stations from Connecticut highways and bridges, beginning with the eight tollbooths on the Connecticut Turnpike along with the toll on the Bissell Bridge in Windsor, all of which were eliminated by December 31, 1985. Likewise, the three toll stations along the Merritt Parkway were removed by June 1988, and the following year the last two toll collection points in the state (on the Buckeley and Charter Oak bridges) were removed, making Connecticut a toll-free state for the first time since 1923. In a nostalgic turn of events, it was arranged for the same man who had paid the first toll on the Charter Oak Bridge, as a child of thirteen, to pay the last toll, which was in fact the last toll collected in Connecticut during the expressway era.[28]

Together the state's fourteen toll points contributed $66 million a year toward a balanced state budget (more than $50 million from the Connecticut Turnpike alone), and to compensate for this loss of revenue legislators chose to raise the state gas tax instead. And raise it they did, from eleven cents per gallon at the time of the tollbooth crash in 1983 to twenty-six cents by 1992.[29]

No sooner had gas tax revenues accumulated in the STF than the General Assembly began to raid the fund to deal with some of the state's other budgetary needs. It was then that questionable costs previously paid from the general fund (such as pension and fringe benefits for transportation employees) were first paid from the Special Transportation Fund instead. As these questionable costs themselves increased (and of course they did), "the General Assembly looked to the fuel tax as the means to keep the STF in balance." As raising revenue through the collection of tolls was no longer feasible, the state excise tax on gasoline became a mainstay for transportation funding and was repeatedly increased by the legislature, in small increments at first then more quickly and more noticeably to a high of thirty-nine cents per gallon by 1997.[30]

Confounding the problem of transportation finance still further was something called the gross receipts tax. Begun in 1981, the gross receipts tax was a percentage tax added to the price of all petroleum products entering Connecticut. It was levied as a wholesale tax to be paid directly by petroleum distributors, but when the courts struck down that provision of the law, the tax levy was simply passed on to the retailer, who in turn passed it along to the consumer at the pump. In effect, the gross receipts tax became a gasoline tax by another name. As such, one might reasonably suppose that the revenue derived from it would go to support transportation. However, the legislators who created the tax had something different in mind. As first conceived, the gross receipts tax was to help pay for the cleanup of oil spills, leaks, and other oil-related damage to the environment. As such, revenue from the tax was deposited in the state's general fund. As the gross receipts tax itself was raised from 2 percent in 1981 to more than 7 percent over a twenty-year period, its effect was to raise the price of gas at the pump by ten, fifteen, or as much as twenty cents per gallon.[31]

Clearly the impact of the two I-95 tragedies muddied the waters of transportation finance in Connecticut. While the collapse of the Mianus River Bridge led to the recreation of a separate transportation fund intended to protect transportation-related revenues from being co-opted for nontransportation purposes (a good thing), the fiery toll-booth crash led to the elimination of tolls as a major source of transportation revenue (not a good thing) and replaced them with higher gas taxes that only tempted legislators to raid transportation funds to balance the state budget (a bad thing). This dilemma was compounded by the unexplained practice of assigning revenue from other taxes more directly related to transportation, such as the gross receipts tax on petroleum products and the sales tax collected on all motor vehicles in the state, to the general fund for nontransportation uses.

In 1995, following completion of the ten-year improvement program undertaken after the collapse of the Mianus River Bridge, the General Assembly established a legislative task force to look into these very issues and determine the long-term stability of the Special Transportation Fund. After reviewing the history of the fund and the inexplicable use of transportation-related taxes for nontransportation purposes, the task force concluded that the future viability of the Special Transportation Fund demanded that the state either "transfer some or all of the expenses for the state agencies not specifically related to . . . the transportation program back to the General Fund from which they came," or "move into the [transportation] fund those . . . transportation-related user fees that currently go to the General Fund [such as the gross receipts tax] that have never been made available to support the STF." In addition, the task force recommended that the state do whatever it could to lower the per gallon excise tax on gasoline.[32]

By the time the expressway era (and the first phase of ConnDOT's multimodal existence) came to a close, transportation financing in Connecticut had become a nightmarish web of political intrigue that not even the most savvy state legislator could easily untangle. In addition to the problems associated with balancing traditional modes of transport in one system, the state also faced the more difficult task of balancing finances so as to pay for future transportation improvements as well as the state's ongoing social commitments.

A New Vision for a Postinterstate Era

As the interstate system neared completion in the 1990s, Congress revised its highways-only transportation policy to favor intermodal surface transportation, and thereafter three Connecticut governors worked to reform ConnDOT so as to keep the state competitive in a new world of global commerce.

A NEW FEDERAL POLICY

As the 1980s came to a close and with the end of construction on the interstate system in sight, Congress began to consider how to change federal transportation policy in a more permanent way so as to better incorporate into its transportation programs the multimodal and environmental lessons learned since passage of the Interstate Highway Act in 1956. What was the federal government's role in ground transportation to be once the interstate system was completed? The answer to that question came in 1991 with the Intermodal Surface Transportation Efficiency Act (ISTEA), commonly pronounced "ice tea." Then and now, ISTEA was considered landmark legislation that modified federal transportation policy so as to increase the flexibility of states in planning, financing, and designing surface transportation projects. As usual, this was done through the designation of funding amounts for specific transportation programs, each with their own prerequisites. Therefore, while the overall impact of the legislation was to make it easier for states to use federal funds for either transit or highway projects, the end result was yet another complicated jumble of bureaucratic programs, acronyms, and funding allocations through which states could partner with Washington in creating the transportation system they believed fostered their best interests.

Written in page after page of stilted legalese, the main provisions of the ISTEA legislation can be more simply stated. In summary, the act

- Appropriated the final $7.2 billion to be used for completion of the interstate highway system by 1996;
- Created a new program allotting funds for the preservation and maintenance of the interstate system at the same 90:10 funding ratio used to build the system (prior to ISTEA, the maintenance of interstate highways was considered a state responsibility);
- Combined four federal highway programs—interstate, primary, secondary, and urban highways—into one new National Highway System (NHS) containing 160,000 miles of federally funded highways (including the entire interstate system) that carried about 40 percent of the nation's highway traffic;
- Initiated a Surface Transportation Program (STP) that promoted multimodal transportation solutions by allowing program funds to be used for either highway or transit projects at the discretion of the states;
- Began a Congestion Mitigation and Air Quality Improvement Program (CMAQIP) that directed federal funds to those transportation projects that specifically helped states meet air quality standards (as set by the 1990 Clean Air Act), thereby for the first time linking transportation funds directly to the attainment of environmental standards;
- Encouraged states to seek more creative means for financing their share of project costs by allowing tolls to be collected on interstate highways, anathema for so long, and even permitting public-private partnerships that made it possible to transfer ownership of interstate highways to private corporations for long-term maintenance; and
- Increased the power of metropolitan planning organizations to determine which specific transportation improvements to include in their regional plans (the aim here was to broaden public participation in the planning process and thereby ensure that transportation solutions arose

from a grassroots consensus, and were not imposed from above through the power of the state).[33]

ISTEA marked a new federal vision for transportation planning that stressed multimodal—rail, bus, highway—networks, greater connectivity between all modes (including air and water ports), greater funding flexibility for states, and expanded public involvement in transportation decision-making. Here were new standards that clearly reflected the lessons learned from generations of highways-only policy.

An integral component of this new vision for transportation planning was a change in perspective that emphasized transportation not simply in terms of mobility as an end in itself, but rather as a means to a greater social good: economic competitiveness. One of the stated purposes of ISTEA was to "provide the foundation for the Nation to compete in the global economy." Traffic congestion was to be thought of no longer as only a sign of inconvenience and lost time but also as economic opportunities missed and economic growth stunted. Transportation arteries were to be considered arteries of commerce as crucial to a healthy society as unobstructed blood flow is to a healthy individual. As President George H. W. Bush said on signing ISTEA into law, "An efficient transportation system is absolutely essential for a productive and efficient economy."[34] It was a simple shift in perspective, but not an easy one for transportation planners to comprehend. Given their history of scientific management, planners were trained to see traffic congestion in engineering terms and therefore to provide engineering solutions that focused on the safe movement of people and goods, not on the economic ramifications of obstructed flow.

As with assembling the state's first multimodal network under ConnDOT in the 1970s, adapting to the postinterstate world would take time. It would also take the efforts of three consecutive Connecticut governors (Rowland, Rell, and Malloy) over nearly two decades to literally re-form ConnDOT, that is, realign its internal organization and retrain its engineers in the realities of the postinterstate era as defined by the Intermodal Surface Transportation Efficiency Act. It was a task in some ways more difficult than assembling the state's intermodal network. This was a shift in cultural perspective not easy to accomplish but one that would become increasingly important as the phenomenon of globalization captured public attention.

In 1999, a coalition of public, private, and institutional leaders came together "to develop a framework for understanding the economic activity and organizations" in Connecticut. The group named themselves the Connecticut Regional Institute for the 21st Century, and later that year released a report called *Connecticut: Strategic Economic Framework* (commonly referred to as the Gallis Report after its author, Michael Gallis & Associates) that startled the region with the new economic realities of globalization. Following the collapse of the Soviet Union in 1991, the economies of the world realigned themselves in new patterns of connectivity; the Gallis Report aimed to show the economic leaders of Connecticut how to compete successfully in this modern age of globalization. According to Gallis, in this new scheme of things Connecticut was positioned as part of a New Atlantic Triangle defined at its corners by the metropolitan centers of New York, Boston, and Albany. Within the state itself, Connecticut was subdivided into three economic regions: a coastal corridor from New York to New Haven that served 1.3 million persons; a north-south corridor from New Haven to Northampton, Massachusetts, that contained two million people, or 60 percent of the state's population; and a southeast coastal corridor from New London to Newport, Rhode Island, with some 300,000 persons. The report emphasized the need within these corridors to maintain the economic vitality of each of the state's metropolitan centers, which it considered "the building blocks of global economic activity."[35]

With Connecticut thus defined, the group went on to discuss what it saw as the main stumbling block to Connecticut being a full participant in the global marketplace: transportation. In its view, *effective transportation was the key to a successful economy at any scale,* between metropolitan centers, within the New Atlantic Region, and around the world. In the case of Connecticut, this meant in particular an effective transportation link to New York City where the state gained access to the main economic grid, nationally and internationally. But the state's transportation links to New York were overwhelmed and had been for some time. Gallis warned in no uncertain terms that if this situation was not corrected sooner rather than later, Connecticut was in danger of becoming "a giant cul-de-sac, an eddy in the economic stream,"[36] unable to compete and grow in the new world economy.

To ease this risk, the Gallis Report made several recommendations: that the state emphasize a multimodal transportation strategy; that it reverse the trend of suburbanization wherever possible; that it revitalize its aging urban centers; and that it establish ways for the state's three economic regions to interact to address these problems. The report also singled out Bradley International Airport as an undervalued transportation hub for the entire state, one that must be better utilized if Connecticut wished to be a vital part of the Northeast region.[37]

These results should have come as no surprise to anyone familiar with Connecticut history. As we saw in the first volume of this study, financier J. P. Morgan and railroad president Charles Mellen, captains of the New Haven Empire at the start of the twentieth century, faced a similar reality, and their drive to create a New Haven monopoly was based on similar thinking. Recognizing that geography had made New England a fringe economic region attached to the mainland of North America at the Hudson River, Morgan saw that his road's connection to the rest of the nation depended on trunk line railroads owned by other corporations, including the New York Central and the Pennsylvania Railroad. "By creating a regional monopoly, Mellen could ensure that the New Haven obtained the best competitive rates from these trunk line railroads, while within New England a monopoly of railroad, steamboat, and electric railway operations would allow him to eliminate redundant lines, lower rates on high traffic routes, and ensure the best integrated service overall."[38] Morgan and Mellen knew that they did not have the incoming revenues necessary to achieve such a regional rail monopoly honestly, so instead they amassed the profits they needed through a maze of shadow corporations, financial shenanigans, and corporate debt that ultimately led to their downfall. The experience of the New Haven Railroad might indeed be a cautionary tale for a state transportation monopoly that found itself in a similar position a century later.

The Gallis Report was a wakeup call for Governor Rowland and other state leaders, and soon after its publication the governor convened a transportation summit at Central Connecticut State University to see what might be done about the plight of Connecticut transportation. As a solution to the cultural difficulties at ConnDOT, Governor Roland proposed the creation of a new Connecticut Transportation Strategy Board composed of business leaders and state officials who would be able to identify a new strategy for solving the state's transportation difficulties. Working with and not for ConnDOT—whose narrow-minded engineering solutions were still considered an obstacle to seeing transportation as a means to economic growth—the board was considered a quick and easy way to reform the transportation planning process from outside the ConnDOT bureaucracy.

In June 2011, Governor Roland and the state legislature created the fifteen-member Connecticut Transportation Strategy Board (CTSB) tasked with identifying a comprehensive strategy to improve and expand all aspects of the state's transportation system in a way that enhanced the state's economic growth. Like the Gallis Report, the CTSB divided the state into transportation corridors (four this time instead of three) that it called transportation investment areas. These included coastal I-95, midstate I-84, north-south I-91, and in eastern Connecticut, I-395. To meet its objective, the board proposed a four-point strategy by which the state should prioritize future transportation investments in each area: first, make the most of existing infrastructure, especially in urban centers; second, reduce congestion by providing more options to driver-only automobile travel, especially in the I-95 corridor to New York City; third, reduce truck traffic statewide by providing more options for the movement of freight; and last, establish a plan to finance capital and operating expenses with revenue dedicated to transportation improvements only, which would provide adequate financing for transportation improvements in the long term. To ensure that this strategy was followed, CTSB was given the power to "review the Department of Transportation's proposed operating and capital budgets as they relate to implementation of the strategy and make recommendations" to the legislature.[39]

With regard to Bradley International Airport, Governor Rowland and the legislature also created (as part of the same public act) a new seven-member board of directors for Bradley Airport that included, along with several state officials, three persons from the business community and a representative of the Strategy Board. The resulting Bradley International Community Advisory Board was empowered to develop an effective management program for the airport, establish a set of strategic goals, monitor their effectiveness, approve the airport's annual capital and operating budget, and "establish and review policies and plans for marketing the airport and determining the best use of airport property." Though the new board was to be located within ConnDOT for administrative purposes, like the CTSB the Bradley Advisory Board would report directly to the governor and the legislature.[40]

Together the Connecticut Transportation Strategy Board and the Bradley International Community Advisory Board were attempts by

Governor Roland to bring the new economic thinking regarding transportation to Connecticut, not by reforming ConnDOT directly but by reforming the transportation planning process from the outside, using the expertise of business leaders to redirect the entrenched attitudes of a state bureaucracy born of a highways-only policy. As one consultant noted, with regard to Bradley Airport in particular, the lack of "clear accountability and sophisticated management" at ConnDOT was inhibiting the use of Bradley Airport as an economic generator. "We are focused on a mission change. It is not just about transportation any more. It's about economic development." To clarify the distinction, the consultant explained that it was no longer just about serving the passengers who chose to use Bradley Airport. "It's about stealing passengers from the airport next door."[41]

The Connecticut Transportation Strategy Board and the Bradley International Community Advisory Board were important steps in changing attitudes and broadening participation in the planning process. Over the next decade, working with regional planning agencies in prioritizing transportation improvements around the state, the CTSB kept ConnDOT focused on the multimodal strategy integral to Connecticut's economic future, and helped to encourage grassroots involvement. However, the effectiveness of the Bradley Advisory Board waxed and waned over the years, as Governor Rowland appointed members more willing to challenge ConnDOT decisions while Governor Rell was less inclined.

Governor Jodi Rell, however, did address the public's general dissatisfaction with ConnDOT's behavior by tackling agency reform head-on. The catalyst for Rell's unprecedented attack on the department was a scandal that erupted in 2006, when it was discovered that the contractor then widening a portion of I-84 from Southington to Waterbury had installed faulty drains, many of which led "nowhere, while some were clogged with debris and others were apparently connected with substandard, cracked and leaking pipes." Other nonconforming work included "improper installation of the bridge structure that required reconstruction of the deck, improper installation of bridge bearings . . . and defective welds in the mast arms of the median light poles." The problem was compounded when an audit of the project confirmed that "the construction inspection staff most likely observed the flaws but did not report them."[42]

Governor Rell used the scandalous revelations to call for a major reform of ConnDOT. "The I-84 failure was unfortunately the latest in a series of irregularities and problems at DOT that point to the need for cultural and organizational change," Rell said. "The need for change goes to the heart of the organization." As a result, Rell suggested that ConnDOT be broken up into two agencies, one devoted solely to rail and bus transit, the other to highways. To investigate this proposal and other ways of modifying department behavior, Governor Rell in 2007 appointed a legislative Commission on the Reform of the Connecticut Department of Transportation. When the commission submitted its report the following February, its recommendations were grouped into four main areas:

- ConnDOT must become more responsive to public opinion in all its activities;
- ConnDOT must set measurable goals and be held accountable for achieving them;
- Since transportation funding is far from plentiful, ConnDOT must choose its projects strategically, to get the best transportation impact for the dollars spent; and
- ConnDOT should be more active in advocating for transportation funds in Hartford and Washington, with an eye toward discovering innovative sources of new funding.[43]

What the commission did not recommend was breaking the department in two. The commission believed there was much that could be done internally and therefore reform efforts should focus not on changing the organizational structure but instead on changing habits, updating attitudes, and improving leadership within the existing organization.

Both governors Rowland and Rell took important steps to reform ConnDOT, one from without, the other from within, so as to realign its mission with the new multimodal, economically based view of transportation that pervaded the postinterstate era. However, neither governor was willing to tackle the decades-old problem of transportation financing in Connecticut. To fund the transportation initiatives of his administration (including the construction of a new ten-lane cable stay bridge to carry I-95 over the Quinnipiac River in New Haven, and the widening of I-95 through West Haven), Governor Rowland relied mainly on the gas tax. Later, the Rell administration chose to fund the purchase of hundreds of new Metro-North railcars and the construction of a large rail maintenance facility in New Haven by negotiating an increase in the gross receipts tax on petroleum products, with the added revenue directed to those particular projects.[44] Neither addressed the state budget dilemma created by the underfunding of pension benefits and the raiding of transportation revenue to balance a budget heavy with the cost of nontransportation social programs. That task would fall to Dannel Malloy, former mayor of Stamford, who became governor of Connecticut in January 2011.

2015: A New Beginning?

In 2015, Governor Dannel Malloy and ConnDOT commissioner James Redeker initiated a bold thirty-year program to reinvigorate Connecticut's surface transportation system, but ongoing budget difficulties threaten implementation of the program.

LET'S GO CONNECTICUT!

If the budget shortages of the past decades were not problem enough, the Great Recession of 2008 had a substantial and sustained impact on the Connecticut economy, compounding the state's financial difficulties. High unemployment and reduced commercial activity reduced the amount of tax revenues coming into the state coffers, as employers laid off workers and residents tightened their domestic belts, depleted savings, and postponed purchases to make ends meet. Economic conditions also made it difficult if not impossible to raise taxes, either to provide much-needed transportation revenue or to balance the state budget overall. And to make a bad situation even worse, the recession persisted in Connecticut long after its effects had eased elsewhere in the nation. The Great Recession exacerbated the fiscal dilemma Connecticut lawmakers faced in 2015 and made the likelihood of resolving the state's transportation financing difficulties even more remote. As one fiscal report put it, "Connecticut is in quiet crisis by every measure: consistent budget imbalances, growing unfunded liabilities, falling bond ratings, stagnant economic growth, competitive disadvantages compared to neighboring states on most important indices, and increasing out migration."[45]

From the start, Governor Malloy was determined to make transportation and its related issues a priority for his administration. He began boldly by dismantling two of ConnDOT's modal responsibilities and giving them instead to specialized public authorities. First, shortly after taking office in 2011, Malloy created the Connecticut Airport Authority, a new public agency designed to manage Bradley International Airport along with five other state-owned airfields.[46] Likewise, in 2015 the governor created the Connecticut Port Authority, whose sole aim was to attract new maritime commerce to the state's three largest water ports: Bridgeport, New Haven, and New London.[47] With the creation of these agencies, the Connecticut Transportation Strategy Board and the Bradley International Community Advisory Committee were disbanded.

Since both agencies were structured to be administratively and financially independent of ConnDOT, their creation reduced the focus of the state's multimodal transportation agency to the management of ground transportation only—railroads, buses, highways, bicycle paths, and walking trails—consistent with the new federal grouping of surface transportation programs under ISTEA. With the creation of these two authorities, the aspects of Connecticut transportation that might most directly benefit from commercial marketing techniques were put into the hands of business leaders in their respective fields. While the air and water authorities coordinated their activities with the transportation department, ConnDOT's internal focus sharpened considerably. In addition, Malloy appointed James Redeker, chief of the department's own Bureau of Public Transportation and a man with an extensive background in rail transit, as the new commissioner of ConnDOT.

To give some perspective to the situation that Malloy and Redeker inherited, consider the scope of surface transportation in Connecticut at the time of their administration. The highway system alone contained 1,400 miles of roads on the federal highway system, including 350 miles of interstate expressway; 2,300 miles of state highway and expressway routes; and 17,300 miles of local town roads. This amounted to a total highway network of some 21,000 miles for which ConnDOT was responsible in whole or in part. And in 2015, nearly 30 percent of all *expressway* mileage in the state was considered at or near capacity, with the proportion expected to rise to 40 percent by 2035. In addition, there were four thousand highway bridges in the state for which ConnDOT was responsible, four hundred of which were then considered to be in poor condition.[48]

As for rail transportation, ConnDOT then owned and operated 450 rail coach cars, fifty diesel locomotives, and fifty-two railroad stations along a half dozen rail lines, and was also responsible for the maintenance of three hundred railroad bridges in the state. And the system was well utilized. Ridership on the Metro-North New Haven line alone approached forty million persons a year, having nearly doubled in the last twenty years. In addition, ConnDOT together with fifteen regional transit districts around the state operated hundreds of motor buses that provided service to tens of thousands of bus riders each day over hundreds of miles of local and express bus routes in Connecticut.[49] Though ConnDOT no longer had to worry about air and water operations, what ground transportation remained was considerable in both size and scope from an engineering point of view alone, not to mention the costs of operating such a system.

Having re-formed ConnDOT's organizational structure and with a new commissioner at the helm, Malloy in his second term undertook a public initiative he called Transform Connecticut to prepare an all-encompassing long-term plan to revitalize the state's surface transportation system and keep Connecticut an attractive place to live and do business. After two years of study and much public input, a thirty-year plan of transportation improvements prepared by ConnDOT entitled "Let's Go Connecticut!" was released in February 2015.[50]

Rather than a wish list of surface transportation projects that might be built if only we had the money, Let's Go Connecticut was designed to contain only those projects that engineers, politicians, and citizens alike agreed were long overdue or must be implemented if Connecticut was to maintain its status in the global marketplace. Gone were the days of projected expectations of some idealistic future. In their place was a down-to-earth realism born of the gravity of the present moment. Still, the plan was expected to cost $100 billion over thirty years, with two-thirds of the money relegated to bridge and highway improvements, and one third to rail and bus improvements. The plan also dramatized what was for many an astounding, eye-opening fact of transportation life. Consistent with the engineering maxim, "Remember, whatever you build must be forever rebuilt," two-thirds of the cost of Let's Go Connecticut over the next thirty years, or $66 billion, was required *simply to maintain and rebuild the existing system*. Only $34 billion, or one third of the total cost was to be spent on expanding the capacity of the existing system.[51]

To get the balling rolling, Malloy had ConnDOT prepare a short-term, five-year startup program that included only the most urgent improvements, and in the spring of 2015, Malloy asked two things of the legislature: $2.8 billion of state funding over and above ConnDOT's expected budget for that year so that work on the five-year program could begin, and a constitutional amendment (referred to as a lockbox) that would guarantee that all revenue raised to finance Let's Go Connecticut would be used for transportation expenses only (and not to balance general budget deficits as it had in the past). Let's Go Connecticut was meant to mark a new day for ConnDOT and a new beginning for Connecticut transportation. To emphasize the point, Malloy proclaimed, "We cannot afford to repeat history. I will not repeat history."[52]

However, while the legislature voted to bond the additional $2.8 billion Malloy requested for ConnDOT projects, it voted down consideration of a constitutional amendment for transportation financing. As one legislator proclaimed, "As long as other priorities . . . are at risk of being cut to balance state finances, then transportation must be on the table as well."[53] Instead, the legislature enacted a statutory lockbox, a state law that agreed to use transportation funds only for transportation projects. While a step in the right direction, a statutory lockbox was hardly secure, for like any state law it could be changed at any time by a majority vote of the legislature.

Let's Go Connecticut! In 2015, Governor Malloy and ConnDOT unveiled a thirty-year program intended to revitalize all modes of transportation in Connecticut, but budget shortages continued to threaten implementation of the plan. Courtesy of ConnDOT

THE BUDGET CRISIS PERSISTS

With the short-term five-year startup program funded and underway, Governor Malloy appointed a Transportation Finance Panel to address the problems of financing the Let's Go Connecticut plan over the long term, namely to find ways to raise the revenues needed to keep the Special Transportation Fund solvent over the next thirty years. In a report submitted to the governor on January 15, 2016, the finance panel recommended a course of action it said would "double the annual revenues in the STF by 2030."[54] Raising this additional revenue, the panel insisted, would keep the STF solvent for at least the next fifteen years, or halfway through ConnDOT's planned program. Beyond that, the panel did not think it wise to speculate.[55]

Among the panel's recommendations was first and foremost a constitutional amendment to protect transportation revenues. As for raising additional funds, the group proposed several options, all of which it considered necessary to sound transportation financing. First was to steadily raise motor vehicle receipts, licenses, and fees by indexing the existing rate structure to inflation. Second, increase the state gas tax by fourteen cents per gallon over seven years, returning it to its peak of thirty-nine cents per gallon in the 1990s. (Here the report was clear: "If the gas tax had not been reduced . . . the price tag for *Let's Go Connecticut* would be significantly lower."[56]) Third, increase rail and bus fares and station parking rates by 2.5 percent annually to keep pace with inflation. Fourth, institute electronic tolling on Connecticut expressways to help pay for improvements in the I-95 and I-91 travel corridors. The panel also reminded the legislature that by incorporating time-of-day pricing (where toll rates are varied by time of day), electronic tolling could also be used in certain parts of the state to reduce traffic congestion during peak hours. Last, increase the state sales tax by 0.5 percent and direct the added revenue to the STF.[57]

At first it appeared that the legislature would take the finance panel's recommendations to heart. In the summer of 2016, lawmakers enacted a 0.5 percent increase in the sales tax and pledged the revenue to the Special Transportation Fund. That meant a transfer of $130 million in additional revenue to the STF in the first year alone. However, no sooner did yet another deficit in the general fund appear when Governor Malloy was forced to rescind $50 million (40%) of the sales tax pledge for that year and return it to the general fund.[58] Needless to say, the more controversial suggestions made by the finance panel were quietly tabled.

In October 2017, after an extended special session, Connecticut lawmakers surprised everyone by passing their most effective budget bill in many years, and in a most bipartisan manner. In addition to balancing the state budget, the bill contained a bond covenant provision by which lawmakers hoped to reassure bond markets "of Connecticut's seriousness in addressing its fiscal challenges." Effective the following year, "Every bond issued with this covenant will include a pledge that the state will address its long-term liabilities, rein in spending and borrowing, and rebuild its Budget Reserve Fund. This is the clearest message yet that Connecticut is on a much needed disciplined path in managing its fiscal affairs."[59]

To keep the pressure on for significant fiscal reform, Governor Malloy appointed yet another commission—this one called appropriately enough the Commission on Fiscal Stability and Competitive Growth—to investigate measures that would more permanently stabilize the state's precarious fiscal policy. The commission made ten major recommendations, many of which had been heard before. The most significant recommendation with regard to transportation was to raise the gas tax and institute electronic tolling to raise the additional revenue needed to fund the transportation projects proposed in Let's Go Connecticut.[60]

How will Connecticut lawmakers ultimately resolve the ongoing budget crisis that has haunted state finances since the 1960s? Will they, as the Commission on Fiscal Stability and Competitive Growth recommended, restructure the state tax system and eliminate future deficits derived from decades of underpayment to the state employee pension fund? Will they institute electronic tolling and raise the gas tax to help pay for ConnDOT's thirty-year plan of transportation improvements? Will they propose a constitutional amendment to the voters that will effectively keep transportation revenues from being used for other than transportation purposes? No matter how far down the road politicians kick the fiscal can, how Connecticut lawmakers ultimately answer these three fundamental questions will define the future of transportation in Connecticut, and more importantly the state's ability to provide for the common good of all its citizens in the decades ahead.

Conclusion A Historical Perspective: 1614–2015

L ooking back over four centuries of Connecticut transportation history, we can see how transportation policy and technology—as well as the state's geographic position in the region—have shaped the physical and economic evolution of the British colony and the American state called Connecticut.

A UNIQUE WAY OF LOOKING AT THE PAST

Dutch mariner Adrian Block sailed the Connecticut River in 1614, marking the first contact between European colonists and local Ninnimissinuwock natives. To say that since then much has changed in Connecticut would be an understatement for the centuries. Though no one could know at the time, the new agriculture that was established on the Connecticut landscape with colonization, displacing the hunter-gatherer ways of the Native American culture that had been here for several millennia, would itself evolve, slowly at first then with accelerated speed to become the technological culture we live in today, deeply immersed in the money-making of global capitalism and the scientific management of bureaucratic megagovernment. As a result of that transformation, the capacity of the land itself to sustain humankind has changed most of all. Where 120,000 native Ninnimissinuwock once dominated the landscape, today nearly four million descendants of various immigrant groups from around the world endure.

The changes that have occurred have brought with them human comfort and convenience (often mistaken for progress) that have come at a tremendous price, not only in the demands that the complexities of modern living place upon us day in and day out, but more significantly in the impact that such unfathomable growth has had (and continues to have) on the natural environment—the air, the soil, the water, the plants, and the animals—on which *all* life depends. Ironically, comfort and convenience aside, we have after four centuries come full circle, back to the reality of the Ninnimissinuwock people, who knew intuitively that "one must live with nature, not against it. Nature has limits."

As we have seen, transportation has been a key element of economic and social change throughout the centuries, and for that reason the story of Connecticut transportation gives us a unique view of the history of the state. In much the way that engineers and planners have come to think of transportation not as an end in itself but as a means to sustainable growth that is inexorably bound up with our use of the land and the impact of our technologies on the natural environment, so too the transportation history told in this study can give us a unique view of our past, one that makes population growth, land use, technology, and ecology important characters in the story of Connecticut.

Telling the history of a place through the evolution of its transportation modes can help us see certain aspects of our lives in ways we might otherwise miss. For the purposes of this study, let us consider three thematic elements that are woven through the stories told in both volumes. We can call these elements *land, technology,* and *law,* and define them as follows. By *land* we mean the absolute number of people living in a given area, the manner in which they are distributed over the land, and how they live on the land they inhabit. By *technology* we refer to the means used to convert a given form of energy into a mode of transportation, including any vehicle involved and any infrastructure that vehicle may require. Lastly, by the *law* we mean how the construction of a given transportation technology is financed and the governmental policies associated with its operation, including court decisions that establish such policies or settle important transportation-related disputes.

The story of Connecticut transportation told in these two volumes was woven from more than sixty topics related to one or more of these thematic threads. In broad terms, it is the story of the different transportation networks that have been built in Connecticut over the centuries, the men who built them, the technology employed, and the means used to finance each system. What follows are some important points to remember about this fascinating story, grouped according to these three themes.

THE LAND
1. The story of Connecticut transportation unfolds on a physical stage larger than the state itself. It coincides with that portion of Southern New England cornered by four major centers of population: New York City, Albany, Boston, and Providence (and bordered on the south by Long Island Sound). By contrast, Connecticut itself lacks a city of such

magnitude but is instead comprised of numerous small towns and multiple larger cities scattered about the state. The combination of these two facts accounts for the heavily traveled traffic corridors that have arisen at various times during the state's history, and the higher-than-average number of system miles required in the state (regardless of mode) given its small size.

2. The single fact that has most influenced the course of transportation history in Connecticut from colonial times to the present day is the state's geographic position midway between New York City and Boston. The first post road constructed in this travel corridor dates from the early colonial period and traversed Connecticut from Greenwich to New Haven, then north through Hartford to Springfield, and eastward to Boston. As populations grew, two additional post routes were added through Connecticut, one along the shoreline from New Haven to Rhode Island, and another that branched from the first post road at Hartford and ran across the state's eastern highlands to the Massachusetts state line in Union. These three travel corridors, commonly referred to as the upper, lower, and middle post roads to Boston, have formed the spine of every transportation mode in Connecticut for four hundred years. In that time, improvements in transportation technology have reduced the one-way travel time from New York City to Boston from seven days in the colonial period to about four hours today.

3. All three post routes share a common link from Greenwich to New Haven, and this portion of the Boston Post Road has been the most heavily traveled link in many of the state's transportation networks since colonial times. The result has been a nagging dilemma (commonly referred to as the post road problem) over how best to provide for the excessive traffic in this portion of the corridor, much of which originates outside of Connecticut and is destined for points beyond New Haven. As a result, the corridor today is crammed with the remnants of parallel transportation systems built over the centuries to solve that very problem: the four-track New Haven Railroad main line to Grand Central Station, the four-lane Boston Post Road (U.S. Route 1), the four-lane Merritt and Wilbur Cross parkways, and the four-to-six lane Connecticut Turnpike. Yet despite the existence of all these transportation options, congestion along this link persists and remains the single greatest challenge facing the Connecticut Department of Transportation.

4. Connecticut was once home to about 120,000 Native American inhabitants and twice that number of English colonists. Today,

transportation improvements along with the commercial and technological advances of managerial capitalism allow the state to sustain some 3.5 million persons in a lifestyle most would consider a vast improvement over yesteryear. The need to conserve natural resources has been commented on since the mass deforestation of the colonial era, but only recently have we come to more fully realize how much damage population growth and modern consumption levels have done to the natural environment, not just in Connecticut but indeed globally. The main story line in these two volumes concerns the tremendous achievements in industry, wealth, and growth that transportation and technology have made possible during the nineteenth and twentieth centuries, while the climax of that story in the 1960s tells of our growing awareness of the impact of such growth on the natural environment, and our search for smarter, more sustainable ways to live on the land.

5. Human history enacted above ground is directly related to geologic events that happened eons ago below ground, and the state's geologic history has influenced its transportation developments in significant ways. For example, the surface topography of Connecticut consists of several north-south river valleys separated by terrains of rolling hills and valleys, together with a drowned coastline with numerous river and stream crossings. This geologic fact of life made east-west travel across Connecticut more difficult for centuries, until the arrival of the internal combustion engine and the automobile. In addition, the presence of Long Island, a remnant of the most recent ice age, has historically denied Connecticut direct access to the open seas and the possibility of competing with the more accessible ports of New York and Boston. And of course, the lack of a river outlet for the Farmington Valley at New Haven—also likely the result of a blockage created during the last ice age—gave rise to one of the state's grandest (some might say most grandiose) transportation schemes, the construction of the Farmington Canal from New Haven to Northampton, Massachusetts.

THE TECHNOLOGY

1. The bicycle was an important transportation development that paved the way for the automobile by providing elements of the technology required and by stimulating a public desire for a mechanized form of individual travel to replace the horse and wagon. Under the direction of Albert Pope, Hartford became a national center of bicycle production in the 1880s and 1890s.

2. In the way that the external combustion steam engine and the coal that fueled it were the key to the pattern of industrialization and urbanization that occurred in the nineteenth century, the internal combustion engine and the gasoline that fueled it were the key to the pattern of suburbanization and regionalism that occurred in the twentieth century, and that continues to this day.

3. The story of aviation in Connecticut mirrors the history of aviation in general, from early ballooning to twentieth-century gliders and heavier-than-air planes. The one anomaly in Connecticut aviation history is the work of Gustave Whitehead, a Bridgeport resident who some believe achieved heavier-than-air flight in a machine of his own design over Connecticut two years before the Wright brothers. In much the way that Albert Pope made Hartford an important center of bicycle manufacturing in nineteenth-century America, Frederick Rentschler made Hartford a national center of aircraft engine production in the twentieth century.

4. In response to the traffic congestion caused by automobility, engineers designed a new kind of roadway, the controlled-access superhighway that functioned as a paved concrete railroad for the truck and automobile. From 1935 to 1994, the federal-state highway partnership built more than six hundred miles of superhighways in Connecticut.

5. Timing was an important factor in the expressway era. Though the traffic congestion and the outward movement of population from city to suburb created by automobility first appeared in the 1920s, the impact was moderated by the economic conditions of the Great Depression and World War II. When automobility resumed with a vengeance after the war, an unprecedented population boom magnified its impact. The decision to build superhighways through rather than around city centers was a critical aspect of postwar regionalization. That decision was made in the early 1940s, a decade before funding was made available for the interstate highway system in the 1950s, and two decades before the impact of that decision became apparent in the 1960s.

LAW

1. Albert Pope and the bicycle culture he created were influential in the creation of the good roads movement of the 1890s, which led to the formation of the nation's first federal and state highway agencies, including the federal Office of Road Inquiry in 1893 and the Connecticut Highway Commission in 1895. Therefore, Connecticut's first modern

highway program was undertaken in response not to the advent of the automobile but to the bicycle phenomenon of the 1880s and 1890s.

2. The progressive movement revolutionized how engineers thought about highway building by switching their focus from responding to traffic congestion already visible (as along the lower post road in Fairfield County) to providing for the highway needs of the entire state in some target year, typically twenty or more years in the future. This was done by adopting an attitude of futurism that combined the techniques of scientific management with the projection of existing trends into the future. This new attitude of futurism together with the high cost of superhighways led to a necessary shift away from the state's tradition of pay-as-you-go financing and toward a new fiscal future based on the necessity to borrow on credit and repay with interest, which began with the construction of the Merritt Parkway in the 1930s.

3. The policy of the federal and state governments to subsidize the new transportation modes made possible by the internal combustion engine, namely the automobile and the airplane, to the exclusion of existing but privately owned modes of transportation, which included the steamboat, the railroad, and the electric trolley, resulted in decades of unfair competition, the eventual decline of these established transportation services, and the subsequent acquisition and rebuilding of these transportation services by public agencies.

4. Citizen revolts against superhighway construction in the 1960s brought first reforms in highway planning and ultimately the administration of all transportation modes by megagovernmental agencies in Washington and Hartford. The creation of these departments of transportation can be seen as the climax of a multicentury saga of transportation in Connecticut, which began with town responsibility for bridges, ferries, and earthen highways in the colonial period, then reverted to a century of private ownership of steamboat, canal, railroad, and trolley services, then reverted back to public responsibility for highways and airports in the early auto age, and finally culminated with all modes coming under public ownership and responsibility in the 1960s. Since the formation of ConnDOT, the last fifty years represent the beginnings of a new era of transportation in Connecticut, one characterized by multimodal planning and a new view of transportation as a means to economic growth. During those fifty years, two difficulties have arisen as to the administration of a multimodal transportation system in Connecticut: first, the need to reform an ingrained culture of highways-only thinking among

planners and engineers; and second, the need to provide dedicated and sustainable funding for multiyear transportation programs. While ConnDOT has made remarkable progress in overcoming the cultural obstacle, the state has yet to resolve the financial crisis that threatens future transportation funding.

5. Much of Connecticut history has been tainted by the erroneous political idea that the town was the origin of governmental authority in the Connecticut colony, an idea that was carried over into the state's first constitution in 1818 in the practice of representation by town, not population. From the first, this belief in town autonomy has been historically wrong and legally untenable and has been rejected repeatedly by the courts. The exceptional sway of rural towns over the legislature that resulted from this representation clause in the state constitution led to several instances of injustice documented in this study, including the failed constitutional convention of 1902, the Merritt Parkway land fraud scandal of the 1930s, and the failed effort to establish regional governance in Connecticut in the 1960s. Though this pernicious belief has proved mightier than the truth for centuries, its true impact on the state's history has yet to be fully assessed.

HISTORIC OPPORTUNITY OR DAYDREAM?

In 2010, the Federal Railroad Administration (FRA), a bureau of the U.S. Department of Transportation, initiated a multiyear rail planning study of the 450-mile-long Northeast Corridor (NEC) from Washington, D.C., to Boston, Massachusetts. In Connecticut, the NEC traverses the shoreline from Greenwich to New Haven and on to New London and Providence, following the shoreline route of the lower post road. The NEC is the most heavily traveled rail corridor in the United States. Each day, 750,000 persons ride more than two thousand trains along some portion of the route. (The NEC also carries fourteen million car-miles of freight each year.) Home to one of the densest populations in the United States and enough commercial activity to make the states along the NEC the fifth-largest economy in the world, the corridor is expected to grow by an additional seven million persons by 2040, the study's target year. The purpose of the study was to determine the improvements necessary to maintain effective rail service in the region during the growth spurt of the coming decades.[1]

In 2012, the scope of the study was broadened to include the possibility of initiating high-speed rail service between Washington and Boston capable of traveling up to 220 miles per hour. It is estimated that such high-speed service would reduce travel time from Washington to New York (currently two hours and forty-five minutes) by thirty-five minutes, and from New York to Boston (currently three hours and thirty minutes) by forty-five minutes, a 20 percent reduction in travel time over the entire corridor.[2]

In addition to answering questions of increased capacity and reduced travel time along the NEC, the FRA study has inadvertently made an important contribution to Connecticut's transportation future by considering one option, in particular, that might help the state address its thorniest transportation problem, the ongoing congestion along the lower post road from Greenwich to New Haven.

As the study progressed, more than fifteen alternatives were considered; three options emerged as possibilities. The first option was to simply keep pace with demand by adding tracks and reducing bottlenecks to expand the capacity of the existing system as needed. The second option was to grow the rail network at a more aggressive pace by expanding existing two-track sections to four tracks and existing four-track sections to six tracks, and by adding a new route in Connecticut from Hartford eastward to Providence, with a station stop at the University of Connecticut in Storrs. The third option, the most aggressive of all, included in addition to an upgrade of the existing spine through Connecticut the construction of a second, more northerly rail spine from New York to Danbury then east to Waterbury and Hartford and on to Boston via either Springfield, Worcester, or Providence. The estimated cost for the three options ranged from $64 billion for the first to $308 billion for the third, most expensive option.[3]

As part of its planning process, the FRA prepared a report outlining the various options studied and their impacts on the natural environment, and brought this information to public hearings throughout the region in 2015 and 2016. Not surprisingly, comments on the various options were mixed overall and particularly hostile in portions of eastern Connecticut where it was proposed to move existing sections of track that curve along the Connecticut shoreline inland through more developed portions of shoreline communities, from Old Lyme, Connecticut, to Kenyon, Rhode Island, so as to allow for faster running speeds along that portion of the route. The crux of the objections was the lack of detail in the proposed plan. While FRA considered the choice between the three options to be more conceptual than specific, the public reacted to the lack of final route information (which house or business will be affected?) and the high cost

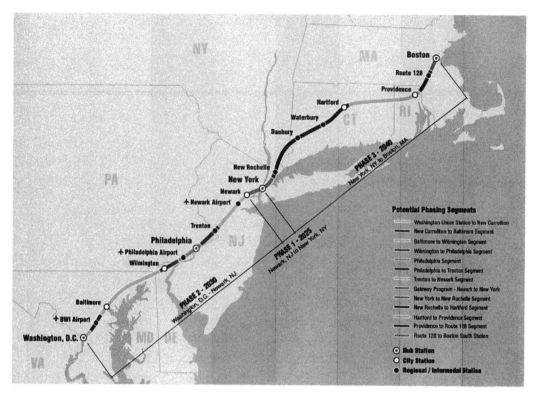

A new post road to Boston? A proposal for a new rail spine across central Connecticut studied by the Federal Railroad Administration could help Connecticut solve its thorniest transportation problem: traffic congestion in the travel corridor from Greenwich to New Haven.
Federal Railroad Administration

of the second spine option. As Connecticut Transportation commissioner James Redeker remarked, "Would I like to see more of Connecticut rail-accessible . . . ? Absolutely. As to whether the costs and impacts are worth those outcomes, we don't know that yet. That's the problem." Like many others, the commissioner thought it was time to slow the whole planning process down. "My gut instinct is that more time would be helpful."[4]

But the study continued (likely in an effort to release a final report before the end of the Obama presidency) and in July 2017 the Federal Railroad Administration unveiled its decision on this conceptual stage of the study. Although some positive comments were received concerning the possibility of a second rail spine across central Connecticut, high cost and right-of-way battles were seen as formidable obstacles. The executive director of the Capitol Region Council of Governments raised his voice with a pessimism typical of other respondents: "When you say 'let's just build something from Danbury to Providence'"—never mind how much it costs and how many eminent domain cases you're going to have to win. It's unconstrained by funding limits, constructability, environmental and community impacts. Well good luck on that."[5]

In the end, the FRA decided that the expansion of the existing system along the shoreline route through Connecticut was the most feasible option to pursue. However, to placate those opposed to the relocations in Old Lyme and elsewhere, the disputed portion of the selected alternative through eastern Connecticut was circled and marked "For Further Study."[6] However, the further study was to be completed not by the FRA but by the states of Connecticut and Rhode Island, without whose approval no federal plan could move forward. In effect, long-term planning for the New England portion of the Northeast Corridor was stalled, until the two states with the most strident objections could devise a way forward.

While the outcome was disappointing to all concerned, it need not be the final word on the matter. Though Connecticut is in no hurry to study the possibilities of establishing high-speed rail service along the shoreline route, history would suggest that the possibility of a second rail spine across central Connecticut should not be so quickly discarded. Increasing the traffic capacity of the lower post road (as in the selected alternative) has been the accepted solution to the post road problem ever since stagecoach service on the state's first earthen turnpikes was supplemented by the construction of the New York & New Haven Railroad in the 1840s. Subsequent improvements aimed at solving the congestion problem in this corridor included double tracking the New Haven main line in the 1880s; widening U.S. Route 1 in the 1920s; building the Merritt Parkway in the 1930s and the Connecticut Turnpike in the 1950s; and widening the Merritt Parkway and the Connecticut Turnpike from the 1980s to the present. Indeed, as recently as February 2018 ConnDOT proposed yet another plan to widen lower portions of I-95 by adding an additional northbound lane between exit 9 in Stamford and exit 28 in Bridgeport, and one southbound lane from exit 7 in Stamford to the New York state line. An advantage of this latest widening option is that it could be done within the road's existing right-of-way, eliminating the need for costly land purchases. Even so, the price tag on the project would be a hefty $2.3 billion. The new proposal was considered "a game-changer for breaking gridlock in Fairfield County,"[7] even though it will take at least eight years to complete. However, like other projects in the state's 2015 master plan, "Let's Go Connecticut," the proposal was given "no chance of proceeding until legislators stabilize Connecticut's cash-starved Special Transportation Fund."[8]

Clearly, it is time to consider a different approach. The true value of the NEC study may be bringing into the ongoing discussion of Connecticut's transportation future the option of opening a second rail spine across central Connecticut from Danbury to Hartford and Providence. Unlike the NEC study, however, state engineers need not specifically consider high-speed rail service. A more traditional, less costly rail line, with who knows what cost savings, may be as effective. In any event, in this age of excess communication, where it is easy enough to be in contact with others for business or pleasure almost any time from almost any place, perhaps it is time to reevaluate the costs and benefits of reducing travel time over hundreds of miles by tens of minutes. Why must we justify transportation improvements only in time saved or other economic terms? Could taking an action that makes sense historically be justification enough?

Pursuit of a second spine option by ConnDOT raises an important related issue worth further discussion. What is the role of a public transportation monopoly, such as that created by the federal-state mega-government, in pursuing a transportation option that may be undertaken not in response to a localized traffic problem but to redirect future growth to another geographic region in an effort to resolve the local problem? Certainly, it poses a risk. Yet either way, growth will occur, and with no effort to reorient land use patterns, growth will follow existing patterns of development as it has in the case of the post road for four centuries. It is a difficult question to answer because it strikes at the heart of the federal-state power-sharing partnership. Is transportation in Connecticut to be merely a reflection of choices made in Washington, resulting in funding for specific federal transportation programs—be it highway, rail, or transit—or can the state's transportation future truly be determined by Connecticut legislators making decisions in Hartford, however risky, that they consider in the best interest of the people they represent?

The possibility of a second rail spine across central Connecticut provides a historic opportunity unprecedented since the opening of the first post road to Boston four centuries ago. Surely, the prospect of a second rail spine, bringing better access to impoverished cities such as Danbury, Waterbury, and Willimantic while providing a direct connection between the state capital and its flagship university at Storrs, should not be casually dismissed as a nigh-on-impossible daydream. Surely, it would be difficult to achieve at whatever the cost. As they say, the devil is in the details. In this case, however, within the details—of a revitalized rail line to Boston across central Connecticut with a direct connection to New York City—may also lie a new solution to Connecticut's thorniest, most historic transportation problem.

THE MORE THINGS CHANGE . . .

There is a popular saying (a sure conversation starter among any gaggle of historians) that "the more things change, the more they stay the same." Surely, dramatic changes have occurred during the four centuries of transportation history recounted in this study, nowhere more so than to the character we call The Land. Where a hunter-gatherer economy had existed among Native Americans for thousands of years in ecological balance, European colonists installed in its place a new agricultural economy where the natural environment was seen as a commodity to be bought and sold, and the best use of the land was inexorably tied to its economic value. Once this new culture was established, a series of revolutions (political, legal, and technological) allowed the population of an expanding nation, with land to spare, to grow in ways no one could have foreseen. In particular, the technology of mass production and mass distribution by rail changed the face of the landscape forever. As industry of all types became concentrated in urban centers with the best rail access, populations soared, until by the end of the nineteenth century, fed by crops grown in distant places, Connecticut was able to sustain nearly one million persons in a dozen or so densely populated urban centers—eight times the number of Native Americans that had lived on the land 250 years before.

With continued technological advancements, including the advent of automobility, the population of the state tripled by the 1960s to three million persons, the new growth being spread out across the landscape in a more suburban pattern. According to engineering projections at the time, the population of Connecticut was expected to climb to five million by the end of the century, with no end in sight. But then something happened. The impacts of population growth and automotive technology were made visible in massive traffic backups, smog-colored skies, and foul-smelling rivers. Cities, instead of being revitalized by urban renewal, became home to a larger number of ghetto dwellers than ever before. Clearly, something had gone wrong, and the more the public became aware of the negative impacts of growth and technology, the more they protested, demanding that something be done.

Concern over human impact on the natural environment did not originate in the 1960s. The *Connecticut Courant* of April 22, 1817, contained an article by the state's own Noah Webster, who was alarmed by the ongoing deforestation taking place throughout New England, which on the arrival of the first Europeans had been fully forested with first-growth timber. Webster reminded his fellow citizens that "our country can not sustain the present consumption of wood for a century to come . . . We must either reduce the annual consumption [then averaging thirty to forty cords per family per year] within the limits of the annual growth, or that time will arrive when we must search the bowels of the earth for fuel."[9] Webster's article was one of the first pleas for conservation in the new nation; it was based not on the intricate interdependencies of ecology, whose principles were as yet unknown, but on the common sense that life and experience had provided him: "It is the ordinance of Providence that men should live within their means—we must come to this sooner or later—and adapt our manner of life to our circumstance."[10]

The disaster that Webster foretold was postponed by the technological inventions that made the mining of coal, oil, and natural gas possible. But neither was his idea forgotten. By the early twentieth century, with the closing of the western frontier, the need to preserve some of the country's most beautiful landscape became obvious and gave rise to the nation's first national parks, along with a broader movement to conserve all of the nation's natural resources. To this was added in the 1930s and 1940s the specifics of a new science called ecology that studied the true function of the natural community and the place of humans in that community. For the first time, the land was seen not as a mere collection of soils, plants, and animals but for what it truly was: a circuit of energy, originating in the sun, that flowed upward through the food chain and thereby sustained all life, including humankind. As this shocking awareness bubbled up in the popular culture of the 1960s, it was embedded in our social consciousness by the photo images provided by the *Apollo* astronauts of the fragile blue marble we call Earth seen against the impenetrable blackness of space.

As a result, much did change. The new consciousness filtered down through existing government bureaucracies, and a new standard was adopted for managing growth: land use planning. For the first time since the concept of zoning had taken hold in the 1920s, large-scale projects such as new expressways were to be reconciled with the use of the land through which they passed. In a process that was to be ongoing, comprehensive, and coordinated with local communities, the impacts of such projects were to be evaluated not only in economic and engineering terms but also with regard to the impact of construction on the natural environment. In an effort to reduce our dependence on automobility, government action rescued a failing rail system, and responsibility for all modes of travel—land, air, and water—was consolidated into mega departments of transportation at the federal and state levels, creating in effect a public transportation monopoly of the kind once aspired to by Connecticut railroad magnates Morgan and Mellen.

However, one thing had not changed. For all our newfound environmentalism, we continued to view the land in mainly economic terms. The dollar value associated with its use was still paramount, and as a result, smart-growth alternatives that were more ecologically balanced were viewed in a similar light and seen only as more costly than other options, less valuable in their own right. What is missing in our evaluation is a more enlightened ethic toward the land, an extension of the civil rights available to most Americans (the securing of which had been the focus of much protest in the 1960s) to the land itself.

The case for a land ethic, a mainstay of the environmental movement in the 1960s, was put forth as early as 1949 by the midwestern conservationist Aldo Leopold in his book *A Sand County Almanac*. Leopold noted that slaves were once considered chattel and treated accordingly, a view that was no longer considered ethical or humane. As slaves were freed from the one-way economic relationship that benefited only their owners, so too must we free ourselves from our one-way economic relationship with the land, which also brings its owners privilege (financial gain) without obligation. Adoption of a land ethic will enlarge our sense of community to include soils, air, water, plants, and animals, while affirming the right of these essential members of our human community to exist in an unspoiled state. Leopold believed that the events of the twentieth century, from the Dust Bowl to suburban sprawl, were proof positive that a land ethic was no longer just an idea to be debated, but one that had become an ecological necessity.[11] What had been unveiled by our new environmental consciousness was what Leopold referred to as the paradox of the twentieth century: "Our tools are better than we are, and grow better faster than we do . . . But they do not suffice for the oldest task in human history: to live on a piece of land without spoiling it."[12] It was time, he believed, for society to affirm that spoiling the land was wrong not only because government regulations made it so; it was, indeed, *morally* wrong.

In Connecticut, the existence of nine regional Councils of Governments (COGs), groups of towns that have voluntarily agreed to tackle growth-related issues on a regional scale, may be seen as a good first step in the evolution of a land ethic in the state. There is considerable evidence that the nation's economy is driven not by individual states but by metropolitan regions within states, and that these regional economies, and not the economies of individual states, are the building blocks of our national economy. So the emphasis on the region as opposed to the city or the state as today's most significant political entity not only makes good planning sense but good economic sense as well. Unfortunately, in Connecticut, regional governance remains voluntary and advisory and

Though Connecticut has nine regional councils of government, the organizations have no political power to implement land use recommendations. Courtesy of the Connecticut Office of Policy and Management

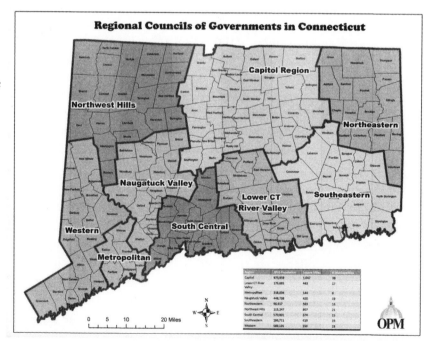

focuses more on the sharing of government services (so as to reduce their cost) than on land use and growth issues per se.

As with individual Connecticut towns, COGs have only those powers that are given to them by the state legislature, and they currently lack the taxing power necessary to fund significant land use decisions. Therefore, in discussing the challenges faced by urban centers in Connecticut, Governor Malloy's Commission on Fiscal Stability and Economic Growth concluded, "Without a large city, Connecticut's best chance for regional economic development might be dynamic and cohesive regions that act like large cities."[13] To that end, the commission suggested giving COGs the option "to levy an additional sales tax of up to 0.5 percent . . . to be used solely for regional economic development and shared services arrangements," and in addition, authorizing COGs "to impose supplemental time-limited sales or property taxes by special referenda to fund discrete capital projects."[14] The commission's goal was to make COGs effective agencies of government, functioning in the modern era of globalization much as counties once did in colonial Connecticut and still do in many other states.

To date, no such legislation has been considered. However, in 2015, the legislature did consider a bill to create a Connecticut Transit Corridor Development Authority whose purpose would be to stimulate economic development within a half-mile radius of all transit stations in the state, a measure the editors of the *Hartford Courant* called "a strategy for smart growth."[15] The bill stirred much controversy, in part because it would have given the proposed Authority the same power of eminent domain entrusted to the state Department of Transportation. The provision was later removed from the bill, yet the bill was ultimately dismissed because the authority was seen as "another layer of government bureaucracy" intended to do "what any town can already voluntarily plan and construct."[16]

Herein lies the heart of the matter, the core reason why it is difficult, despite the adoption of many effective regulations, to advance the cause of a land ethic in Connecticut via strong regional governance. The reason is the very persistence of history, for better or for ill. As the writer James Baldwin once noted, with respect to African American history, "History is not the past. It is the present. We carry our history with us. We are our history."[17] In the case of town autonomy in Connecticut, the believed history is known to be false but remains a pernicious myth.

The value of history, the reason we record it and study it, lies in its ability to help us see the world around us in a broader perspective and as a result change who we are in relation to our surroundings. In our youth and adolescence it is natural to be self-centered, to think that the world was made for us to do with as we please. But as we age and accumulate life experiences, we are meant to mature emotionally and therefore to better align ourselves and our needs with the world around us, rather than in opposition to it.

The study of history can help us make that transformation. But first, we must see our history for what it truly is, and not simply as a nostalgic retelling of yesteryear. For example, for centuries the written history of Connecticut has masked the importance of the state's "rotten borough" system of legislative representation behind a seemingly harmless sobriquet, referring to Connecticut as a "Land of Steady Habits." As we have seen, the idea that the power of state government is derived from each town, and not from the individuals who live in them, has indeed persisted as a steady habit, only to deny Connecticut citizens for nearly two centuries the truly representative government they fought for in the American Revolution. When changes were finally made to the Connecticut constitution in 1965, they were made not voluntarily but by order of the U.S. Supreme Court. In fact, the power of this pernicious idea, repeatedly disavowed by the state Supreme Court, had already undercut an attempt in 1902 to revise the state constitution; fostered the political atmosphere that made the Merritt Parkway scandal of the 1930s possible; and contributed to the defeat of regional governance in the 1960s. Still today it exerts a strong hold on the public's imagination, which begs a question: what other effects has this false but widely held belief had on what is considered the accepted history of Connecticut? Surely, it is time to investigate the matter more thoroughly, to see this erroneous belief for what it really is: not a feel-good affirmation of local power but rather the unrelenting reluctance of Connecticut's colonial and state governments to share power with its constituents.

If we are to promote the cause of a land ethic in Connecticut, it is also necessary to present the land itself as a character in the story of Connecticut (as it has been in this transportation study) and rewrite the state's history accordingly. Acknowledging the ecological aspects of Connecticut history, taking them to heart, and educating future generations accordingly will serve to further our understanding of the importance of the land (and how we treat it) in our history. Indeed today, nearly a century after Leopold first proposed it, the adoption of a land ethic is still considered by many as a necessary step in the resolution of the environmental issues (droughts, melting glaciers, and climate change) that now threaten us on a global scale.

Lest we become daunted by the amount of work ahead, let us remember that the proper study of history can also provide much-needed solace in times of crisis. History can remind us, as with Noah Webster, that we are not the first to identify intractable environmental problems or wrestle with their consequences. History contains the wisdom of all who have come before us, and when taken to heart, the wisdom of the past can motivate us to overcome the problems of the present.

It is appropriate that the last word on the matter be given to Henry David Thoreau, a New England conservationist of the first order who throughout his life sought to understand the role of technology and progress in human history. When the railroad first came to Massachusetts in the 1840s, Thoreau knew instinctively that the public's ready acceptance of the railroad and its steam technology put man in danger of becoming "a tool of his tools." Today, Thoreau's notebooks provide a refresher course in the fundamental principles that can help us to become more humble in the face of technological change. Remember, Thoreau said, "What you get by achieving your goals is not as important as what you become by achieving your goals."

As to the question of progress—whether the more things change, the more they stay the same—Thoreau also provides us with a perceptive insight into how to think about the unending technological changes that impact our daily lives. He believed that when all was said and done, "things do not change, we change." And so it must be with the land. We must change our view of the natural environment, take it to heart as an essential part of the human community, and use this ethical awareness to teach ourselves ways to accomplish what Aldo Leopold considered the most demanding of all human tasks: "to live on a piece of land without spoiling it."

Appendixes

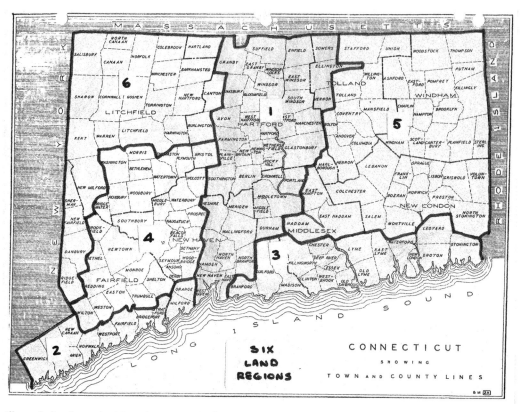

All population figures in this study are organized according to the state's six geomorphic regions, which better reflect the history of the state than artificial regions such as counties.
Author

Appendix A Population by Geomorphic Region 1900–2000

The grouping of Connecticut towns into the six geomorphic regions used in this study is based on the regional plan promoted by the Connecticut Historical Commission in *Historic Preservation: A Cultural Resource Management Plan for Connecticut,* published in 1990. These regions were delineated to reflect the geological and ecological divisions of the state's natural history. These natural regions correspond more closely to the many human activities that comprise the history of Connecticut than administrative divisions such as counties and planning regions imposed on the landscape for other reasons. Moreover the use, and an awareness, of these six geomorphic regions remind us of the importance of the land and its natural history in the telling of the human story.

All the population figures in the following tables are taken from United States Census data. The land areas of individual towns are from the 2003 edition of the *Connecticut State Register and Manual.*

Connecticut Towns' and Cities Populations by Geomorphic Region 1900–2000

Region 1: Central Lowland

	Land Area	1900	1920	1940	1950	1960	1980	2000
Avon	23.1	1302	1534	2258	3171	5273	11201	15832
Berlin	26.5	3448	4298	5230	7470	11250	15121	18215
Bloomfield	26.0	1513	2394	4309	5746	13613	18608	19587
Cheshire	32.9	1989	2855	4352	6295	13383	21788	28543
Cromwell	12.4	2031	2454	3281	4286	6780	10265	12871
Durham	23.6	884	959	1098	1804	3096	5143	6627
East Granby	17.5	684	1056	1225	1327	2434	4102	4745
East Hartford	18.0	6406	11648	18615	29933	43977	52563	49575
East Haven	12.3	1167	3520	9094	12212	21388	25028	28189
East Windsor	26.3	3158	3741	3967	4859	7500	8925	9818
Ellington	34.1	1829	2127	2479	3099	5580	9711	12921
Enfield	33.4	6699	11719	13561	15464	31464	42695	45212
Farmington	28.1	3331	3844	5313	7026	10813	16407	23641
Glastonbury	51.4	4260	5592	6632	8818	14497	24327	31876
Granby	40.7	1299	1342	1544	2693	4968	7956	10347
Hamden	32.8	4662	8611	23373	29715	41056	51071	56913
Hartford (1784)	17.3	79850	138036	166267	177397	162178	136392	121578
Manchester	27.3	10601	18370	23799	34116	42102	49761	54740
Meriden (1867)	23.8	28659	34764	39494	44088	51850	57118	58244
Middlefield	12.7	845	1047	1230	1983	3255	3796	4203
Middletown (1784)	40.9	17486	22129	26495	29711	33250	39040	43167
New Britain (1870)	13.3	28202	59316	68685	73726	82201	73840	71538
New Haven (1784)	18.9	108027	162537	160605	164443	152048	126109	123626
Newington	13.2	1041	2381	5449	9110	17664	28841	29306
North Branford	24.9	814	1110	1438	2017	6771	11554	13906
North Haven	20.8	2164	1968	5326	9444	15935	22080	23035
Plainville	9.7	2189	4114	6935	9994	13149	16401	17328
Portland	23.4	3856	3644	4321	5186	7496	8383	8732
Rocky Hill	13.5	1026	1633	2679	5108	7404	14559	17966
Simsbury	33.9	2094	2958	3941	4822	10138	21161	23234
Somers	28.3	1593	1673	2114	2631	3702	8473	10417
Southington	36.0	5890	8440	9649	13061	22797	36879	39728
South Windsor	28.0	2014	2142	2863	4066	9460	17198	24412

Connecticut Towns' and Cities Populations by Geomorphic Region 1900–2000 (*Continued*)

Suffield	42.2	3521	4070	4475	4895	6779	9294	13552
Vernon	17.7	8483	8898	8978	10115	16961	27974	28063
Wallingford	39.0	9001	12010	14788	16976	29920	37274	43026
West Hartford	22.0	3186	8854	33776	44402	62382	61301	63589
West Haven (1961)	*10.8*	*0*	*0*	*30021*	*32010*	*43002*	*53184*	*52360*
Wethersfield	12.4	2637	4342	9644	12533	20561	26013	26271
Windsor	29.6	3614	5620	10068	11833	19467	25204	28237
Windsor Locks	9.0	3062	3554	4347	5221	11411	12190	12043
Region 1: Total	1007.7	374517	581304	753718	872806	1088955	1248930	1327213

Region 2: Western Coast

	Land Area	1900	1920	1940	1950	1960	1980	2000
Bridgeport (1836)	*16.0*	*70996*	*143555*	*147121*	*158709*	*156748*	*142546*	*139529*
Darien	12.9	3116	4184	9222	11767	18437	18892	19607
Fairfield	30.0	4489	11475	21135	30489	46183	54849	57340
Greenwich	47.8	12172	22123	35509	40835	53793	59578	61101
Milford (1959)	*22.6*	*3783*	*10193*	*16439*	*26870*	*41662*	*50898*	*52305*
New Canaan	22.1	2968	3895	6221	8001	13466	17931	19395
Norwalk (1893)	*22.8*	*19932*	*27743*	*39849*	*49460*	*67775*	*77767*	*82951*
Orange	17.2	6995	16614	2009	3032	8547	13237	13233
Stamford (1893)	*37.8*	*18839*	*40067*	*61215*	*74293*	*92713*	*102453*	*117083*
Stratford	17.6	3657	12347	22580	33428	45012	50541	49976
Westport	20.0	4017	5114	8258	11667	20955	25290	25749
Region 2: Total	266.8	150964	297310	369558	448551	567251	613982	638269

Region 3: Eastern Coast

	Land Area	1900	1920	1940	1950	1960	1980	2000
Branford	22.0	5706	6627	8060	10944	16610	23363	28683
Chester	16.0	1328	1675	1676	1920	2520	3068	3743
Clinton	16.3	1429	1217	1791	2466	4166	11195	13094
Deep River/Saybrook	13.6	1634	2325	2332	2570	2968	3994	4610
East Lyme	34.0	1836	2291	3338	3870	6782	13870	18118
Essex	10.4	2530	2815	2859	3491	4057	5078	6505
Groton (1964)	*31.3*	*5962*	*9227*	*10910*	*21896*	*29937*	*41062*	*39907*

(continued)

Connecticut Towns' and Cities Populations by Geomorphic Region 1900–2000 (*Continued*)

Guilford	47.1	2785	2803	3544	5092	7913	17375	21398
Killingworth	35.3	651	531	531	677	1098	3976	6018
Ledyard	38.1	1236	1161	1426	1749	5395	13735	14687
Lyme	31.9	750	674	717	857	1183	1822	2016
Madison	36.2	1518	1857	2245	3078	4567	14031	17858
New London (1784)	*5.5*	*17548*	*25688*	*30456*	*30551*	*34182*	*28842*	*25671*
Old Lyme	23.1	1180	946	1702	2141	3068	6159	7406
Old Saybrook	15.0	1431	1463	1985	2499	5274	9287	10367
Stonington	38.7	8540	10236	11002	11801	13969	16220	17906
Waterford	32.8	2904	3935	6594	9100	15391	17843	19152
Westbrook	15.7	884	849	1159	1549	2399	5216	6292
Region 3: Total	463.0	59852	76320	92327	116251	161479	236136	263431

Region 4: Southwest Hills

	Land Area	1900	1920	1940	1950	1960	1980	2000
Ansonia (1893)	*6.0*	*12681*	*17643*	*19210*	*18706*	*19819*	*19039*	*18554*
Beacon Falls	9.8	623	1593	1756	2067	2886	3995	5246
Bethany	21.0	517	411	706	1318	2384	4330	5040
Bethel	16.8	3327	3201	4105	5104	8200	16004	18067
Bethlehem	19.4	576	536	715	1015	1486	2573	3422
Bridgewater	16.2	649	481	537	639	898	1563	1824
Bristol (1911)	*26.5*	*9643*	*20620*	*30167*	*35961*	*45499*	*57370*	*60062*
Brookfield	19.8	1046	896	1345	1688	3405	12872	15664
Derby (1893)	*5.0*	*7930*	*11238*	*10287*	*10259*	*12132*	*12346*	*12391*
Easton	27.4	960	1017	1262	2165	3407	5962	7272
Middlebury	17.8	736	1067	2173	3318	4785	5995	6451
Monroe	26.1	1043	1161	1728	2892	6402	14010	19247
Morris	17.2	535	499	606	799	1190	1899	2301
Naugatuck	16.4	10541	15051	15388	17455	19511	26456	30989
Newtown	57.8	3276	2751	4023	7448	11373	19107	25031
Oxford	32.9	952	998	1375	2037	3292	6634	9821
Plymouth	21.7	2828	5942	6043	6771	8981	10732	11634
Prospect	14.3	562	266	1006	1896	4367	6807	8707
Redding	31.5	1426	1315	1758	2037	3359	7272	8270
Roxbury	26.2	1087	647	660	740	912	1468	2136

Connecticut Towns' and Cities Populations by Geomorphic Region 1900–2000 (*Continued*)

Seymour	14.6	3541	6781	6754	7832	10100	13434	15454
Shelton (1915)	*30.6*	*5572*	*9475*	*10971*	*12694*	*18190*	*31314*	*38101*
Southbury	39.1	1238	1093	1532	3828	5186	14156	18567
Thomaston	12.0	3300	3993	4238	4896	5850	6276	7503
Trumbull	23.3	1587	2597	5294	8641	20379	32989	34243
Washington	38.2	1820	1619	2089	2227	2603	3657	3596
Waterbury (1853)	*28.6*	*51139*	*91715*	*99314*	*104477*	*107130*	*103266*	*107271*
Watertown	29.2	3100	6050	8787	10699	14837	19489	21661
Weston	19.8	840	703	1053	1988	4039	8284	10037
Wilton	27.0	1598	1284	2829	4558	8026	15351	17633
Wolcott	20.4	581	719	1765	3553	8889	13008	15215
Woodbridge	18.8	852	1170	2262	5182	5182	7761	8983
Woodbury	36.5	1988	1698	1998	2564	3910	6942	9198
Region 4: Total	767.9	138094	216230	253736	297454	378609	512361	579591

Region 5: Eastern Hills

	Land Area	1900	1920	1940	1950	1960	1980	2000
Andover	15.5	385	389	560	1034	1771	2144	3036
Ashford	38.8	757	673	704	845	1315	3221	4098
Bolton	14.4	457	448	728	1729	2933	3951	5017
Bozrah	20.0	799	858	904	1154	1590	2135	2357
Brooklyn	29.0	2358	1655	2403	2652	3312	5691	7173
Canterbury	39.9	876	896	992	1321	1857	3426	4692
Chaplin	19.4	529	385	489	712	1230	1793	2250
Colchester	49.1	1991	2050	2338	3007	4648	7761	14551
Columbia	21.4	655	706	853	1327	2163	3386	4971
Coventry	37.7	1632	1582	2102	4043	6356	8895	11504
Eastford	28.9	523	496	496	598	746	1028	1618
East Haddam	54.3	2485	2312	2217	2554	3637	5621	8333
East Hampton	35.6	2271	2394	2955	4000	5403	8572	13352
Franklin	19.5	546	552	667	727	974	1592	1835
Griswold	35.0	3490	4220	5343	5728	6472	8967	10807
Haddam	44.0	2015	1736	2069	2636	3466	6383	7157
Hampton	25.0	629	475	535	672	934	1322	1758

(*continued*)

Connecticut Towns' and Cities Populations by Geomorphic Region 1900–2000 (*Continued*)

Hebron	36.9	1016	915	999	1320	1819	5453	8610
Killingly	48.5	6835	8178	9547	10015	11298	14519	16472
Lebanon	54.1	1521	1343	1467	1654	2434	4762	6907
Lisbon	16.3	697	867	1131	1282	2019	3279	4069
Mansfield	44.5	1827	2574	4559	10008	14638	20634	20720
Marlborough	23.3	322	303	476	901	1961	4746	5709
Montville	42.0	2395	3411	4135	4766	7759	16455	18546
North Stonington	54.3	1240	1144	1236	1367	1982	4219	4991
Norwich (1784)	*28.3*	*24637*	*29685*	*34140*	*37633*	*38506*	*38074*	*36117*
Plainfield	42.3	4821	7926	7613	8071	8884	12774	14619
Pomfret	40.3	1831	1454	1710	2018	2136	2775	3798
Preston	30.9	2807	2743	4206	1775	4992	4644	4688
Putnam	20.3	7348	8397	8692	9304	8412	8580	9002
Salem	29.0	468	424	504	618	925	2335	3858
Scotland	18.6	471	391	478	513	684	1072	1556
Sprague	13.2	1339	2500	2285	2320	2509	2996	2971
Stafford	58.0	4297	5407	5835	6471	7476	9268	11307
Sterling	27.2	1209	1266	1251	1298	1397	1791	3099
Thompson	46.9	6442	5055	5577	5585	6217	8141	8878
Tolland	39.7	1036	1040	1192	1659	2950	9694	13146
Union	28.7	428	257	234	261	383	546	693
Voluntown	38.9	872	656	723	825	1028	1637	2528
Willington	33.3	885	1200	1233	1462	2005	4694	5959
Windham	27.1	10137	13801	13824	15884	16973	21062	22857
Woodstock	60.5	2095	1767	1912	2271	3177	5117	7221
Region 5: Total	1430.6	109374	124531	141314	164020	201371	285155	342830

Region 6: Northwest Highlands

	Land Area	1900	1920	1940	1950	1960	1980	2000
Barkhamsted	36.2	864	719	724	946	1370	2935	3494
Burlington	29.8	1218	1109	1246	1846	2790	5660	8190
Canaan	33.0	820	561	555	708	790	1002	1081
Canton	24.6	2678	2549	2769	3613	4783	7635	8840
Colebrook	31.5	684	492	547	592	791	1221	1471
Cornwall	46.0 46.0	1175	834	907	896	1051	1288	1434

Connecticut Towns' and Cities Populations by Geomorphic Region 1900–2000 (*Continued*)

Danbury (1889)	*42.1*	*19474*	*22325*	*27921*	*30337*	*39382*	*60470*	*74848*
Goshen	43.7	835	675	778	940	1288	1706	2697
Hartland	33.0	592	448	300	549	1040	1416	2012
Harwinton	30.8	1213	2020	1112	1858	3344	4889	5283
Kent	48.5	1220	1086	1245	1392	1686	2505	2858
Litchfield	56.1	3214	3180	4029	4964	6264	7605	8316
New Fairfield	20.5	584	468	608	1236	3355	11260	13953
New Hartford	37.0	3424	1781	1836	2395	3033	4884	6088
New Milford	61.6	4804	4781	5559	5799	8318	19420	27121
Norfolk	45.3	1614	1229	1333	1572	1827	2156	1660
North Canaan	19.5	1803	1933	2304	2647	2836	3185	3350
Ridgefield	34.4	2626	2707	3900	4356	8165	20120	23643
Salisbury	57.3	3489	2497	3030	3132	3309	3896	3977
Sharon	58.7	1982	1585	1611	1889	2141	2623	2968
Sherman	21.8	658	533	477	549	825	2281	3827
Torrington (1923)	*39.8*	*12453*	*22055*	*26988*	*27820*	*30045*	*30987*	*35202*
Warren	26.3	432	350	328	437	600	1027	1254
Winsted/Winchester (1917)	*32.3*	*7763*	*9019*	*8482*	*10535*	*10496*	*10841*	*10664*
Region 6: Total	909.8	75619	84936	98589	111008	139529	211012	254231
State Total	4845.8	908420	1380631	1709242	2010090	2537194	3107576	3405565

Cities in *italics*. Year formed in
(parentheses).

Appendix B Controlled-Access Expressways

This appendix lists all controlled-access highways built in the state from the opening of the first section of the Merritt Parkway in 1938 to the completion of the northeast quadrant of I-291 from South Windsor to Manchester in 1994. The list includes parkways, interstate highways, and state expressways, for a total of six hundred system miles. The opening of the Connecticut Turnpike (I-95) in 1958 is considered the beginning of interstate highway construction in Connecticut, while the opening of I-291 in 1994 marked the completion of the 347-mile Interstate Highway System in the state. All mileage figures refer to the length of the expressways and do not reflect the number of lane miles on each highway, which have varied over time as portions of expressways are widened. As of 1994, the total system of controlled-access highways in Connecticut contained approximately 1,500 lane miles, or an average of 2.5 lanes per mile of expressway. Opening dates and segment descriptions are taken from Kurumi.com, a privately operated website devoted to Connecticut roads, and should be considered approximate.

ROUTE	SECTION	OPENED
2	Main Street to Route 17	1952
2	Route 32 to Route 169	1959
2	Pitkin Street to Main Street	1961
2	Scott Hill Road to Route 32	1961
2	Route 17 to West Road, Marlborough	1964
2	Route 66 to South Main Street	1964
2	Mixmaster interchange East Hartford	1965
2	West Road to Route 66	1966
2	South Main Street to Exit 17, Colchester	1967
2	Exit 17 to Route 354	1967
2	Route 354 to Scott Hill Road	1971
3	Wethersfield to Glastonbury	1987
7	I-95 to Route 123, Norwalk	1971
7	Danbury and Brookfield	1977
8	Beacon Falls	1942
8	Derby	1951
8	Seymour	1961
8	Waterbury to Thomaston, Torrington	1964
8	Waterbury, including I-84 interchange	1967
8	Torrington to Winsted	1970
8	Shelton	1975
8	Beacon Falls	1982
9	Route 17 to Achenson Drive, Middletown	1950
9	Middletown	1956
9	Route 154 to Route 17	1959
9	Berlin Turnpike to Route 71	1962
9	Old Saybrook to Essex	1966
9	Higganum to Route 154	1966
9	Essex to Higganum	1968
9	Middletown to I-91	1969
9	Route 71 to Ellis Street, New Britain	1969

ROUTE	SECTION	OPENED
9	Ellis Street to Route 72	1978
9	Route 72 to Route 175	1986
9	I-91 to Berlin Turnpike	1989
9	Route 175 to I-84	1992
11	Colchester to Salem	1972
15	Greenwich to Route 7	1938
15	Route 7 to Milford	1940
15	Wilbur Cross: Sikorsky Bridge to Route 34	1941
15	Connector to Route 1, Milford	1942
15	Connector to Charter Oak Bridge	1942
15	Berlin Turnpike, Meriden to Hartford	1942
15	Wilbur Cross: Route 5 to Berlin Turnpike	1946
15	Wilbur Cross: Whitney Avenue to Route 5	1947
15	Wilbur Cross: Route 34 to Whitney Avenue	1949
15	Charter Oak Bridge to Union	1950
20	I-91 to Bradley Airport	1961
25	Bridgeport	1972
25	Bridgeport to Route 111	1982
34	New Haven	1960
72	Berlin Turnpike to Route 71	1962
72	New Britain to Plainville	1973
72	New Britain	1978
72	Plainville to Route 177	1986
I-84	Danbury to Route 302 Newtown	1961
I-84	West Hartford; Plainville to Southington	1965
I-84	Manchester to Bolton Notch	1971
I-84	Manchester	1972
I-84	Columbia, Coventry, Windham and Mansfield	1973
I-84	Widening in Newtown underway	1973
I-84	Route 302 to Southbury	1976
I-84	Reconstruction in Waterbury	1980

ROUTE	SECTION	OPENED
I-84	Danbury and east Hartford	1985
I-84	Various sections	1986
I-84	interchange with I-91	1990
I-86	Ashford and Union	1976
I-86	Reconstruction in Vernon, Tolland and Willington	1977
I-86	Reconstruction in Vernon, Tolland and Willington	1980
I-91	Charter Oak Bridge to Whitehead Highway	1945
I-91	I-84 to Route 159	1950
I-91	Hartford to Windsor Locks	1958
I-91	Windsor Locks to Massachusetts State Line	1959
I-91	Wetherfield to Rocky Hill	1964
I-91	Meriden to Rocky Hill	1965
I-91	New Haven to Meriden	1966
I-95	Greenwich to Killingly	1958
I-95	Greewich to New York Thruway	1958
I-95	Waterford to Rhode Island StateLline	1964
I-291	Windsor to Manchester	1994
I-384	East Hartford and Manchester	1971
I-395	I-95 to Route 6 (built as Connecticut Tpke)	1958
I-395	Route 6 to Route 101(built as state route 12)	1962
I-395	Route 101 to Mass. Line (built as state route 12)	1968
I-691	Route 5 to Middlefield	1966
I-691	Route 322 to Route 5	1971
I-691	Route 322 to I-84	1987

Appendix C Notable Highway Bridges

NOTABLE BRIDGES OF THE EARLY AUTO AGE

NAME	ROUTE	OVER	TOWNS
Warehouse Point Bridge	140	Connecticut River	Windsor–South Windsor
Thompsonville Bridge	190	Connecticut River	Suffield–Enfield
Middletown Bridge	66	Connecticut River	Middletown–Portland
Hartford (Buckeley)Bridge	6	Connecticut River	Hartford–East Hartford
Old Saybrook Bridge	1	Connecticut River	Old Saybrook–Old Lyme
Haddam Bridge	82	Connecticut River	Haddam–East Haddam
New London Bridge	1	Thames River	New London–Groton
Washington Street Bridge	1	Housatonic River	Stratford–Milford
Mystic Bridge	1	Mystic River	Mystic
Tomlinson Bridge	1	Quinnipiac River	New Haven

NOTABLE BRIDGES OF THE EXPRESSWAY ERA

NAME	ROUTE	OVER	TOWNS
Middletown (Aragoni) Bridge	66	Connecticut River	Middletown–Portland
Merritt Parkway Bridge	15	Housatonic River	Stratford–Milford
Charter Oak Bridge	15	Connecticut River	Wethersfield–East Hartford
New London (Gold Star Memorial) Bridge	I-95	Connecticut River	New London–Groton
Old Saybrook (Baldwin) Bridge	I-95	Connecticut River	Old Saybrook–Old Lyme
Commodore Hull (Sikorsky) Bridge	15	Housatonic River	Stratford–Milford
General Rochambeau Bridge	I-84	Housatonic River	Newtown–Southbury
State Street (Founders) Bridge	State Street	Connecticut River	Hartford–East Hartford
Putnam Bridge	3	Connecticut River	Rocky Hill–Glastonbury
Bissell (Wolcott Avenue) Bridge	I-291	Connecticut River	Windsor–South Windsor
Hartford (Buckeley) Bridge	I-84	Connecticut River	Hartford–East Hartford

OPENED	TYPE OF STRUCTURE	OWNER	COMMENTS
1886	Iron suspension bridge	Privately-owned toll bridge	Freed 1907; new bridge by county in 1921
1892	Iron truss bridge	Privately-owned toll bridge	Freed 1907; given to county in 1907
1896	Iron truss draw bridge	Privately-owned toll bridge	Freed 1907; to county in 1907; to CHD in 1919
1908	Stone arch bridge	Bridge & Highway District	Low-level bridge with no draw
1911	Steel truss with lift draw	Special Bridge Commission	to CHD in 1915
1913	Low-level swing bridge	Special Bridge Commission	to CHD in 1915
1919	Low-level swing bridge	CHD	existing railroad bridge converted to highway use
1921	Double-leaf bascule bridge	CHD	note open-spandrel concrete arches
1922	Bascule draw bridge	CHD	external balanced-bean design
1924	Double-leaf bascule bridge	City of New Haven	new lift bridge in 2002

OPENED	TYPE OF STRUCTURE	OWNER	COMMENTS
1938	steel arch	CHD	
1940	steel girder	CHD	
1942	steel girder	Special Bridge Commission	to CHD in 1959
1943	steel truss	Special Bridge Commission	to CHD in 1951
1948	prestressed concrete	Special Bridge Commission	to CHD in 1951
1940	deck truss	CHD	open steel deck
1953	steel girder	CHD	
1957	steel girder	Greater Hartford Bridge Authority	to CHD in 1959
1959	steel girder	Greater Hartford Bridge Authority	to CHD in 1959
1960	prestressed concrete	Greater Hartford Bridge Authority	to CHD in 1959
1963	multiple stone arch	Greater Hartford Bridge Authority	to CHD in 1959, widened to carry I-84

Notes

Introduction: The Bicycle Leads the Way

1. Official Catalogue of the International Exposition, 1876.

2. *A Facsimile of FRANK LESLIE'S Illustrated Historical Register of the Centennial Exposition, 1876* (New York: Paddington Press, 1976), 65.

3. Ibid., 77.

4. "The Progress of the Century," Currier & Ives lithograph, 1876.

5. Lyle Cumming, *Internal Fire: The Internal Combustion Engine 1673–1900* (Lake Oswego, Oreg.: Carnot Press, 1976).

6. Bruce D. Epperson, *Peddling Bicycles to America: The Rise of an Industry* (Jefferson, N.C.: McFarland, 2010), 23.

7. "Welcome to Pope," *Hartford Courant*, July 3, 1903, 1.

8. Epperson, *Peddling,* 55.

9. David V. Herlihy, *Bicycle: The History* (New Haven, Conn.: Yale University Press, 2004), 190–98.

10. Karl Kron, *Ten Thousand Miles on a Bicycle* [1887] (reprinted by Emil Rosenblatt, Croton-on-Hudson, New York, 1982), 398.

11. Herlihy, *Bicycle,* 44–45.

12. Ibid., 102.

13. Ibid., 202.

14. Samuel Clemens, "Taming the Bicycle," unpublished essay, 1884.

15. Epperson, *Peddling,* 109.

16. Richard Buel Jr. and J. Bard McNulty, *Connecticut Observed: Three Centuries of Visitors' Impressions 1676–1940* (Hartford, Conn.: Acorn Club, 1999), 186.

17. Kron, *Ten Thousand Miles,* 769–70.

18. Philip Mason, "League of American Wheelmen and the Good-Roads Movement, 1880–1905" (PhD thesis, University of Michigan, Ann Arbor, 1957), 47.

19. "Official Programme, Third Annual Cycling Tournament, the Hartford Wheel Club, Charter Oak Park, Hartford, Connecticut, September 2 & 3, 1889."

20. Kron, *Ten Thousand Miles,* 132–33.

21. *The Cyclist's Road-Book of Connecticut,* rev. ed. (Hartford, Conn.: Brown & Gross, 1890).

22. Charles L. Dearing, *American Highway Policy* (Washington, D.C.: Brookings Institution, 1941), 231.

23. Federal Highway Administration, *America's Highways 1776–1976* (Washington, D.C.: U.S. Government Printing Office, 1976), 44–45.

24. *Hartford Courant,* January 12, February 16, and August 31, 1894.

25. Connecticut Highway Commissioner, *First Report of the State Highway Commission,* January 1, 1896, 6.

26. Hiram Percy Maxim, *Horseless Carriage Days* (New York: Harper & Brothers), 1936.

27. Ibid.

1. The Early Auto Age

1. George J. Bassett, "Derby Turnpike," *New Haven Colony Historical Society Papers* 10 (1951), 102–8.

2. *Report of the Special Committee Appointed by the General Assembly of 1897 to Investigate the Subject of State Road Improvement, 1899.*

3. James H. MacDonald, "Address by James H. MacDonald, State Highway Commissioner, at a Joint Hearing of the Committees on Appropriations and Roads & Bridges & Rivers," March 21, 1907.

4. "Proposed Charter for New York and Boston Automobile Boulevard," 1907 (further information can be found in the weekly magazine *The Automobile,* January 31, 1907, 236); "Proposed New York and Boston Automobile Boulevard Map," Frank Mead, engineer, n.d.

5. "Senate Rejects Auto Parkway Resolution," *Hartford Courant,* July 19, 1907, 13.

6. James H. MacDonald, "Address."

7. Bureau of Public Roads, U.S. Department of Agriculture; and Connecticut State Highway Department, *Report of a Survey of Transportation on the State Highway System of Connecticut,* 1926, 21–24.

8. Ibid., 21.

9. "The Toll Bridge Question," *Hartford Courant,* May 3, 1887, 2.

10. Ibid.

11. "An Act to Establish a Free Public Highway across the Connecticut River in Hartford County," *Public Acts of the State of Connecticut,* 1881–87, 746.

12. "East Hartford Bridge," *Hartford Courant,* August 15, 1888, 8.

13. "An Act Amending an Act to Establish a Free Public Highway across the Connecticut River in Hartford County," *Public Acts of the State of Connecticut,* 1889, 110–11.

14. "Free at Last," *Hartford Courant,* September 12, 1889, 5.

15. "The Old Bridge Weak," *Hartford Courant,* July 14, 1892, 4.

16. "An Act Concerning the Hartford Bridge," *Public Acts of the State of Connecticut,* 1893, 395. State ownership was a reasonable request for two reasons: first, the original bridge charter had the crossing ultimately being freed into the hands of the state; and second, the state was responsible for bridge crossings over navigable waterways such as the Connecticut River.

17. "Where Is the Money?" *Hartford Courant,* October 4, 1893; see also October 7, 10, and 24, 1893. For Buckley's repeal of state ownership, see "An Act Concerning the Hartford Bridge," *Public Acts of the State of Connecticut,* 1895, 530.

18. Mabel H. Goodwin, *Journal of Mabel H. Goodwin,* East Hartford, Conn., May 19, 1895.

19. Ibid., May 26, 1895.

20. "An Act Concerning the Hartford Bridge," *Public Acts of the State of Connecticut,* 1895, 530; "Creating the Connecticut River Bridge and Highway District," *Public Acts of the State of Connecticut,* 1895, 485. "The Bridge Bill," *Hartford Courant,* June 13, 1895, 3.

21. Connecticut Supreme Court, *Connecticut Reports,* 68 Conn 131, June 1896. Italics added.

22. "An Act to Authorize the Board of Commissioners for the Connecticut Bridge and Highway District to Construct a Bridge across the Connecticut River at Hartford, in the State of Connecticut," *U.S. Statutes at Large* 32, ch. 562 (1903) 836; ch. 1314, 844. The debate over the Hartford crossing led the Congress to adopt general legislation concerning the regulation of bridges over navigable rivers. See *U.S. Statutes at Large* 34, ch. 1130 (1906), 84. As a result of the second ruling, the Hartford Bridge was built without a draw section. However, the piers on the western end of the span had already been relocated to accommodate a draw span, and it was this configuration that was in fact built. As a result, the intended symmetry of the structure was permanently ruined, as can still be seen today.

23. "Report on Bridge," *Hartford Courant,* February 11, 1892, 7; *Public Acts of the State of Connecticut*, 1899, 296; and 1907, 188.

24. E. W. Wians, "The New Stone Bridge over the Connecticut River at Hartford," *Cassier's Magazine* 33 (November 1907–April 1908), 530.

25. "Hartford Bridge Souvenir Number 1818–1908" (East Hartford, Conn.: American Enterprise, October 6, 7, 8, 1908).

26. Connecticut Department of Transportation, *Spanning a Century: The Buckeley Bridge 1908–2008*, 2008, 49–53.

27. George E. Wright, *Crossing the Connecticut* (Hartford, Conn.: Smith-Linsley Co., 1908), 95.

28. Arthur Jerome Eddy, *Two Thousand Miles on an Automobile* (Philadelphia: J.B. Lippincott & Co., 1902), 267.

29. Ian Hubbard, *Crossings: Three Centuries from Ferry Boats to the New Baldwin Bridge* (Lyme, Conn.: Greenwich Publishing Group, 1993), 22–25.

30. Edward W. Bush, "The Saybrook Bridge over the Connecticut River," *Papers of the Connecticut Society of Civil Engineers* (1911), 63.

31. Bruce Clouette and Matthew Roth, *Connecticut Historic Highway Bridges* (Newington: Connecticut Department of Transportation, 1991), 13.

32. Bruce Clouette, *Where Water Meets Land: Historic Moveable Bridges of Connecticut* (Newington: Connecticut Department of Transportation, 2004), 15.

33. Connecticut Highway Department, "Forty Years of Highway Development in Connecticut 1895–1935," Tercentenary Commission of the State of Connecticut, publication no. 46, 1935.

34. Tom Lewis, *Divided Highways: Building the Interstate Highways, Transforming American Life* (New York: Viking Press, 1997), 31–33.

35. Frank Coffey and Joseph Layden, *America on Wheels: The First 100 Years, 1896–1996* (Los Angeles: General Publishing Group, 1996), 24, 38–41.

36. "All for Good Roads," *Hartford Courant,* February 11, 1904, 13.

37. Wilson v. Shaw, 204 US 24, 1907.

38. Richard F. Weingroff, "Building the Foundation," *Public Roads* 60, no. 1.

39. Ibid.

40. Ibid.

41. Frederic L. Paxson, "The Highway Movement 1916–1935," *American Historical Review* 51, no. 2 (1946), 247.

42. "Forty Years of Highway Development in Connecticut," 13.

43. Ibid.

44. Ibid., 14–15.

45. Ibid., 14.

46. Michael McGerr, *The Rise and Fall of the Progressive Movement 1870–1920* (New York: Free Press, 2003).

47. Austin T. Ceasare, *Connecticut and the Progressive Movement* (master's thesis, Southern Connecticut State University, 2004), 123.

48. Frederick W. Taylor, *The Principles of Scientific Management* (New York: Norton & Co., 1911).

49. *Report of a Survey of Transportation on the State Highway System of Connecticut,* 1926.

50. Ibid., 40.

51. Kenneth T. Jackson, *Crabgrass Frontier: The Suburbanization of the United States* (London: Oxford University Press, 1985), 118–31.

52. Ibid., 175–85, 290–96.

53. Statistics from "Appendix A: Population by Geomorphic Region 1900-2000" in this volume.

54. Ibid.

55. Regional Plan Association of New York, *Regional Survey of New York and Its Environs,* vol. 1, 1929.

56. American Institute of Architects, Committee on Town Planning, *City Planning Progress in the United States* (Washington, D.C.: The Octagon, 1917); Connecticut Development Commission, "Planning and Zoning in Connecticut," April 1946.

57. *Town of Windsor v. Henry D. Whitney, et al.,* 95 Conn 357, 358. A second zoning case that same year added to the staying power of the Windsor decision when the Court decided against a town trying to enforce a permit regulation against a particular defendant precisely because the procedures used in that community allowed the town warden to grant or refuse a building permit at his own discretion, which the Court deemed unreasonable, and therefore unconstitutional, for violating "due process of law." See: 95 Conn 317, 318.

58. "Planning and Zoning in Connecticut," 4; *Regional Survey of New York and Its Environs,* vol. 2, 386.

59. Christopher Collier, "New England Specter: Town and State in Connecticut History, Law and Myth," *Connecticut Historical Society Bulletin* 60, nos. 3–4 (1995), 172–73.

60. Ibid., 179.

61. New York, New Haven & Hartford Railroad, *Annual Report of the New Haven Railroad,* 1925.

62. Howard E. Boardman, "Recommendations of Special Committee of the Connecticut Society of Civil Engineers with Respect to the Consolidation of New England Railroads," *Proceedings of the Connecticut Society of Civil Engineers* 9 (1930–33), 60–72.

63. Andrew J. Pavlucik, *The New Haven Railroad: A Fond Look Back* (New Haven, Conn.: Pershing Press, n.d.), 36–37.

64. "N.E.T.'s Operations Growing Rapidly," *Railway Age* (1981).

65. Pavlucik, *New Haven Railroad,* 25.

66. "Trolley Company Adopts Policy of Substituting Busses . . ." *Fairfield News,* August 8, 1931.

67. "Decisions of the Interstate Commerce Commission of the United States," *Interstate Commerce Commission Reports* 220 (1937), 510.

2. Connecticut Takes to the Sky

1. Donald S. Lopez, *Aviation,* Smithsonian Guides (Washington, D.C.: National Air and Space Museum, 1995), 18.

2. Ezra Stiles, *Diary of Ezra Stiles,* April 19–25, 1785, 157.

3. Ibid., May 3–13, 1785, 161.

4. "Patent Federal BALLOONS," *Connecticut Courant,* June 9 and June 30, 1800, 1.

5. Evidence exists that at least one such flight did occur. In mid-November 1819, the *Connecticut Courant* reported that a Frenchman named Pelubit took off on a free balloon flight from State House Square in Hartford "in the presence of a large multitude of spectators." The balloon "ascended in handsome style, and soon disappeared, in a southerly direction," only to be discovered later six miles away in Wethersfield. While Pelubit offered the spectacle to the public for free, he did have six men on hand to pass the hat among the crowd for "what may be given to an old industrious man who has a large family."

6. In the 1840s, Brooks was assigned by Barnum to create one of the showman's most popular hoaxes, a band of Druid musicians dressed in authentic Druid ceremonial garb and playing ancient Druid instruments. In reality, the strange-looking garb and odd-looking hornlike instruments had been fashioned by Brooks himself, who trained the five-man band, most of whom spoke little English, to play music while holed up in a hotel in Bristol. The Druid Band made its debut on Christmas Day 1849, marching down Broadway to Barnum's New York City museum, where the band played to sellout crowds for several months.

7. "Once Famous Showman Dead," *New York Times,* April 8, 1906.

8. Broadside, "Cherry Hill Park, July 4, 1884," Connecticut Historical Society.

9. "The Flying Machine Exhibition," *Hartford Daily Courant,* June 7, 1878.

10. Harvey H. Lippincott, "Air Transportation and the Development of the Aviation Industry in Connecticut," United Technologies Corporation, May 7, 1977, 2.

11. "Connecticut Pioneers in Aviation," Connecticut Aeronautical Historical Association, 1963.

12. Ibid.

13. Ibid.

14. *Bridgeport Sunday Herald,* August 18, 1901.

15. John Brown, *Gustave Whitehead and the Wright Brothers: Who Flew First?* (Munich: Fleck Future Concepts, 2016), 18, 478. Italics in original.

16. Paul Jackson, *Jane's All the World's Aircraft* (foreword), March 8, 2013.

17. David C. Schlenoff, "Connecticut Proclaims Gustave Whitehead Flew before the Wright Brothers," *Scientific American* (June 13, 2013), 5.

18. Harvey H. Lippincott, "Gustave Whitehead: An Objective Analysis," Connecticut Aeronautical Historical Association, August 15, 1964.

19. Ibid.

20. Richard DeLuca, "Gustave Whitehead's Flying Machine," *Connecticut History* (Fall 2003), 222.

21. Wright Brothers Aeroplane Co., "History of the Airplane," www.wright-brothers. org/History_Wing/History_of_the_Airplane/History_of_the_Airplane_Intro/History_of_ the_Airplane_Intro.htm, accessed August 15, 2019.

22. "C. K. Hamilton Flew High over Home City," *New Britain Daily Herald,* July 2, 1910, 3.

23. "Connecticut Pioneers in Aviation," Connecticut Aeronautical Historical Association, 1963.

24. "Frank Coffyn in a Wright Biplane Circling over Charter Oak Park Enclosure," *Hartford Courant,* September 6, 1910, 1.

25. Albert A. LeShane, "Hardware City Fliers: Early Aviation in New Britain" (reprinted by the Plainville [Conn.] Historical Society, 1996), 17–20.

26. Lippincott, "Air Transportation," 4.

27. Ibid., 4–5.

28. Connecticut Aeronautical Historical Society, "Aviation Laws of Connecticut," 1961.

29. Hartford Aviation Commission, "Program of the 1922 Aviation Meet at the Hartford Municipal Airport," November 10–12, 1922; Connecticut National Guard, "Program of the Fourth Annual Hartford Air Meet," October 24, 1925; Hartford Aviation Commission, "Minutes of Meetings," 1920–25.

30. Commissioner of Aviation, *Biennial Reports of the Commissioner of Aviation, 1927–28,* 16.

31. *Report of the Commissioner of Motor Vehicles, 1924–26,* 19–20.

32. "Hartford Crowd Greets Lindbergh," *New York Times,* July 21, 1927, 3.

33. Pratt & Whitney Aircraft, *The Pratt & Whitney Aircraft Story,* 2nd ed., July 1952, 15–20.

34. Frederick B. Rentschler, *An Account of the Pratt & Whitney Aircraft Company 1925–50* (East Hartford, Conn.: Pratt & Whitney Aircraft, 1950), 10–11.

35. Ibid., 11–15.

36. Ibid., 15–17.

37. Pratt & Whitney Aircraft, *Pratt & Whitney Aircraft Story.*

38. Mark P. Sullivan, *Dependable Engines: The Story of Pratt & Whitney* (Reston, Va.: American Institute of Aeronautics and Astronautics, 2008), 10.

39. Ibid., 11–20.

40. Ibid., 11–20.

41. It is interesting to note that as airline travel was emerging as a reliable mode of transportation, the New Haven Railroad, while in reorganization in the 1940s, considered the possibility of competing directly in the air transport market between New York and Boston. As a way to protect its major transportation corporation against the negative impact of emerging airline service in the region, Connecticut enacted legislation in 1933 to allow the New Haven to own aircraft and provide air service for passengers and freight. After debating the matter internally for several years and hiring consultants to gauge existing air traffic in the New York to Boston corridor—more than six thousand passengers per month in the fall of 1937, and rising—the railroad in 1941 partnered with Transcontinental & Western Airlines (TWA) to form a new corporation, TWA–New England (later renamed New England Airlines), and applied to the Civil Aviation Board (CAB) for a "Certificate of Convenience and Necessity" to fly from Newark, New Jersey, to Boston, Massachusetts. However, with the cost of an airline ticket set at $9.90 by the CAB (and rail fare between the two cities at $5.06), the New Haven decided it could not compete effectively in the aviation business. In 1946, the New Haven requested that its application to the CAB be withdrawn, and the following year New England Airlines was dissolved as a corporation without the New Haven's attempt at air travel ever getting off the ground. See: Secretary's File #A-13-15, Record Group 1, Series 1, Box 20, Secretary's Records, New England Airlines, New Haven Railroad archives, University of Connecticut, Storrs.

42. Pratt & Whitney Aircraft, *Pratt & Whitney Aircraft Story.*

43. Sullivan, *Dependable Engines,* 32.

44. Stephen L. McFarland, "Higher, Faster and Farther: Fueling the Aeronautical Revolution, 1919–45," in Roger Launius, *Innovation and the Development of Flight* (College Station: Texas A&M University Press, 1999).

45. Sullivan, *Dependable Engines,* 34–35.

46. "Mr. Horsepower," *Time,* May 28, 1951, 91–92.

47. Sullivan, *Dependable Engines,* 34–39.

48. Sullivan, *Dependable Engines,* 42–44.

49. Thomas C. Palshaw, *Bradley Field: The First 25 Years* (Windsor Locks, Conn.: New England Air Museum, 2000), 4–32.

50. Ibid., 69–74.

51. Ibid., 81–83.

3. Parkways, Expressways & Interstates, Part I

1. Gabrielle Esperdy, *Connecticut's Merritt Parkway: History and Design* (National Park Service, 1992), 7–11.

2. Esperdy, *Connecticut's Merritt Parkway,* 7.

3. Ibid., 7.

4. Ibid., 13.

5. Ibid., 13.

6. Ibid., 16.

7. Ibid., 16.

8. Ibid., 15–16.

9. Bruce Radde, *The Merritt Parkway* (New Haven, Conn.: Yale University Press, 1993), 83, 94, 97.

10. Esperdy, *Connecticut's Merritt Parkway,* 28–29.

11. Radde, *Merritt Parkway,* 28–31.

12. Esperdy, *Connecticut's Merritt Parkway,* 30.

13. John A. MacDonald, "The Merritt Parkway," *Journal of the Connecticut Society of Civil Engineers* (1938), 32.

14. Radde, *Merritt Parkway,* 33–34.

15. Ibid., 24.

16. Ibid., 84–85.

17. Ibid., 52–63.

18. Esperdy, *Connecticut's Merritt Parkway,* 37.

19. Ibid., 37.

20. Radde, *Merritt Parkway,* 29–30.

21. *Bridgeport Post,* November 14, 1937, 4.

22. Connecticut Supreme Court, *Connecticut Reports*, 124 Conn 20, February 1938, 20.

23. Radde, *Merritt Parkway,* 30.

24. Ibid., 31, 128n.

25. Esperdy, *Connecticut's Merritt Parkway,* 33–34.

26. Esperdy, *Connecticut's Merritt Parkway,* 40; *Hartford Courant,* February 3, 1937.

27. Radde, *Merritt Parkway,* 91.

28. Ibid., 100.

29. Walter C. Maynard, "West Rock Tunnel," *Journal of the Connecticut Society of Civil Engineers* 65 (March 16, 1949).

30. Ibid.

31. Radde, *Merritt Parkway,* 85.

32. Connecticut Highway Department, *Biannual Reports of the Connecticut Highway Department,* 1945–46, 11.

33. Earl Swift, *The Big Roads: The Untold Story of the Engineers, Visionaries and Trailblazers Who Created the American Superhighways* (Boston: Houghton Mifflin, 2011), 121–44.

34. Lewis Mumford, *The Highway and the City* (New York: Harcourt, Brace & World, 1963), 234–46.

35. Richard F. Weingroff, "The Genie in the Bottle: The Interstate System and Urban Problems 1939–1957," *Public Roads* 64, no. 2, 5.

36. Ibid., 5.

37. Italics added.

38. Weingroff, "Genie in the Bottle."

39. Ibid.

40. Ibid.

41. Ibid.

42. Ibid.

43. G. Albert Hill, "Banquet Address by State Highway Commissioner G. Albert Hill," *Journal of the Connecticut Society of Civil Engineers* (March 18, 1953).

44. Ibid. Approximate mileage scaled from map in Hill's article.

45. H. R. Lochner & Co., "A Plan for the Solution of the Post Road Congestion Problem," February 1952, viii.

46. Walter C. McKain Jr., "Non-user Benefits and the Connecticut Turnpike," *Journal of the Connecticut Society of Civil Engineers* (January 18, 1961), 135.

47. Ibid.

48. Ammann & Whitney, "An Engineering Report on the Estimated Cost for Greenwich-Killingly Expressway," November 1953, 4.

49. "Turnpike Largest Project Ever Undertaken by State," *New Haven Evening Register*, October 23, 1957.

50. With this provision, the federal law begged the question of whether states such as Connecticut should now be reimbursed for the cost of building these toll roads in the first place. The question was debated for decades. In 1991, as the interstate era came to an end, the federal government capitulated, and states such as Connecticut were indeed repaid 90 percent of the cost of constructing toll roads such as the Connecticut Turnpike.

51. Arthur C. England, "The National System of Interstate and Defense Highways in Connecticut," *Journal of the Connecticut Society of Civil Engineers* (April 7, 1960).

52. Jane Jacobs, *The Death and Life of Great American Cities* (New York: Random House 1961), 145–46.

53. "Careful Planning Held Answer to Highways, Urban Renewal," *Hartford Courant,* September 10, 1957, 1.

54. Lewis Mumford, "Address of Lewis Mumford: Connecticut General Life Insurance Co.," September 11, 1957, Manuscript Collection 2, Folder 7568, Mumford Archives, University of Pennsylvania.

4. Parkways, Expressways & Interstates, Part II

1. See appendix A.

2. Ibid.

3. Jacobs, *Death and Life of Great American Cities,* 15.

4. Ta-Nehisi Coates, *We Were Eight Years in Power: An American Tragedy* (New York: One World, 2017), 188.

5. Ibid., 191.

6. Horace Brown, "Highlights of Connecticut State Planning History," *Connecticut Planning: Newsletter of the Connecticut Chapter of the American Planning Association* (April–June 2006), 4–11.

7. Connecticut Interregional Planning Program, *Connecticut: Choices for Action,* 1966.

8. "Where Will Connecticut People Live in Year 2000?" *Hartford Courant,* September 3, 1967, 31.

9. Connecticut Interregional Planning Program, *Connecticut: Choices for Action.*

10. Mumford, "Address."

11. Judy A. Watson, "County Government Abolishment," Office of Legislative Research Report, January 30, 1998.

12. *The State's Biggest Business: Local and Regional Problems,* Report of the Connecticut Commission to Study the Necessity and Feasibility of Metropolitan Government, January 1967.

13. "The Commission to Study Metropolitan Government," *Hartford Courant,* February 17, 1966, 14.

14. *State's Biggest Business,* 11.

15. "Metro Setup Dropped as Plan," *Hartford Courant,* November 10, 1966, 51.

16. "Meskill Endorses Plan to Guide Urban Spread," *Hartford Courant,* September 28, 1974, 11.

17. Christopher Collier, "New England Specter: Town and State in Connecticut, History, Law and Myth," *Connecticut Historical Society Bulletin* 60, nos. 3–4 (1995), 184.

18. "Metro Setup Dropped As Plan," *Hartford Courant,* November 10, 1966, 51.

19. "Visionary 70s Plan Reimagined Region," *Hartford Courant,* March 13, 2011.

20. Ibid.

21. "Act Concerning the Creation of the Greater Hartford Bridge Authority for the Financing and Construction of Five Bridges across the Connecticut River in the Greater Hartford Area, and Other Purposes," *Public Acts of the State of Connecticut,* 1955, 556.

22. Connecticut Department of Transportation, *Spanning a Century: The Buckeley Bridge 1908–2008,* 2008, 71.

23. England, "The National System of Interstate and Defense Highways in Connecticut."

24. See appendix B.

25. Ibid.

26. Ibid.

27. *Hartford Courant,* May 17, 1961, 10.

28. *Hartford Courant,* May 19, 1961, 28.

29. Richard DeLuca, *We, The People! Bay Area Activism in the 1960s* (San Bernardino, Calif.: Borgo Press, 1994), 54.

30. Ibid., 69.

31. Ibid., 73.

32. Charles F. Barnes Jr., "Traffic Studies and the Highway Network in the Greater Hartford Area," *Journal of the Connecticut Society of Civil Engineers* (April 11, 1961), 30–57.

33. Second interstate program.

34. *Hartford Times,* September 26, 1969.

35. Connecticut Highway Department, "Public Hearing Transcript I-291, Farmington, West Hartford, Bloomfield," September 25, 1969, 59.

36. "Charlotte Kitowski: Riding Down the Highways," *Hartford Courant,* November 12, 1978, 37.

37. Citizens to Preserve Overton Park v. Volpe, 1971.

5. A Public Monopoly: The First 50 Years

1. Harvard Law Review Association, "The New Haven Railroad Reorganization Proceedings; Or the Little Railroad That Couldn't," *Harvard Law Review* (February 1965), 861–80.

2. Ibid., 863. Italics added.

3. Joseph R. Daughen and Peter Binzen, *The Wreck of the Penn Central* (Boston: Little, Brown, 1971).

4. Gregg M. Turner and Melancthon W. Jacobus, *Connecticut Railroads . . . An Illustrated History* (Hartford: Connecticut Historical Society, 1989), ch.15.

5. Paul Frisman, "OLR Backgrounder: Transit Districts," OLR Research Report, October 17, 2012.

6. Ibid.

7. Connecticut Department of Transportation, "Connecticut Today: Bus Service," August 1980.

8. Mark Pazniokas, "Donna Parson, Longtime Connecticut Activist, Dies," *Connecticut Mirror,* December 17, 2014.

9. Richard L. Madden, "Connecticut Drops Plan to Extend I-84 to Border with Rhode Island," *New York Times,* August 21, 1983, 47.

10. "Route 10 Bypass Proposals Met with Unanimous Opposition," *Cheshire Herald,* September 25, 2014, 14.

11. Connecticut Department of Transportation, "Managing Travel in Connecticut: 100 Year History," July 1995, 78.

12. Ibid.

13. *Hartford Courant,* January 11, 1957, 16.

14. Adam Stern, "Connecticut's Income Tax Wars, Part 1: A Brief History of the State's Personal Income Tax 1915–1991," *Connecticut History* (Fall 2009), 140.

15. Ibid., 141.

16. Ibid., 142.

17. Ibid., 144–45.

18. *Report of the Task Force on the Future of the Special Transportation Fund,* February 6, 1996, 3.

19. Ibid., 4.

20. "Repairs Start on I-95 Span amid Inquiry," *New York Times,* June 30, 1983.

21. National Transportation Safety Board, *Report on the Collapse of the Mianus River Bridge,* December 19, 1983, 13, 40.

22. "Bridge Inspector Given Probation," *New York Times,* September 20, 1983.

23. *Report of the Task Force on the Future of the Special Transportation Fund,* February 6, 1996, 1.

24. Ibid., 4.

25. Stern, "Connecticut's Income Tax Wars," 147–51.

26. "Anti-toll Movement in Connecticut Attracts Support," *New York Times*, February 25, 1983.

27. "6 Die in Crash at Toll Station in Connecticut," *New York Times*, January 20, 1983.

28. Connecticut Department of Transportation, "Managing Travel in Connecticut," 67–68.

29. Ibid., 81.

30. *Report of the Task Force on the Future of the Special Transportation Fund,* February 6, 1996, 10.

31. Levied as a percentage rather than a flat tax, the gross receipts tax fluctuated almost daily. As a result, signs that listed the state flat tax on gasoline were removed from gas station pumps, leaving only the total price per gallon on display, thereby hiding the impact of the gross receipts tax on gasoline prices from the driving public.

32. *Report of the Task Force on the Future of the Special Transportation Fund,* February 6, 1996, 10.

33. Richard F. Weingroff, "Creating a Landmark: The Intermodal Surface Transportation Act of 1991," *Public Roads* 65, no. 3 (2001).

34. Ibid.

35. Michael Gallis & Associates, *Connecticut: Strategic Economic Framework,* Report of the Connecticut Regional Institute for the 21st Century, 1999.

36. Ibid.

37. Ibid.

38. Richard DeLuca, *Post Roads & Iron Horses: Transportation in Connecticut from Colonial Times to the Age of Steam* (Middletown, Conn.: Wesleyan University Press, 2011), 176.

39. "An Act Implementing the Recommendations of the Transportation Strategy Board," Public Act 01-5, June 2001.

40. Ibid.

41. "Consulting Firm Criticizes Lack of Strategic Planning at Bradley," *New Haven Register,* December 16, 1999, A6.

42. Connecticut Department of Transportation, "I-84 Construction Oversight and Audit Services: Task 3—Construction Audit," May 18, 2007, as amended May 23, 2007, 7.

43. *Report of the Governor's Commission on the Reform of the Connecticut Department of Transportation,* February 2008, 1–11.

44. "Budget," *Hartford Courant,* June 29, 2005, B7.

45. *Report of the Commission on Fiscal Stability and Economic Growth,* March 2018, 6.

46. "An Act Establishing the Connecticut Airport Authority," Public Act 11-84, June 2011.

47. "Board of Connecticut Port Authority to Meet for First Time," *The Day,* February 12, 2016.

48. Connecticut Department of Transportation, "Transportation in Connecticut: The Existing System," 2014.

49. Ibid.

50. Connecticut Department of Transportation, "Let's Go Connecticut! Connecticut's Bold Vision for a Transportation Future," February 2015.

51. Transportation Finance Panel, *Transportation Finance Panel Final Report,* January 15, 2016.

52. Connecticut Department of Transportation, "Let's Go Connecticut! 5 Year Transportation Ramp-Up Plan," February 2015, 2.

53. "Transportation Funding Debate Still Centered on 'Lockbox,'" *Connecticut Mirror*, February 6, 2017.

54. Transportation Finance Panel, *Transportation Finance Panel Final Report,* January 15, 2016, 2.

55. Ibid., 11.

56. Ibid., 12.

57. Ibid, 14–16.

58. Keith M. Phaneuf et al., "A Handshake, Then a Vote on Connecticut's Next Budget," *Connecticut Mirror*, May 12, 2016.

59. "Connecticut 'Locks' into New Budgetary Restraints in Three Weeks," *Connecticut Mirror,* May 25, 2018.

60. *Report of the Commission on Fiscal Stability and Economic Growth,* with Executive Summary, March 2018, 7.

Conclusion: An Historical Perspective: 1614-2015

1. NEC Master Plan Working Group, "Northeast Corridor Infrastructure Master Plan," Executive Summary, ES-2, May 2010.

2. Ana Radelat, "Northeast Rail Plan Stymied by Lack of Funding, Concerns in Fairfield County," *Connecticut Mirror,* December 11, 2017.

3. Ana Radelat, "New Federal Study Proposes Overhaul of Connecticut Railroads—At a Cost," *Connecticut Mirror,* November 11, 2015.

4. Jan Ellen Spiegel, "Massive Rail Plan Leaves Connecticut Hopeful but Mystified," *Connecticut Mirror,* January 4, 2016.

5. Ibid.

6. Federal Railroad Administration, "NEC FUTURE: Highlights of the FRA's Record of Decision," July 2017.

7. Keith M. Phaneuf, "ConnDOT Pitches 'Astounding,' Cheaper Plan to Break I-95 Gridlock," *Connecticut Mirror,* February 22, 2018.

8. Ibid.

9. "Domestic Economy," *Connecticut Courant*, April 22, 1817, 1.

10. Ibid.

11. Aldo Leopold, *A Sand County Almanac & Other Writings on Ecology and Conservation* (New York: Library of America, 2013), 171–89.

12. Ibid., 410.

13. "Want to Prosper? Act Like a Region, Proponents Say," *Connecticut Mirror*, February 28, 2018. Three-part series on regionalism continues on March 2 and 3, 2018.

14. Ibid.

15. *Hartford Courant*, April 7, 2015, editorial page.

16. Mark Pazniokas, "ConnDOT's Early Stumbles, Successes in Development," *Connecticut Mirror*, July 13, 2015.

17. Raoul Peck (dir.), *I Am Not Your Negro,* 2017.

Bibliography

"An Act Amending an Act to Establish a Free Public Highway across the Connecticut River in Hartford County." *Public Acts of the State of Connecticut,* 1889.

"An Act Concerning the Creation of the Greater Hartford Bridge Authority for the Financing and Construction of Five Bridges across the Connecticut River in the Greater Hartford Area, and Other Purposes." *Public Acts of the State of Connecticut,* 1955.

"An Act Concerning the Hartford Bridge." *Public Acts of the State of Connecticut,* 1893.

"An Act Concerning the Hartford Bridge." *Public Acts of the State of Connecticut,* 1895.

"An Act Establishing the Connecticut Airport Authority." Public Act 11-84, June 2011.

"An Act Implementing the Recommendations of the Transportation Strategy Board." Public Act 01-5, June 2001.

"An Act to Authorize the Board of Commissioners for the Connecticut Bridge and Highway District to Construct a Bridge across the Connecticut River at Hartford, in the State of Connecticut." *U.S. Statutes at Large* 32, ch. 562 (1903).

"An Act to Establish a Free Public Highway across the Connecticut River in Hartford County." *Public Acts of the State of Connecticut,* 1881–87.

American Institute of Architects, Committee on Town Planning. *City Planning Progress in the United States.* Washington, D.C.: The Octagon, 1917.

Ammann & Whitney. "An Engineering Report on the Estimated Cost for Greenwich-Killingly Expressway." November 1953.

Barnes, Charles F., Jr. "Traffic Studies and the Highway Network in the Greater Hartford Area." *Journal of the Connecticut Society of Civil Engineers* (April 11, 1961).

Bassett, George J. "Derby Turnpike." *New Haven Colony Historical Society Papers* 10 (1951).

Boardman, Howard E. "Recommendations of Special Committee of the Connecticut Society of Civil Engineers with Respect to the Consolidation of New England Railroads." *Proceedings of the Connecticut Society of Civil Engineers* 9 (1930–33).

Brown, Horace. "Highlights of Connecticut State Planning History." *Connecticut Planning: Newsletter of the Connecticut Chapter of the American Planning Association* (April–June 2006).

Brown, John. *Gustave Whitehead and the Wright Brothers: Who Flew First?* Munich: Fleck Future Concepts, 2016.

Buel, Richard, Jr., and J. Bard McNulty. *Connecticut Observed: Three Centuries of Visitors' Impressions 1676–1940.* Hartford, Conn.: Acorn Club, 1999.

Bureau of Public Roads, U.S. Department of Agriculture; and Connecticut State Highway Department. *Report of a Survey of Transportation on the State Highway System of Connecticut.* 1926.

Bush, Edward W. "The Saybrook Bridge over the Connecticut River." *Papers of the Connecticut Society of Civil Engineers.* 1911.

Ceasare, Austin T. *Connecticut and the Progressive Movement.* Master's thesis, Southern Connecticut State University, 2004.

Clemens, Samuel. "Taming the Bicycle." Unpublished essay, 1884.

Clouette, Bruce. *Where Water Meets Land: Historic Moveable Bridges of Connecticut.* Newington: Connecticut Department of Transportation, 2004.

———, and Matthew Roth. *Connecticut Historic Highway Bridges.* Newington: Connecticut Department of Transportation, 1991.

Coates, Ta-Nehisi. *We Were Eight Years in Power: An American Tragedy.* New York: One World, 2017.

Coffey, Frank, and Joseph Layden. *America on Wheels: The First 100 Years, 1896–1996.* Los Angeles: General Publishing Group, 1996.

Collier, Christopher. "New England Specter: Town and State in Connecticut History, Law and Myth." *Connecticut Historical Society Bulletin* 60, nos. 3–4 (1995).

Commissioner of Aviation. *Biennial Reports of the Commissioner of Aviation.* 1927–28.

Connecticut Aeronautical Historical Association. "Connecticut Pioneers in Aviation." 1963.

Connecticut Aeronautical Historical Society. "Aviation Laws of Connecticut." 1961.

Connecticut Department of Transportation. "Connecticut Today: Bus Service." August 1980.

———. "I-84 Construction Oversight and Audit Services: Task 3—Construction Audit." May 18, 2007, as amended May 23, 2007.

———. "Let's Go Connecticut! Connecticut's Bold Vision for a Transportation Future." February 2015.

———. "Let's Go Connecticut! 5-Year Transportation Ramp-Up Plan." February 2015.

———. "Managing Travel in Connecticut: 100 Year History." July 1995.

———. *Spanning a Century: The Buckeley Bridge 1908–2008.* 2008.

———. "Transportation in Connecticut: The Existing System." 2014.

Connecticut Development Commission. "Planning and Zoning in Connecticut." April 1946.

Connecticut Highway Commissioner. *First Report of the State Highway Commission.* January 1, 1896.

Connecticut Highway Department. *Biannual Reports of the Connecticut Highway Department.* 1945–46.

———. "Forty Years of Highway Development in Connecticut 1895–1935." Tercentenary Commission of the State of Connecticut, publication no. 46. 1935.

———. "Public Hearing Transcript I-291, Farmington, West Hartford, Bloomfield." September 25, 1969.

Connecticut Historical Society. "Cherry Hill Park, July 4, 1884," broadside.

Connecticut Interregional Planning Program. "Connecticut: Choices for Action." 1966.

Connecticut National Guard. "Program of the Fourth Annual Hartford Air Meet." October 24, 1925.

Connecticut Supreme Court. *Connecticut Reports,* 68 Conn 131, June 1896.

Connecticut Supreme Court. *Connecticut Reports,* 124 Conn 20, February 1938.

"Creating the Connecticut River Bridge and Highway District." *Public Acts of the State of Connecticut.* 1895.

Cumming, Lyle. *Internal Fire: The Internal Combustion Engine 1673–1900.* Lake Oswego, Oreg.: Carnot Press, 1976.

The Cyclist's Road-Book of Connecticut, rev. ed. Hartford, Conn.: Brown & Gross, 1890.

Daughen, Joseph R., and Peter Binzen. *The Wreck of the Penn Central.* Boston: Little, Brown, 1971.

Dearing, Charles L. *American Highway Policy.* Washington, D.C.: Brookings Institution, 1941.

"Decisions of the Interstate Commerce Commission of the United States." *Interstate Commerce Commission Reports* 220 (1937).

DeLuca, Richard. "Gustave Whitehead's Flying Machine." *Connecticut History* (Fall 2003).

———. *Post Roads & Iron Horses: Transportation in Connecticut from Colonial Times to the Age of Steam.* Middletown, Conn.: Wesleyan University Press, 2011.

———. *We, The People! Bay Area Activism in the 1960s.* San Bernardino, Calif.: Borgo Press, 1994.

Eddy, Arthur Jerome. *Two Thousand Miles on an Automobile.* Philadelphia: J.B. Lippincott & Co., 1902.

England, Arthur C. "The National System of Interstate and Defense Highways in Connecticut." *Journal of the Connecticut Society of Civil Engineers* (April 7, 1960).

Epperson, Bruce D. *Peddling Bicycles to America: The Rise of an Industry.* Jefferson, N.C.: McFarland, 2010.

Esperdy, Gabrielle. *Connecticut's Merritt Parkway: History and Design.* National Park Service, 1992.

A Facsimile of FRANK LESLIE'S Illustrated Historical Register of the Centennial Exposition, 1876. New York: Paddington Press, 1976.

Federal Highway Administration. *America's Highways 1776-1976.* Washington, D.C.: U.S. Government Printing Office, 1976.

Federal Railroad Administration. "NEC FUTURE: Highlights of the FRA's Record of Decision." July 2017.

Frisman, Paul. "OLR Backgrounder: Transit Districts." *OLR Research Report.* October 17, 2012.

Goodwin, Mabel H. *Journal of Mabel H. Goodwin.* East Hartford, Conn., May 19, 1895. East Hartford Historical Society.

Hartford Aviation Commission. "Minutes of Meetings." 1920–25.

———. "Program of the 1922 Aviation Meet at the Hartford Municipal Airport." November 10–12, 1922.

"Hartford Bridge Souvenir Number 1818–1908." East Hartford, Conn.: American Enterprise, October 6, 7, 8, 1908.

Harvard Law Review Association. "The New Haven Railroad Reorganization Proceedings; Or the Little Railroad That Couldn't." *Harvard Law Review* (February 1965).

Herlihy, David V. *Bicycle: The History.* New Haven, Conn.: Yale University Press, 2004.

Hill, G. Albert. "Banquet Address by State Highway Commissioner G. Albert Hill." *Journal of the Connecticut Society of Civil Engineers* (March 18, 1953).

Hubbard, Ian. *Crossings: Three Centuries from Ferry Boats to the New Baldwin Bridge.* Lyme, Conn.: Greenwich Publishing Group, 1993.

Jackson, Kenneth T. *Crabgrass Frontier: The Suburbanization of the United States.* London: Oxford University Press, 1985.

Jackson, Paul. "Foreword." *Jane's All the World's Aircraft* (March 8, 2013).

Jacobs, Jane. *The Death and Life of Great American Cities.* New York: Random House, 1961.

Kron, Karl. *Ten Thousand Miles on a Bicycle* [1887]. Reprinted by Emil Rosenblatt, Croton-on-Hudson, New York, 1982.

Leopold, Aldo. *A Sand County Almanac & Other Writings on Ecology and Conservation.* New York: Library of America, 2013.

LeShane, Albert A. "Hardware City Fliers: Early Aviation in New Britain." Reprinted by Plainville [Conn.] Historical Society, 1996.

Lewis, Tom. *Divided Highways: Building the Interstate Highways, Transforming American Life.* New York: Viking Press, 1997.

Lippincott, Harvey H. "Air Transportation and the Development of the Aviation Industry in Connecticut." United Technologies Corporation, May 7, 1977.

———. "Gustave Whitehead: An Objective Analysis." Connecticut Aeronautical Historical Association, August 15, 1964.

Lochner, H. R., & Co. "A Plan for the Solution of the Post Road Congestion Problem." February 1952.

Lopez, Donald S. *Aviation.* Smithsonian Guides. Washington, D.C.: National Air and Space Museum, 1995.

MacDonald, James H. "Address by James H. MacDonald, State Highway Commissioner, at a Joint Hearing of the Committees on Appropriations and Roads & Bridges & Rivers." March 21, 1907.

MacDonald, John A. "The Merritt Parkway." *Journal of the Connecticut Society of Civil Engineers* (1938).

Mason, Philip. "League of American Wheelmen and the Good-Roads Movement, 1880–1905." PhD thesis, University of Michigan, Ann Arbor, 1957.

Maxim, Hiram Percy. *Horseless Carriage Days.* New York: Harper & Brothers, 1936.

Maynard, Walter C. "West Rock Tunnel." *Journal of the Connecticut Society of Civil Engineers* 65 (March 16, 1949).

McFarland, Stephen L. "Higher, Faster and Farther: Fueling the Aeronautical Revolution, 1919–45." In Roger Launius, *Innovation and the Development of Flight.* College Station: Texas A&M University Press, 1999.

McGerr, Michael. *The Rise and Fall of the Progressive Movement 1870–1920.* New York: Free Press, 2003.

McKain, Walter C., Jr. "Non-user Benefits and the Connecticut Turnpike." *Journal of the Connecticut Society of Civil Engineers* (January 18, 1961).

Michael Gallis & Associates. *Connecticut: Strategic Economic Framework.* Report of the Connecticut Regional Institute for the 21st Century, 1999.

Mumford, Lewis. "Address of Lewis Mumford: Connecticut General Life Insurance Co." September 11, 1957. Manuscript Collection 2, Folder 7568, Mumford Archives, University of Pennsylvania.

———. *The Highway and the City.* New York: Harcourt, Brace & World, 1963.

National Transportation Safety Board. *Report on the Collapse of the Mianus River Bridge.* December 19, 1983.

NEC Master Plan Working Group. "Northeast Corridor Infrastructure Master Plan." Executive Summary, ES-2, May 2010.

"N.E.T.'s Operations Growing Rapidly." *Railway Age* (1981).

New York, New Haven & Hartford Railroad. *Annual Report of the New Haven Railroad.* 1925.

"Official Programme, Third Annual Cycling Tournament, the Hartford Wheel Club, Charter Oak Park, Hartford, Connecticut, September 2 & 3, 1889." Connecticut State Library.

Palshaw, Thomas C. *Bradley Field: The First 25 Years.* Windsor Locks, Conn.: New England Air Museum, 2000.

Pavlucik, Andrew J. *The New Haven Railroad: A Fond Look Back.* New Haven, Conn.: Pershing Press, n.d.

Paxson, Frederic L. "The Highway Movement 1916–1935." *American Historical Review* 51, no. 2 (1946).

Peck, Raoul (dir.). *I Am Not Your Negro.* 2017.

Pratt & Whitney Aircraft. *The Pratt & Whitney Aircraft Story,* 2nd ed. July 1952.

"Proposed Charter for New York and Boston Automobile Boulevard." 1907. Further information can be found in the weekly magazine *The Automobile,* January 31, 1907, 236.

"Proposed New York and Boston Automobile Boulevard Map." Frank Mead, engineer, n.d.

Public Acts of the State of Connecticut, 1899, 296.

Public Acts of the State of Connecticut, 1907, 188.

Radde, Bruce. *The Merritt Parkway.* New Haven, Conn.: Yale University Press, 1993.

Regional Plan Association of New York. *Regional Survey of New York and Its Environs,* vols. 1 and 2. 1929.

Rentschler, Frederick B. *An Account of the Pratt & Whitney Aircraft Company 1925–50.* East Hartford, Conn.: Pratt & Whitney Aircraft, 1950.

Report of the Commissioner of Motor Vehicles. 1924–26.

Report of the Commission on Fiscal Stability and Economic Growth, with Executive Summary. March 2018.

Report of the Governor's Commission on the Reform of the Connecticut Department of Transportation. February 2008.

Report of the Special Committee Appointed by the General Assembly of 1897 to Investigate the Subject of State Road Improvement. 1899.

Report of the Task Force on the Future of the Special Transportation Fund. February 6, 1996.

Schlenoff, David C. "Connecticut Proclaims Gustave Whitehead Flew before the Wright Brothers." *Scientific American* (June 13, 2013).

Secretary's File #A-13-15, Record Group 1, Series 1, Box 20. Secretary's Records, New England Airlines, New Haven Railroad archives, University of Connecticut, Storrs.

The State's Biggest Business: Local and Regional Problems. Report of the Connecticut Commission to Study the Necessity and Feasibility of Metropolitan Government. January 1967.

Stern, Adam. "Connecticut's Income Tax Wars, Part 1: A Brief History of the State's Personal Income Tax 1915–1991." *Connecticut History* (Fall 2009).

Stiles, Ezra. *The Literary Diary of Ezra Stiles,* entries of April 19–25, 1785. Edited by Franklin B. Dexter. New York: C. Scribner's Sons, 1901.

Sullivan, Mark P. *Dependable Engines: The Story of Pratt & Whitney.* Reston, Va.: American Institute of Aeronautics and Astronautics, 2008.

Swift, Earl. *The Big Roads: The Untold Story of the Engineers, Visionaries and Trailblazers Who Created the American Superhighways.* Boston: Houghton Mifflin, 2011, 121–44.

Taylor, Frederick W. *The Principles of Scientific Management.* New York: Norton & Co., 1911.

Town of Windsor v. Henry D. Whitney, et al., 95 Conn 357.

Transportation Finance Panel. *Transportation Finance Panel Final Report.* January 15, 2016.

Turner, Gregg M., and Melancthon W. Jacobus. *Connecticut Railroads . . . An Illustrated History.* Hartford: Connecticut Historical Society, 1989.

U.S. Reports. Citizens to Preserve Overton Park v. Volpe. 401 U.S. 402 (1971).

Watson, Judy A. "County Government Abolishment." Office of Legislative Research Report. January 30, 1998.

Weingroff, Richard F. "Building the Foundation." *Public Roads* 60, no. 1 (1996).

———. "Creating a Landmark: The Intermodal Surface Transportation Act of 1991." *Public Roads* 65, no. 3 (2001).

———. "The Genie in the Bottle: The Interstate System and Urban Problems 1939–1957." *Public Roads* 64, no. 2 (2000).

Wians, E. W. "The New Stone Bridge over the Connecticut River at Hartford." *Cassier's Magazine* 33 (November 1907–April 1908).

Wilson v. Shaw, 204 US 24, 1907.

Wright Brothers Aeroplane Co. "History of the Airplane." www.wright-brothers.org/History_Wing/History_of_the_Airplane/History_of_the_Airplane_Intro/History_of_the_Airplane_Intro.htm. Accessed August 15, 2019.

Wright, George E. *Crossing the Connecticut.* Hartford, Conn.: Smith-Linsley Co., 1908.

Index

Note: Page numbers in italics refer to illustrations and captions.

policy and, 152, 189–90; Merritt Parkway and, 92, 93
engine knock, 81
engines, 80–82; air-cooled radial, 74–78, *77*; automobile, 19; liquid-cooled aircraft, 78. *See also* internal combustion gasoline engine; steam engine
Enlightenment, the, 58
environment, natural, 149–50, 191–92, 196; consciousness of, *147*; effects of economic growth on, 184, 187; pollution of, 19, 201; protection of, 146–48, 169
Environmental Impact Statements, 146, 162, 197
environmentalism and environmental movement, 196–97; interstate highway system and, 116–18; *Silent Spring* and, 140–41
Environmental Protection Agency, 146
Euclid (village), 50
Europe, 1, 4, 5, 6, 9, 119
Expressway Bond Committee, 112
Expressway Era, 134–37, 188
Expressway Reserve Fund, 112
expressways and parkways, 42, 87, 103, 108, 153; construction of, 137–40, 143, 161–63; controlled-access, 101, 102, 111; interstate, 109, 111; intrastate, 109, 139. *See also* highways and roads; superhighways

FAA (Federal Aviation Agency), 84, 85
Fairfield, 67, 93
Fairfield, George A., 8, 10
Fairfield County, 26, 48, 88, 93, 111; Merritt Parkway and, 90, 91; traffic congestion in, 87, 89, 110, 189, 193–94
Farmington, 48, 139
Farmington Canal, 187
Farmington Valley, 187
Federal-Aid Highway Acts, 84; of 1916, 38–39; of 1921, 39, 40; of 1944, 105; of 1956 (FAHA 56), 113–15, 134–35; of 1973, 148, 159, 162
Federal Airport Act of 1946, 84
Federal Aviation Act of 1958, 84
Federal Aviation Agency (FAA), 84, 85

Federal Emergency Relief, 91
federal government, 72, 82, 128; flight to suburbs and, 124–25; funding by, 38–40, 57, 84, 91, 108, 112, 124, 141, 146, 152; Hartford Bridge and, 31–32; highways standards of, 39–40, 102; railroads and, 53–54; roads and highways and, 16–17, 20, 87; as state aviation partner, 58, 83–86; as state transportation partner, 20, 37–42, 151, 188, 194; transportation policy of, 140, 170–72
Federal Highway Administration (FHWA), 115–16, 145, 146, 148
Federal Housing Acts: of 1949, 107, 122; of 1954, 122, 125
Federal Housing Administration (FHA), 124
Federal Railroad Administration (FRA), 190–92, *192*, 193
Federal Works Agency, 106
ferries, 30, 35, 36, 37, 136, 189
FHA (Federal Housing Administration), 124
FHWA (Federal Highway Administration), 115–16, 145, 146, 148
Fleming, Philip B., 106–7
flivver aircraft, 77
Fokker, Anthony, 71
Foote, Franklin, 145
Forbes, A. Holland, 72
Ford, Henry, 37, 44
Ford Motor Company, 80
Founders Bridge, 135
FRA (Federal Railroad Administration), 190–92, *192*, 193
France, 58, 60; Paris, 59, 68, 73
Freeway Revolt, 141–42, 146
freeways, 103, 141
Fundamental Orders of 1639, 132
futurism, 46, 189

Gallis, Michael, 173
Gallis Report (*Connecticut: Strategic Economic Framework*), 173–74
gasoline, 1, 81, 188. *See also* gas tax; internal combustion gasoline engine
gas tax, 40, 142, 170, 177, 230n31; federal, 114; hidden, 230n31; increase in, 168–69, 182, 183

Herring, Augustus, 67
high-speed rail service, 190–91, 194
Highway Commission, 17, 18, 22, 43, 188
Highway Commissioner, 23, 36, 40, 108; MacDonald as, 22–23, 88, 96
Highway Department (CHD), 17, 20, 39, 40–43, 87–88, 92–94, 99, 102, 111, 136, 139, 163; creation of, 36–37; Merritt Parkway and, 90, 91; postwar initiatives of, 107–8; scientific management of, 44–45
Highway Fund, 40
highwaymen, 37–38, 40, 116
Highway Patrol, 167
highways and roads, 17, 148; financing of, 112, 118; gradients of, 15, 40; improvements to, 37, 40, 88, 101; local control over, 18, 189; nonuser benefits of, 111–12; paved, 14, 15, 19; Progressive movement and, 42–46; system of, 20, 23, 44–45, 48, 103, 164. See also expressways and parkways; superhighways; and route names and numbers
highways-only policy, *143*, 151, 162, 172, 176; adverse impacts of, 140, 142; reform of, 189–90
Highway Trust Fund, 114, 118, 162
Hill, G. Albert, 108, 109, 111
hills, 15, 40, 93
history, 199, 200
Hitler, Adolf, 104
Hooker, Thomas, 33
Hornet engine, 77–78
horseless carriages, 1, 5–6, 18. See also automobiles; automobility
horses, 5, 29, 30, 89, 187
Housatonic River bridges, 26, 98
housing, 105, 107, 122, 146
Hudson River, 155, 174
Hurley, Robert A., 95, 96
Hutchinson River Parkway, 89, 94, 99
hydrogen gas, 59, 60

ICC. See Interstate Commerce Commission
immigrants, 58, 119, 184; Whitehead as, 64, 65
industrialization and deindustrialization, 5, 6, 8, 12, 55, 80, 111, 119, 129, 188, 195;

industrial revolution and, 2, 125; manufacturing and, 8, 18, 125, 126
inflation, 182
infrastructure, 53, 58, 149, 166, 175
interchanges, 42, 93, 113, 136–37, *137*
Intermodal Surface Transportation Efficiency Act (ISTEA) of 1991, 151, 170–72, 179
internal combustion gasoline engine, 4, 63, 76, 149, 187–89; as competitor of railroads, 154–55; Daimler and, 1, 5; horseless carriage and, 5–6; powered flight and, 58, 66, 74. See also gasoline; and under names of specific models
Interstate Commerce Commission (ICC), 20, 155; New Haven Railroad and, 53, 54, 57
Interstate Highway Act of 1956, 170
interstate highways, 38, 39, 108. See also construction of highways; interstate highway system; U.S. Interstate Routes; and specific route numbers, e.g., U.S. I-95
interstate highway system, *106*, 107, 109, 114, 118, 138, 154, 159; completion of, 151, 171; Congress and, 144; funding of, 105, 113–14, 188. See also National Highway System
ISTEA (Intermodal Surface Transportation Efficiency Act) of 1991, 151, 170–72, 179
Italian Americans, 122, *123*

J-57 jet engine, 82–83
Jacobs, Jane, *The Death and Life of Great American Cities*, 122, 124
Jane's All the World's Aircraft, 65
jet propulsion engines: longer runways for, 84, 85; Pratt & Whitney and, 82–83
Johnson, Lyndon B., 126, 153, 163

Kaunitz, Rita, 132
Kemp, Leroy "Jack," and Merritt Parkway scandal, 92, 93, 95–96, *97*
Kennedy, John F., 124, 139
Kent State University, 140
Kenyon, Rhode Island, 191
kickbacks, 92
Killingly, 25, 39, 111, 112

Garnet Books

Titles with asterisks (*) are also in the
Driftless Connecticut Series

*Garnet Poems: An Anthology of
Connecticut Poetry Since 1776*
Dennis Barone, editor

*The Connecticut Prison Association and
the Search for Reformative Justice*
Gordon Bates

*Food for the Dead: On the Trail of New
England's Vampires*
Michael E. Bell

*The Long Journeys Home: The
Repatriations of Henry ʻŌpūkahaʻia
and Albert Afraid of Hawk*
Nick Bellantoni

Sol LeWitt: A Life of Ideas
Lary Bloom

*The Case of the Piglet's Paternity: Trials
from the New Haven Colony, 1639–1663*
Jon C. Blue

Early Connecticut Silver, 1700–1840
Peter Bohan and Philip Hammerslough

*The Connecticut River: A Photographic
Journey through the Heart of New
England*
Al Braden

*Tempest-Tossed: The Spirit of Isabella
Beecher Hooker*
Susan Campbell

Connecticut's Fife & Drum Tradition
James Clark

Sunken Garden Poetry, 1992–2011
Brad Davis, editor

*Rare Light: J. Alden Weir in Windham,
Connecticut, 1882–1919*
Anne E. Dawson, editor

*The Old Leather Man: Historical Accounts
of a Connecticut and New York Legend*
Dan W. DeLuca, editor

*Paved Roads & Public Money: Connecticut
Transportation in the Age of Internal
Combustion*
Richard DeLuca
*Post Roads & Iron Horses: Transportation
in Connecticut from Colonial Times to the
Age of Steam*
Richard DeLuca

*The Log Books: Connecticut's Slave Ships
and Human Memory*
Anne Farrow

Birding in Connecticut
Frank Gallo

Dr. Mel's Connecticut Climate Book
Dr. Mel Goldstein

*Forever Seeing New Beauties: The
Forgotten Impressionist Mary Rogers
Williams*
Eve M. Kahn

Hidden in Plain Sight: A Deep Traveler
Explores Connecticut
David K. Leff

Maple Sugaring: Keeping It Real in New
England
David K. Leff

Becoming Tom Thumb: Charles Stratton,
P. T. Barnum, and the Dawn of American
Celebrity*
Eric D. Lehman

Homegrown Terror: Benedict Arnold and
the Burning of New London*
Eric D. Lehman

The Traprock Landscapes of New England*
Peter M. LeTourneau and Robert Pagini

Westover School: Giving Girls a Place of
Their Own
Laurie Lisle

Heroes for All Time: Connecticut's Civil
War Soldiers Tell Their Stories*
Dione Longley and Buck Zaidel

The Listeners: U-boat Hunters During the
Great War
Roy R. Manstan

Along the Valley Line: A History of the
Connecticut Valley Railroad*
Max R. Miller

Crowbar Governor: The Life and Times of
Morgan Gardner Bulkeley*
Kevin Murphy

Fly Fishing in Connecticut: A Guide for
Beginners
Kevin Murphy

Water for Hartford: The Story of
the Hartford Water Works and the
Metropolitan District Commission
Kevin Murphy

African American Connecticut Explored
Elizabeth J. Normen, editor

Henry Austin: In Every Variety of
Architectural Style
James F. O'Gorman

Breakfast at O'Rourke's: New Cuisine from
a Classic American Diner
Brian O'Rourke

Ella Grasso: Connecticut's Pioneering
Governor*
Jon E. Purmont

The British Raid on Essex: The Forgotten
Battle of the War of 1812*
Jerry Roberts

Making Freedom: The Extraordinary Life
of Venture Smith
Chandler B. Saint and George Krimsky

Under the Dark Sky: Life in the Thames
River Basin
Steven G. Smith

Welcome to Wesleyan: Campus Buildings
Leslie Starr

Barns of Connecticut
Markham Starr

Gervase Wheeler: A British Architect in
America, 1847–1860*
Renée Tribert and James F. O'Gorman

Forgotten Voices: The Hidden History of a
Connecticut Meetinghouse
Carolyn Wakeman

Connecticut in the American Civil War:
Slavery, Sacrifice, and Survival*
Matthew Warshauer

Inside Connecticut and the Civil War: One
State's Struggles
Matthew Warshauer, editor

Connecticut Architecture: Stories of 100 Places
Christopher Wigren, Connecticut Trust for Historic Preservation

Prudence Crandall's Legacy: The Fight for Equality in the 1830s, Dred Scott, *and* Brown v. Board of Education*
Donald E. Williams Jr.

Riverview Hospital for Children and Youth: A Culture of Promise*
Richard Wiseman

Stories in Stone: How Geology Influenced Connecticut History and Culture
Jelle Zeilinga de Boer

New Haven's Sentinels: The Art and Science of East Rock and West Rock*
Jelle Zeilinga de Boer and John Wareham

Richard DeLuca is the author of *Post Roads and Iron Horses: Transportation in Connecticut from Colonial Times to the Age of Steam*. He is also the author of *We the People! Bay Area Activism in the 1960s*. DeLuca has worked as a transportation planner in Connecticut for fifteen years and has written on regional transportation for *Connecticut History* and the *Encyclopedia of Connecticut History Online*. He lives in Cheshire, Connecticut.

About the Driftless Connecticut Series

The Driftless Connecticut Series is a publication award program established in 2010 to recognize excellent books with a Connecticut focus or written by a Connecticut author. To be eligible, the book must have a Connecticut topic or setting or an author must have been born in Connecticut or have been a legal resident of Connecticut for at least three years.

The Driftless Connecticut Series is funded by the Beatrice Fox Auerbach Foundation Fund at the Hartford Foundation for Public Giving. For more information and a complete list of books in the Driftless Connecticut Series, please visit us online at http://www.wesleyan.edu/wespress/driftless.